I0820268

CLASS OF '99

TRIUMPH AND TRAGEDY IN THE 1999 CART INDY CAR SERIES

JOHN OREOVICZ

Octane Press, Edition 1.0, October 2025

On the cover: (Left to Right) Tony Kanaan, Hélio Castroneves, Greg Moore, Dario Franchitti, and Juan Pablo Montoya injected Indy car racing with a new generation of star power in the late 1990s. *Michael Levitt*

On the front endpapers: Paul Tracy and Dario Franchitti revel in a postrace champagne spray. *Michael Levitt*

On the rear endpapers: Greg Moore and Hélio Castroneves share a moment on the pit wall. *Michael Levitt*

Hardcover ISBN: 978-1-64234-181-2
ePub ISBN: 978-1-64234-182-9
LCCN: 2025931463

Project Edited by Faith Garcia
Interior Design by Tom Heffron
Cover Design by Linsey Dodaro
Proofread by Peter Schletty

octanepress.com

Octane Press is based in Austin, Texas

Printed in China

For Lacey, who showed me the
power of a strong group of friends.

Note to the reader: The so-called "Indy Split" between Championship Auto Racing Teams (CART) and the Indy Racing League (IRL) caused a lot of confusion. In fact, in 1999, neither the "CART FedEx Championship Series" nor the "Pep Boys Indy Racing League" was legally permitted to use the term "Indy car." For the sake of clarity, let's call it what it was: a pair of competing Indy car championships with different cars. As such, "Indy car" and "IndyCar" should generally be viewed here as generic terms for top-level American open-wheel racing.

CONTENTS

Juan Pablo Montoya leads Dario Franchitti and Paul Tracy early in the Detroit GP.
Michael Levitt

PREFACE

Writing the book *Indy Split* almost felt like a duty—someone had to take on that daunting topic, and I suppose I volunteered for the job. *Class of '99* is a far more personal story, because the 1999 CART season was every bit as important to me as it was to the drivers celebrated in these pages. It turned out to be, in my opinion, the most compelling single season in the long history of Indy car racing. It's amazing in retrospect to have been at the center of it all. And it was very emotional to revisit the events of that remarkable year and document it all in detail in this book.

I had spent the 1997 and '98 seasons working public relations for PacWest Racing with drivers Mark Blundell and Mauricio Gugelmin. While I valued and enjoyed the experience, my preference was to be on the media side, writing about the entire series rather than pitching stories or being beholden to one team. The two years at PacWest enhanced my profile in the paddock, and I was able to return to the media at a higher level than where I had been in 1996. It was a gamble to give up a secure PR job to go back to the media, but I bet on myself and started contributing features to *On Track* in 1999, before landing the CART beat for *National Speed Sport News*. The real key is when Pam Miller—now the producer of Fox Sports' IndyCar broadcasts—brought me on board with Quokka Sports to provide coverage for CART.com. The work included stand-up video as well as writing, and one of my few career regrets is not expanding my skill set of video presentation and production.

From the time I started attending the Indianapolis 500 in the late 1970s, it was the people—not the politics—that drove my interest in Indy car racing. Unfortunately, from the moment I started working professionally in the sport in 1993, politics were the dominant story. Despite that turbulent backdrop, the CART series of the '90s somehow produced a core group of star drivers every bit as influential as the generation of Indy car legends led by A. J. Foyt and Mario Andretti.

It all peaked in the 1999 CART season, which ended after twenty races in a 212-point deadlock between Dario Franchitti and Juan Pablo Montoya resolved by a tiebreaker in Montoya's favor. It couldn't have been any closer, but the ending could not have been any sadder, as their friend and rival Greg Moore crashed to his death in the climactic championship finale at California Speedway.

Moore's passing at age twenty-four on October 31, 1999, created one of Indy car racing's most debatable bench racing scenarios. Within hours, Roger Penske contracted Hélio Castroneves to drive the No. 3 car intended for Moore starting in 2000. Separated in age by just eighteen days from the driver he replaced, Hélio had shown plenty of potential as a young Indy car driver in 1998 and '99. But he wasn't a can't-miss prospect like Moore. Castroneves is now one of only four men to have won the Indianapolis 500 four times; what could Moore have achieved in top-shelf Team Penske equipment?

As it stands, Castroneves and the group of young drivers Moore competed (and often partied) with went on to create a generational impact on Indy car racing. Now that the older legends are passing on, they are considered the sport's modern era heroes.

Franchitti won four IndyCar championships and added three Indianapolis victories before a 2013 accident at the Houston street course ended his career at age forty. After winning the 1999 CART title in a tiebreaker over Franchitti, Montoya went on to have a hugely diverse career that included race wins in Formula 1, the NASCAR Cup Series, and an IMSA sports car championship, plus a pair of Indianapolis 500 victories spanning fifteen years. Tony Kanaan's career statistics fall short of the others, but he won an Indy 500 and an IRL championship and is arguably the most popular driver of his generation.

Greg Moore was the biggest personality and may have had more talent than any of them. After breaking free of his awkward, bespectacled teen years, Greg could have passed for a Hollywood star like his pal Jason Priestley. But once in a race car, the polite Canadian native from the Vancouver suburb of Maple Ridge was a no-holds-barred badass—especially on ovals, where his daredevil ability to master a loose car in the outside groove eventually contributed to his demise.

I've long believed that no single figure was capable of saving Indy car racing after it destroyed itself in the 1990s, but if anyone stood a chance, it was Greg. He had the potential to be the kind of dynamic, dominant champion Indy car racing is still searching for. But because fans and media were more focused on Tony George and Andrew Craig and the so-called "leaders" who were tearing down a proud sport, Moore and his peers, including Franchitti, Castroneves, Kanaan, and Montoya, received a fraction of the attention and accolades they deserved.

The biggest impact Moore left on Indy car racing was the way he lived his life—running wheel to wheel with his rivals on the track, then matching them beer for beer at the celebratory afterparty, a party he usually organized. It didn't matter who won. Moore taught a generation of young drivers trained on distrust that they could—and should—really be friends.

The drivers who competed in CART in the late 1990s—when Indy car racing reached its zenith in terms of speed and technology, but prior to breakthrough safety developments like the HANS Device and the SAFER Barrier—share a special bond. Moore is no longer among his peers, but he created and continues to strengthen those lifelong bonds.

The hardest days on the job as a racing journalist are the ones involving death, and thankfully, there were a lot fewer of those in the '90s and into the 2000s than there were for previous generations who covered the sport. October 31, 1999, was by far the most emotionally difficult workday I ever experienced, because everybody loved Greg Moore. Other racing drivers have died over the last twenty-five years, but none had Moore's combination of spirit and potential.

It's fair to say that CART and its tight-knit community never really recovered from the tragedy in Fontana, but Greg Moore's positive energy continues to resonate today. This book celebrates his memory, his potential, and the camaraderie he created among a group of drivers who became Indy car racing's greatest twenty-first century legends.

Greg Moore (left) and Jimmy Vasser (right) after Moore's victory in the 1998 U.S. 500 at Michigan Speedway. *Paul Webb*

PROLOGUE

MOORE'S LOST MILLION

NOVEMBER 1, 1998

Greg Moore sat quietly on the pit wall at California Speedway, where the twenty-three-year-old Canadian had just completed podium celebrations after finishing second to Jimmy Vasser in the Marlboro 500 Presented by Toyota. There were twenty-five lead changes and a frantic one-lap green flag sprint to the finish, and a few minutes after the checkered flag fell, the race was already being called an instant IndyCar classic.

Conceived and constructed by Penske Motorsports, the track—colloquially known as Fontana for its location on the site of a former Kaiser steel mill near Ontario—was immediately established as the fastest circuit in IndyCar racing. One year earlier when it opened, Mauricio Gugelmin qualified on pole position for the 1997 Marlboro 500 at a world closed-course speed record of 240.942 miles per hour, and he unofficially turned an even faster practice lap averaging 242.333 mph.

Concerned by the rising speeds that were driven by intense competition between engine and tire manufacturers, CART (Championship Auto Racing Teams), the sanctioning body for the FedEx Championship Series, mandated an innovative and radical rear wing for its superspeedway races in 1998 at Fontana and Michigan Speedway, the two-mile track that California Speedway was cloned from. The so-called Handford Device made its debut in July at Michigan, and while it achieved its goal of reducing top speeds, it also had the unexpected and unintended effect of creating a huge draft or wake behind the leading car.

That turned the 1998 U.S. 500 at Michigan into a true spectacle, with an Indy car record sixty-two lead changes. Moore, who despite his young age had already demonstrated tremendous skill as an oval racer in his third year in the CART series, was masterful in adapting to the Handford wing and the driving style and race craft it demanded. He emerged victorious for Player's/Forsythe Racing after a tense battle down the stretch with Vasser and his Target Chip Ganassi Racing teammate, 1997 and '98 CART champion Alex Zanardi.

"With five laps to go, I was in fourth," Moore recalled, talking to the author in the summer of 1999. "Jimmy was leading, Alex was second, Scott Pruett was third, and I was fourth. I was a little concerned about getting ahead of Scott because he was very quick on the straightaway. I managed to get by him right away, and luckily Alex and Jimmy started to fight for it. They both wanted to win the race and that allowed me to get by Alex.

"I passed Jimmy with three laps to go, thinking to myself, 'OK, I can hold him off now, no problem,'" Moore continued. "But he passed me on the next lap easily going into Turn One. I had a good run on him going into Three and Four, and I thought 'Maybe I should try to pass him into One and Two this time on the last lap.' I passed him into One and Two and, seeing as it was the last lap, I took the air off his front wing once I passed him. I let the car drift up the track to take the air off so he'd have to lift. It was good, because that got me enough of a lead at the end of the back straight that I was able to get through Three and Four and win the race."

That sequence of events from three months earlier at Michigan no doubt rattled through Moore's mind during the final laps at Fontana in the '98 season finale, and maybe even more so as he decompressed after the race. But that wasn't why he was more upset than he normally would have been. Sure, he was hypercompetitive, and he had just come up short in a thrilling three-way battle for a 500-mile race win. But there was one other key difference between the Michigan and California Speedway races in 1998—or maybe more accurately, about nine hundred thousand.

Desperate to create a "Major Event" given the absence of the Indianapolis 500 from its schedule since 1995, CART awarded a $1 million jackpot for the winner of the season finale at Fontana. The winner's prize money for every other race on the calendar—including Moore's victory three months earlier in the U.S. 500—was $100,000.

Vasser's margin of victory at Fontana of 0.36 seconds therefore came at a huge cost to Moore and the Forsythe team.

"They always say that second is the first loser, but wow, on that day it sure was!" Moore managed to laugh. "I mean, Jimmy won a million bucks, and all we won was sixty grand. It's tough to swallow that pill. But on the other hand, we had a great race."

Indeed, it was. Vasser and Moore combined to lead nearly half of the 250 laps, while Gugelmin and Michael Andretti also led significant chunks. A late caution produced what set up to be a four- or five-lap shootout, but leader Paul Tracy inexplicably spun and crashed while warming his tires. That extended the final caution to create a one-lap, two-mile sprint for the $1 million, with the green and white flags displayed simultaneously. Moore, who inherited the lead from Tracy, takes up the story.

"I had a good restart," he said. "I had a good jump on the guys through Turns Three and Four and I think if I'd had a worse restart maybe I'd have been better off because they wouldn't have had such a run on me going into One. Jimmy got by me and then Alex got by me, and Alex gave me a big slide job going into One—kind of like I did to Jimmy at Michigan, a little bit. But I think Alex was trying to save his ass in the car a little bit through Turn One, because he went in there awfully low and slid up the track. His car was all over the place and that allowed Jimmy to break free. I had to lift, and that was the end of it.

"That allowed Jimmy to go on and win a million bucks," Moore sighed. "Another half a lap and I would have had Jimmy, because I caught his draft into Three and Four, and I was catching him a lot going across the start-finish line, but not enough to win the race. It's unfortunate, but it shows if you've got a good team, good teamwork can win some races for sure."

The 1998 season had been challenging for Moore and every other driver and team that utilized Mercedes-Benz engines. Ilmor

Engineering, Mercedes's racing engine partner, attempted to create the smallest, lightest engine to ever power an Indy car. The so-called IC108E engine met those ambitious packaging goals, but it was also unreliable and difficult to drive smoothly on road and street courses.

Only one driver ever won races with the unloved Mercedes "E" engine: Greg Moore. In 1998, he triumphed in May on the unique "roval" called Emerson Fittipaldi Speedway in Rio de Janeiro, Brazil—stunning Zanardi with a daring outside pass for the lead—and again in July at Michigan. The second-place finish to end the season at Fontana elevated Moore to a career-best fifth place in the CART championship standings, and he was set to continue as the face of a successful Canadian driver development program for Player's/Forsythe Racing.

But Moore knew he had an even higher ceiling. By the summer of 1999, at age twenty-four, he and Gil de Ferran were secure in the knowledge that they would lead a rebuilding Marlboro Team Penske into the twenty-first century. They were part of an emerging group of Indy car drivers who, over the next twenty years, would make the same kind of generational impact that the likes of A. J. Foyt, Mario Andretti, and the Unser brothers did from the 1960s all the way into the '90s.

But as he reflected on the disappointment of losing out on a $1 million prize in the 1998 season finale, Moore had no way of knowing he wouldn't live to see his twenty-fifth birthday.

JIMMY VASSER

"We talked in the Ganassi team prerace meeting at Fontana in '98 about how we didn't want a repeat of what happened at Michigan. The three of us were battling, and Zanardi and I were going back and forth towards the end. Greg snuck up on us, and maybe we were too preoccupied with each other, because Greg snookered us and won that race at Michigan.

"A group of drivers made a plan ahead of the Fontana '98 race; I rented this limousine bus that would take us to Las Vegas that night. After I won the race, I brought along that big fake check they give you in Victory Lane, this big cardboard thing that said, 'One million bucks, Pay to the Order of Jimmy Vasser.' Of course, Greg was on the bus, and we obviously had some beers on the way. He was still upset about losing the race, and I can only go from what Greg was telling us about why he was so pissed.

"He wasn't happy about his contract that he had with Jerry Forsythe at the time. He wanted to make more money, right? But I guess Jerry wouldn't renegotiate his contract for '99. He had one more year, and Jerry was kind of leaving it where it was for Greg. But Jerry said, 'You go out and win that race at Fontana, and you can keep all the money.'

"Greg got second place, and instead of getting 100 percent of a million, he got 40 or 50 percent or whatever his cut was of $60,000. I put that big million dollar check up in the bus there, and he just kept looking at it. That's a lot of money for a young man—for anybody. We razzed him about it for days to come."

DARIO FRANCHITTI

"Jimmy had that big check front and center the whole time. Greg was so pissed, because he had snookered them at Michigan and Jimmy returned the favor when there was a million bucks on the line. Oh, Greg was mad! But we spent a great few days at Jimmy's house, that whole brotherhood."

Indy car's greatest generation came to the fore in the 1970s. From left to right: Mario Andretti, Al Unser, Mark Donohue, Bobby Unser, A. J. Foyt. *Indianapolis Motor Speedway*

CHAPTER 1

INDY CAR RACING'S GREATEST GENERATION

Wally Dallenbach was by no means a household name, but he was an unsung hero among Indy car racing's greatest generation—a core group of drivers that competed over a span of nearly five decades who represented the human face of the sport when the Indianapolis 500 was at its popular peak.

Between 1958 and 1994, Dallenbach and his more famous peers—A. J. Foyt, Mario Andretti, Al Unser, Bobby Unser, Johnny Rutherford, and Gordon Johncock—combined to win 250 Indy car races (seventeen at the all-important Indianapolis 500) and eighteen national championships. They represented and guided American open-wheel racing through technological, cultural, organizational, and political revolutions into the modern era. As a group, they rewrote the record books, and while all but Johncock remained involved in Indy car racing in some capacity late into their lives, their departure as on-track competitors left an enormous void as the 1990s progressed.

Foyt was the most successful, and when restricting the conversation to the USA, the most famous; his sixty-seven Indy car victories and seven United States Auto Club (USAC) sanctioned titles still stand as all-time records. Of course, A. J.'s most famous achievement was being the first driver to record four wins at the Indianapolis 500, a feat he accomplished in 1977.

What made Foyt's fourth Indianapolis win even more significant than the obvious historical aspect was the fact that he accomplished it in a chassis that he commissioned and fabricated from scratch with his loyal team, powered by a Ford-derived engine that spelled out F-O-Y-T on the cam covers. Far beyond owner/driver, A. J. often functioned as his own mechanic and engineer.

But even as a driver, Foyt was no one-trick pony. He won the 1967 24 Hours of Le Mans with Dan Gurney and Ford, and later codrove a Porsche 935 to victory at the Daytona 24 Hours. Foyt also won seven NASCAR Cup Series races, including the 1972 Daytona 500 for the Wood Brothers and seven USAC-sanctioned stock car championships.

Foyt remained competitive driving Indy cars into the late 1970s. His last win came against a diminished field at the 1981 Pocono 500, the final race staged by USAC during the original 1979–81 USAC-CART split. He stubbornly continued competing full time in the CART series into the '90s, notching the occasional top-five finish before suffering severe leg injuries in a devastating crash at Road America in 1990. But A. J. Foyt wasn't about to quit on any terms but his own. Barely able to walk, he qualified in the middle of the front row for the 1991 Indianapolis 500. He was fifty-six years old.

Exactly two years later, Foyt drove his familiar No. 14 car into the Indianapolis Motor Speedway pits prior to Pole Day qualifying and shocked the world by announcing his retirement as a driver. But he didn't quit as a racer. Foyt's team never did win a CART-sanctioned race, but it doggedly kept trying, and Robby Gordon earned the team's first podium results in more than a decade in 1993. And while the formation of the Indy Racing League in 1996 was intended to benefit American short track drivers, it also offered afterthought CART teams like A. J. Foyt Racing a path back to the front of the field. Not surprisingly, Foyt was one of the IRL's most staunch proponents and his team's No. 14 maintains an eternal presence on the IndyCar Series grid. Racing's ultimate survivor, A. J. celebrated his ninetieth birthday in early 2025.

Equally unsurprising, Andretti strongly aligned himself with the upstart CART side. Mario broke into Indy cars in 1964/65 at the height of the rear-engine revolution; by the dawn of the '70s, he had earned three USAC-sanctioned championships and won the Indy 500, sparking a lifelong rivalry with Foyt that wasn't always friendly. Like A. J., Mario was also a Daytona 500 winner and part of the Ford sports car program. But Andretti had even wider aspirations—worldwide. He started his first Grand Prix for Lotus from pole position in 1968 and claimed his first F1 race win in a Ferrari in 1971. He finally teamed with another American racing hero, Parnelli Jones, to tackle F1 full time, but the program foundered after a single season. Undaunted, he rejoined a struggling Lotus team in 1976 and helped develop the basic ground effect aerodynamic principles that still influence racing car design today.

Andretti won a total of twelve Grands Prix and earned the 1978 Formula 1 World Championship in the beautiful John Player Special-liveried Lotus 78 and 79. Along with Phil Hill (1961) he is the only American driver to have won the F1 crown. Remarkably, Mario's victory nearly fifty years ago in the 1978 Dutch Grand Prix remains the last GP triumph for the Stars and Stripes.

Andretti returned to Indy cars full time in 1982 just as the PPG IndyCar World Series was really starting to thrive under CART's management. Mario won the 1984 championship and remained a front-runner into the early 1990s, taking his final win at Phoenix Raceway in 1993. His son Michael quickly rose through the ranks to emerge as a regular Indy car race winner by the mid-80s before claiming the 1991 CART championship, the latter achieved during a four-year run when Mario and Michael were teammates at Newman/Haas Racing.

Mario reluctantly stepped out of the car at the end of the '94 season at the age of fifty-four, following an appropriately elaborate "Arrivederci, Mario!" tour, but he remains heavily involved with the sport to this day, giving demonstration rides in a two-seat Indy car and serving as a spokesman for Firestone. While Foyt's history at Indianapolis resonates strongly with American racing fans and he does own a Le Mans triumph, Andretti's accomplishments in Formula 1 made him a much more acclaimed figure on an international level. The rivalry between the two legends mellowed as they aged, but the needle remains sharp, even in their eighties and nineties.

Because their driving careers extended into the 1990s, Mario and A. J. retain most of the major Indy car records. But it is important to note that longtime devotees of the sport—including the late, much-loved writer Robin Miller—include Parnelli Jones and Dan Gurney among the all-time Indy greats. Miller even commissioned artist Roger Warrick to produce a "Mount Rushmore" sweatshirt that featured Andretti, Foyt, Gurney, and Jones. Even though Parnelli and the "Big Eagle" won fewer races than other star drivers of the era like Johncock, Rutherford, and the Unser brothers, Gurney and Jones still cultivated an elevated stature in the sport—and more importantly, in American popular culture.

Jones (1933–2024) made just seven Indianapolis 500 starts from 1961 to '67, starting on the pole twice on the way to winning in 1963 and adding a pair of second-place finishes. On pavement or dirt, he and Foyt were usually USAC's drivers to beat in the first half of the decade, but by early '67, Parnelli had mostly stepped away from open-wheel competition and Andretti had emerged as Foyt's most credible rival. Parnelli went on to win the 1970 Trans-Am championship and claim a pair of victories in the Baja 1000 off-road race.

Gurney (1931–2018) advanced quickly through West Coast sports car racing to land a factory Ferrari ride in 1959. He won Formula 1 races for Porsche and Brabham and was the man responsible for bringing Team Lotus and the Ford Motor Company together in 1963 to ignite the rear-engine revolution that redefined Indy car racing's competitive parameters. Three years later, Gurney was a manufacturer in his own right, with his All American Racers firm building Formula 1 and Indy cars. He won the 1967 Belgian Grand Prix at Spa-Francorchamps in one of his own Eagles.

Gurney never competed full time in Indy car racing, but his influence as a car builder grew in the 1970s and he drafted the "White Paper" that ultimately led to the formation of Championship Auto Racing Teams (CART). Jones also became a car constructor in the 1970s, but his team's greatest contribution to the sport was the development of the first turbocharged version of the Cosworth DFV Formula 1 engine. The Cosworth DFX finally dethroned the venerable old Offenhauser and dominated Indy car racing in the late '70s and much of the '80s.

The Unser brothers represented the second generation of a family of racers from Albuquerque best known for their mastery of the Pikes Peak Hill Climb staged annually near Colorado Springs. Louis Unser, uncle to Bobby and Al, claimed the first of the family's twenty-six overall victories at "The Mountain" in 1934. Bobby, who was Al's senior by five years, started his first Indianapolis 500 in 1963 in the fearsome Novi before settling into a conflict-ridden but highly successful relationship with Gurney and All American Racers that netted two USAC championships and victories at Indianapolis in 1968 and '75.

Unser joined Penske Racing for the last three years of his career and picked up ten wins, including a disputed triumph in the 1981 Indianapolis 500. Set to drive for Patrick Racing in '82, Unser lost heart after testing the car and retired at age forty-eight to a colorful career in the television booth. He made a brief comeback behind the wheel at Pikes Peak in 1986 to drive an Audi Quattro to the overall triumph, explaining, "A girl [rally champion Michèle Mouton] holds the record? I just couldn't let it go."

Al Unser didn't have the gift of gab like his brother. But he was an equally adept wheelman, taking thirty-nine Indy car wins to Bobby's thirty-five, in a career that outlasted his brother's by more than a decade. Al achieved his initial success driving for the Vel's/Parnelli Jones team, winning the 1970 USAC crown and consecutive Indy 500s in '70 and '71. In 1978, while driving for Jim Hall, he added a third Indy triumph and became the only man to ever sweep the "Triple Crown" of five-hundred-mile races at Indianapolis, Pocono, and Ontario.

Like Bobby, Al enjoyed a late career renaissance with Team Penske. He claimed the 1985 CART championship (his third) by a single point over his son, Al Jr., then drove a backup car that was on display in a hotel lobby to a fourth Indianapolis win in 1987. Unser continued to compete at Indy before quietly calling it quits when he struggled to get up to speed in 1994. Loyal to Indianapolis, "Big Al" later served as a driver coach and steward for the Indy Racing League. The rivalry between Al and Bobby was as fierce as any between siblings, though Al arguably got the last laugh when "Little Al" achieved far more success on the racetrack than Bobby's sons Bobby Jr. and Robby. Intrinsically linked, the Unser brothers died within seven months of each other in 2021.

Rutherford took an Indy car win at Atlanta in 1965, but he acquired the unfortunate nickname "Wreckaford" and did not taste victory again until he joined the McLaren team eight years later. A revitalized "Lone Star J. R." won sixteen races and finished in the top four of the championship standings every year for McLaren through the end of the '70s, including victories at Indianapolis in 1974 and '76. He then claimed a third Indy trophy and the CART-sanctioned championship in 1980 driving the John Barnard–designed Chaparral 2K.

Rutherford's competitiveness waned in the '80s, but like Foyt, he proudly hung on in the face of younger competition, taking his last win in 1986. He tearfully stepped away from the cockpit in 1994; in an odd but endearing gesture, fellow Texan Foyt rolled out the exact 1993 Lola in which A. J. had driven a couple slow, celebratory laps of IMS when he retired a year earlier for Rutherford to do the same. J. R. was a pace car driver for CART for many years and now serves as a brand ambassador for McLaren.

Throughout his driving career, Johncock operated a logging business in Michigan and shared an economy of words with Al Unser. Gordy's Indy car career spanned four decades, from winning at the Milwaukee Mile as part of the vaunted 1965 USAC rookie class to finishing sixth at Indy in 1991 at the age of fifty-four. Most notably, it included victories at the Indianapolis 500 in 1973 and '82, and the 1976 USAC National Championship. Johncock's 1973 Indy win is often overlooked because the month of May was blighted by misfortune, including the death of drivers Art Pollard and Swede Savage, and the race was delayed multiple times and shortened by rain. But his memorable triumph in 1982, when he prevailed in a tense duel with Mears, offered some vindication. Johncock competed at Indianapolis through 1992, when he left racing behind for good and returned to his logging business. He's still working as he approaches his ninetieth birthday.

Most of Johncock's racing success came when he was driving for Patrick Racing, operated by Michigan oil prospector U. E. "Pat" Patrick. From mid-1973 through '79, Gordy's teammate was Wally Dallenbach. Wally had also broken into the USAC field in 1965 but never held down a full-time ride until he got the call from Patrick to replace the gravely injured Savage following the tragic events of the '73 Indy 500. Dallenbach claimed his first win at Milwaukee in his fourth start for Patrick and added the California 500 at Ontario to his trophy case by the end of the year to finish second in the USAC standings despite missing the first five races of the season. Wally won a total of

BOBBY UNSER

"I just wish some of these younger guys could have seen how bad Foyt wanted to win races when he was young. And therefore, set our bar a lot higher. Of course, Foyt doesn't talk to anybody. He was grouchy when I met him and he's still grouchy. He's just fat and grouchy now. But I can say that because he was a hell of a competitor. One hell of a race car driver when he was young.

"I think it was a better atmosphere in the old days. That's not to say these young guys don't have talent and aren't trying hard or driving hard. Franchitti and Castroneves, if they had to have run sprint cars or midgets, they'd have run them. And they would have liked it, and they would have run really good. Hey Castroneves—screw the dancing and come and run a sprint car! It would open their eyes like you would not believe. But they would have been okay. You do what you have to do, when you have to do it.

"Today's drivers are soft, and the conditions are *waaaay* too easy. But that's just coming from an old has-been. The difference is the environment was different. Dario has a lot of desire. He went to NASCAR and he failed. But by the same token, if you don't fail occasionally, you don't succeed occasionally. So, when he came back to Indy cars, he came back a better driver than when he left."

---

five Indy car races and was a solid front-runner, finishing in the top six of the USAC championship every year except 1974.

Along with fellow team owners Dan Gurney and Roger Penske, Pat Patrick was one of the driving forces behind the formation of CART in 1979. At the same time, Dallenbach started an organization called the Championship Drivers Association while also assisting Doctors Stephen Olvey and Terry Trammell to build the CART Safety Team. Recognizing that Dallenbach was in his mid-forties and likely nearing the end of his driving career, Patrick approached him with a proposition.

"He said, 'We need a chief steward. We've been talking and I'm making you an offer on behalf of CART,'" Dallenbach recalled.

After discussing the opportunity during a hunting trip with Al Unser, Wally agreed to try it for a year as co-chief steward with the retiring Don Garner. He wound up staying on the job for more than two decades. Along with Trammell, Olvey, and CART technical director Kirk Russell, Dallenbach pushed forward safety initiatives that moved drivers back in the car to reduce leg injuries. Most importantly, Wally earned and maintained the attention and respect of the fraternity of Indy car drivers. For incoming younger generations, he came across as a kind, grandfatherly figure, but the fact that he was an experienced former Indy car competitor gave him immense credibility. Wally may have ruled with an iron fist, but he somehow used a velvet hammer to ease the blow.

"I think Wally was good for everyone and the perfect chief steward—the right guy for the times," said four-time Indianapolis 500 winner Mears. "He was an old race car driver with a wise head on his shoulders.

RICK MEARS

"They were two opposites in a sense, Bobby and Al. Bobby was more of a developing guy as far as working on the chassis, taking it home and coming up with ideas, changing this, changing that. He spent a lot more time really focusing on making the car work. Bobby felt if he did not have a 10 percent advantage, he was 5 percent behind. He's a racer through and through, and he understood that life's a lot easier if you get that advantage. I've said through the years that I've been basically lazy all my life so the better the car works, the easier it is on me. Which is why I always tried to make the car better.

"Al worked hard at it too, but Al wasn't into the detail as much as Bobby was, as far as taking it home, building his own little wind tunnel, all that kind of stuff. Al was not quite as technical in the mechanics of the car; he still worked on it very hard, but it was more that he would relay the information to the team about what the car was doing and then the team would work on figuring it out more, where Bobby would try to figure it out himself. Where Al came into play more so was in the race. When it's time to go racing, he's got his head screwed on straight. He made very few mistakes. He was on top of it in that respect. When it came time to race, if that car was anywhere close, he put it there."

TONY KANAAN

"There are different types of personalities, and some aren't as likeable or approachable or for the fans. They're there to do business, they'll go to the track, think 'I have to be the fastest guy.' Michael Andretti was business. And once he's done, he didn't want to talk to anybody, he didn't want to be around. He didn't like any of that stuff. He wanted to race cars and go home. Everything else was a pain or a problem if it wasn't about making the car go fast. We still have some people like this way nowadays, but things change, and now you also have some people who have personality, and they don't mind spending the time. By default, those people become more popular. But that generation, coincidence or not, didn't have anybody like that. There was kind of a void. The big names were all unapproachable.

"When I worked for A. J., I had no idea how the perception developed that he's a nice guy. People wanted an autograph, he'd say 'Fuck that!' I thought, 'A. J., how the hell do you have fans?' He doesn't care. But that was that era. He's a badass. That's A. J., and people know how he is. He doesn't get blamed. But then you can sit and talk to Mario for five hours. He'll give you the time. I know they're old now, but they still hate each other, in a competitive way, even though they are old farts. Foyt used to complain, 'Mario Andretti, he's all over the place, I won a lot more.' I said, 'Yeah, but you're an asshole! People know your stats, and you're a badass. But as far as being likable? You don't give people the time of day!' So, Mario is going to be more famous, that's the way it is."

He was always very calm, very relaxed, and in the moment. You never saw Wally go off half-cocked. He didn't get rattled, and he had everyone's respect because he had been there on track. He was a good, calming influence on everybody and played a tremendous leadership role in Indy car racing."

Dallenbach's credibility as a racer and firm but genial manner made him the perfect man to enforce the unwritten code of ethics among drivers. It's fair to say that as cars and circuits got safer, driving standards got rougher in every form of racing over the decades. Dale Earnhardt in NASCAR and Ayrton Senna and later Michael Schumacher in Formula 1 basically burned the rulebook when it came to ethics. But their popularity and charisma somehow legitimized their dirty driving, not only for fans but for an increasingly ruthless younger generation of drivers.

In Indy car racing, Michael Andretti was considered extremely aggressive throughout the 1980s, and Al Unser Jr. was involved in a series of controversial incidents in the latter part of the decade. Emerson Fittipaldi and later Nigel Mansell brought hardcore blocking tactics with them from Formula 1, but their offenses were often overshadowed by the sport's latest bad boy, the edgy young Canadian Paul Tracy. Even champions weren't exempt from Wally's judgement; Alex Zanardi incurred fines and was put on probation several times during his successful three-year run with Chip Ganassi Racing in the late '90s.

"Punishing people wasn't part of Wally's make-up," observed longtime CART technical director Kirk Russell, who would later learn just how tough the job of chief steward was. "In those situations, Wally always got the message across in a manner that was appropriate and very understandable. His manner was always right on the point and correct. Everyone learned. Zanardi was a prime example. He was overly aggressive, and he hit a lot of people on track. Wally sat him down and told him, 'We don't do it this way.' There was never any punishment or intimidation from Wally. He would just be very clear about what was accepted and what wasn't."

Dallenbach started putting drivers on probation in 1996, and over the next three years, Tracy, Andretti, Zanardi, Greg Moore, and Bryan Herta all spent time on probation for causing on-track incidents. During his dominant championship run in 1998, Zanardi was fined $50,000 and parked for the opening qualifying session at Laguna Seca after causing two avoidable incidents at Mid-Ohio. He was livid, and as a lame duck in the CART series (Zanardi had already agreed to terms to return to Formula 1 in 1999), he went public with his grievance.

"I'm disappointed, because I am certainly not an angel," he remarked. "But my performance has been analyzed in the past three years with a microscope. Every time I have had an encounter with a car I have been put on probation and fined, so this is unacceptable. This series is a jungle. There are racing accidents every week, and I am not saying it is not right to take action. But I don't feel I deserve the biggest fine in CART history."

Few drivers chose to speak out like Zanardi, but when they did, Dallenbach always held his ground. "Some of the calls are not easy to make, but they're the calls that have to be made," he said. "My job gets very tough when I have to look at an incident and make a call as to whether it was an accident or intentional. That's the thin line that I—and I alone—decide. It's not easy but based on my experience in the car and out of the car, having done it and having had it done to me, I have a pretty good feeling of what a driver is doing out there. It's bad enough when the accidents are accidents. That will happen in racing. But when it becomes a deliberate act, I'm the guy. I'm your best friend and your worst enemy.

"Thirty or forty years ago, drivers didn't live to see their kids growing up," Dallenbach reasoned. "In the '70s, drivers started living long enough to see their kids become teenagers. By the '80s, drivers were living long enough to get beat by their sons. That's totally a credit to all aspects of the sport—the technology of building the cars, the safety of the racetracks, the emergency care. I can testify to all aspects of it because I started my career in a roadster, and I finished my career in a ground effect car. I've been burned, and I've been hurt. Years ago, if you so much as touched somebody with your car, you had a better than even chance of taking yourself out—or worse."

It can be argued that Indy car racing developed a greater generational gap than any other form of motorsport. Aside from Tom Sneva and Mears, Indy car racing produced no new superstars throughout the 1970s and into the '80s, until Bobby Rahal and legacy name drivers Al Unser Jr. and Michael Andretti began to emerge as race winners. Think about it: Foyt was a few years ahead of them, but the Unsers, Rutherford, Johncock, Dallenbach, and Mario Andretti all graduated to the USAC National Championship level between 1962 and '65. Sneva's first full season was 1974; Mears didn't complete a full campaign until 1979, the year he won his first Indianapolis 500 and the inaugural CART-sanctioned championship. Rahal arrived in 1982, followed within a year by Al Jr. and Michael.

That state of affairs was largely the product of the sport's mismanagement throughout the '70s. USAC, and by extension the Indianapolis Motor Speedway, failed to react to the rear-engine revolution at the Indianapolis 500 from the mid-60s by modernizing or altering the traditional path to Indy cars of midgets and sprint cars. While the Indianapolis 500 remained strong, the rest of the USAC Championship Trail stagnated. That led to the creation of CART, originally intended as an owner's group to spur commercial growth in the industry, but which ultimately became the sanctioning body that grew the sport from the Indy 500 and a handful of poorly promoted and attended oval races into a diverse and successful championship with worldwide appeal.

The presence of Indianapolis and a few other ovals in CART's increasingly road racing–based championship prolonged the careers of Foyt, Rutherford, and their generation, but it also exposed the disconnect between modern Indy car racing and the USAC short oval ladder system. That created an opening for a new breed of American Indy car drivers primarily raised as road racers, like Rahal and Danny Sullivan. Both competed in Europe and caught a brief taste of Formula 1 before finding the evolving Indy car scene back at home under CART much more to their liking.

"When I came up in CART, most of the drivers were American and most had been around for a long time," observed Rahal. "You had the Unser brothers, Andretti, Foyt, Johncock, Rutherford, and those guys had twenty years in the limelight and brought a lot of interest to the series. From an American standpoint, it's gone through a little bit of a trough, but I believe Americans can compete. I think having American stars is very important.

"Americans seem acceptive of foreigners in other sports, but racing seems to be a little different," he continued. "Baseball, the most American of sports, embraces its international aspects, yet in racing, somehow being from Brazil isn't good. Hockey has more players from Russia and Finland than the US or even Canada. It's not necessarily an aspect of our country that I'm particularly proud of. It seems quite xenophobic in a lot of ways. But that's part of the fabric of it, I guess. I think NASCAR used that 'We're all American so we're better' and 'America this, America that' and tried to draw the separation between the two by making clear that difference. To me, who cares what country you're from as long as you get the job done. A lot of people think Kenny Bräck is an American."

Legacy drivers Unser Jr. and Michael Andretti also trained as road racers, helping them make the leap into Indy cars in 1983 by the time they were in their early twenties. But most of the key newcomers to the CART series in the '80s were foreigners, including Teo Fabi, Arie Luyendyk, and of course, Emerson Fittipaldi. Along with them came more aggressive international driving tactics. Fittipaldi—a two-time F1 World Champion—quickly recognized the power that Dallenbach commanded as chief steward.

"When I started racing Indy cars in 1984, I realized right away that Wally was very good at keeping the drivers under control," Fittipaldi observed. "Racing drivers are not an easy group of people to control. We have very strong personalities and most of the time on the track we are full of adrenaline. Wally was always able to control those things in a very diplomatic way but also very clear. People respected him. He made a big contribution to motor racing."

Dallenbach's five Indy car race wins didn't elevate him into the sport's pantheon of greats like Andretti, Foyt, and the Unsers, but he made a significantly different mark over the long-term. "Not many people could point him out, but he's a giant in the industry," said racer-turned-team-owner Chip Ganassi. "He had a larger impact on the sport than 99 percent of people in racing."

By the time Mario Andretti, Rutherford, and Al Unser were the last of Indy car's Greatest Generation to reluctantly retire from driving in 1994, the generation that followed them was also already nearing the end of their careers. In fact, Mears had already walked away in 1992 at the age of forty-one after accomplishing more at Indianapolis in a fifteen-year run than his fellow four-time winners did in twice as many starts. Sullivan and Fittipaldi's Indy car days were ended by serious accidents at Michigan Speedway in 1995 and '96, while Rahal took his "Last Ride" in 1998. Nigel Mansell and Jacques Villeneuve briefly injected some star power to the CART series before heading off (returning, in Mansell's case) to chase the riches in F1. By the late '90s, Michael Andretti and Al Unser Jr. were already in their late thirties and their careers were starting to wane. Indy car racing, it could be said, somehow managed to skip an entire generation of stars.

After winning fifteen races and a pair of CART championships from 1996 to '98, Alex Zanardi should have been a superstar in America. But his success was overshadowed by the CART-IRL split, and he never got to race at Indianapolis, so it was no surprise that he was eager to return to Formula 1 in 1999. Still, CART appeared to be flying high, with $100 million in the bank generated by a successful initial public offering, record levels of sponsorship and manufacturer participation, and a robust schedule of twenty races spread across the US, Canada, Japan, Brazil, and Australia, with plans to expand into Mexico, England, and Germany on the horizon. The adverse effects of the split with the Indianapolis Motor Speedway were not yet glaringly obvious. With Federal Express as the CART Series title sponsor, it seemed a strong foundation was in place to launch an impactful new wave of Indy car stars as the millennium approached, with half a dozen promising young drivers poised to battle with veterans like Tracy, Andretti, Unser, and Jimmy Vasser to take over departing champion Zanardi's crown.

Among the younger set, Greg Moore was convinced that the CART series was not missing anything in terms of star power. "As far as the series lacking charisma, I don't think you can really say that," Moore opined. "The only thing it's going to lack compared to NASCAR is someone doing big, smoking burnouts if they won a race. Look at Max Papis—if anyone has got some charisma, that's a guy that's got a lot of charisma. Just different personalities: myself, Jimmy—the most laid-back guy of the series, just goes with the flow of things—Dario. There's a whole group of us. I think that the age of the drivers seems to be coming down a little bit, and so do the personalities. I'm twenty-three years old. Some of the other guys are twenty-three, twenty-four, twenty-five, twenty-six years old. We've got more of a younger person's attitude toward our series, which is go out, have a good time, and do the best you can. But also, off the racetrack try and maintain a friendship, which I think quite a few of us have done."

The responsibility of maintaining order and ensuring a fair fight among those contenders would fall on Wally Dallenbach's shoulders. And it would be for the last time. Dallenbach started plotting his retirement in 1996, eager to spend more time at his 200-acre Wood'n Handle ranch in Colorado that he financed with the prize money from his 1973 California 500 victory. But Wally was a difficult man to replace, and CART struggled to find a man with his unique blend of judgement, leadership, and humility. After a couple delays, it was finally determined that Dallenbach would step down at the end of the 1999 season, with the Marlboro 500 at California Speedway set to be his final event as Chief Steward, keeping those young lions in check.

MARIO ANDRETTI

"What makes a star in the public's eyes? It's hard to explain and yet it's clear. When you look back, all sports have these periods—mainly through the characters. There's the performance, but there's also how interesting certain people are. Look at golf, in the period of Jack Nicklaus and Arnold Palmer and so on and so forth. When you had rivalries, there was a lot of nasty talk that would be written about, and all that plays huge on how you impact the fans. Today, I was watching Scottie Scheffler. He's considered the number one golfer in the world, and he's got the personality of a brick. He makes a putt for an eagle and gets a big reaction from the fans, and he doesn't even acknowledge them or say thank you.

"A lot of it is about characters—the Bobby Unsers of this world—it all carries. That's what gets people interested. But here's the other thing to me: Just like you cannot teach fast, you cannot teach somebody to be charismatic. They either are or they're not. And that plays huge in many ways. You could be rough around the edges like A. J., but you were making a mark. Then on top of that, he wins, and he's a character like that. And people say, 'Oh, let's see what he's up to now.' It all comes down to the individual, him or herself, in my opinion.

"Hélio's character of showing so much emotion after a race really works for the fans. You could see other guys trying to copy climbing the fences and everything else, and that's a good thing. He carved his own niche. Montoya won right away, but he was a great character too. He was outspoken and everything else. You could not deny that Montoya was a force to be reckoned with, no question. Some of his attitudes along the way didn't help him. He ruffled feathers with

MARIO ANDRETTI

(CONT.)

Michael and other drivers along the way. Zanardi was another one that really took Indy car by storm. A great talent, with the right team at the right time. Tony Kanaan, another guy who cultivated something, especially at Indianapolis. All of that plays.

"I think Franchitti is a total class act in every way. A great race driver, a great ambassador. Unfortunately, I don't think he got his due credit as a race driver, mainly because of the times. That's what cheated him out of achieving more star power. Nevertheless, from my standpoint, my thoughts on Dario are totally positive. He was good for the sport; he was correct and a gentleman and a great champion that never got his due stardom that he deserved.

"The split is a fundamental aspect that threw a wrench into the situation. All of a sudden, you're talking about politics instead of the real racing itself. There were some changes that were hard to swallow. Where do you put the golden years in Indy car? I would say during the CART years, the '80s and early '90s. Then it all went to shit. Why? Because the attention was so focused on the negative. You pay a big price for that, and I think a lot of the powers that be probably don't realize once you sink a product how long it takes to get it back. That's what the generation that came on after the split had to deal with. They suffered, those poor guys, because too much attention was paid on that side, on the politics rather than the racing and everything that was going on at the tracks.

"A lack of promotion played in as well. I think all those things have to go hand in hand. Everything means something, either positive or negative. You've got to have all the shit together. You can't just have a good driver and not a good car. For any series to flourish, you must have good management. Look at what NASCAR did when Indy car hit the toilet with the split—they were smart enough to take advantage, and they became the supreme factor in motorsports in America. You talk to any non-racing fan, they know that racing exists, but they think of NASCAR. They don't think Indy car, which pisses me off. But those are the facts.

"Today, it's getting better, but it so tragic that you have unprecedented talent lined up in the series, but nobody knows about it.

If you take Scott Dixon somewhere, he probably won't be recognized. You don't know how much of a shame that is. When the cop stopped you and said, 'Who do you think you are, Stirling Moss?' All that is gone. I don't hear 'Who do you think you are, Dario Franchitti?' And these guys have won their share. They've won championships, they've won Indy . . . how do you explain that? Is there not an impact with the fans? What is it? I don't know what the formula is."

Alex Zanardi celebrates his last Indy car win at Surfers Paradise in 1998. *Paul Webb*

CHAPTER 2

THE DEPARTING KING

Alessandro Zanardi entered 1995 as an unemployed twenty-nine-year-old racing driver. He was broke and dispirited, fearful that his brief driving career was already over.

An inspired run to second place in the 1991 FIA Formula 3000 championship created the opportunity for Zanardi to compete in the final three races of the season in Formula 1 for the Jordan team. In one of those stories too bizarre to be true, Jordan's regular driver Bertrand Gachot was jailed in August 1991 for spraying CS gas (Mace) at a London taxi driver. His replacement for the Belgian Grand Prix was a relatively unknown German named Michael Schumacher who was driving Sauber-Mercedes sports cars at the time. Schumacher created a sensation by qualifying the Jordan-Ford seventh at Spa-Francorchamps, an intimidating circuit he had never seen before. Such a sensation, in fact, that Benetton F1 team boss Flavio Briatore immediately signed Schumacher to a long-term contract, and he duly appeared in a Benetton for the next F1 race, the Italian Grand Prix. He replaced Roberto Moreno, who drove the next two races for Jordan before being moved aside for Zanardi to finish out the season.

Schumacher finished fifth in his Benetton debut at Monza, and of course, went on to win the 1994 and '95 F1 World Championships for Benetton before adding five additional F1 crowns between 2000 and '04 with Ferrari. Meanwhile, Zanardi showed a lot of speed in his three-race Jordan cameo, but he also had substantial crashes in Japan and Australia, correlating a longtime stereotype about wild Italian drivers. Formula 1 is a cutthroat game, and Zanardi was branded fast but erratic after scoring only one point (for a sixth-place finish in the 1993 Brazilian Grand Prix) in twenty-five F1 starts between 1991 and '94, driving for Jordan, Minardi, and Lotus.

Zanardi had almost given up on himself, but Rick Gorne, the managing director of Reynard Racing Cars, kept the faith. Zanardi had entered the '91 F3000 campaign as an unheralded newcomer before winning two races to emerge as a favorite of Reynard, an aggressive emerging chassis constructor. Under the savvy leadership of Gorne and company founder Adrian Reynard, Reynard had grown in the space of a few years into the world's leading supplier of production racing cars. The company expanded into Indy cars in 1994. Gorne, at the same time, operated as an agent promoting Reynard-affiliated drivers to Indy car teams. Although Zanardi ran only one race in 1995 (a Porsche Supercup event that he won), Gorne encouraged him to travel to America to get his name and face out there at a couple races in the PPG IndyCar World Series.

The first driver Gorne helped get established in the US was Gil de Ferran (born November 11, 1967), who rose through the European formula car ladder (Formula Ford, Formula 3, Formula 3000) with Reynard and was a protégé of legendary Formula 1 champion Jackie Stewart. De Ferran pounded the pavement at Indy car races in 1994 and landed a ride in a Reynard with iconic American racer and car builder Jim Hall of Chaparral fame. As a rookie in 1995, the Paris-born Brazilian took a win at Laguna Seca Raceway to wrap up the season and was considered a rising hot prospect.

Chip Ganassi was the key investor that helped Reynard break into the US market. A Duquesne University graduate and son of a well-known Pittsburgh businessman, Ganassi's driving career was adversely affected by a serious Indy car accident at Michigan International Speedway in 1984. He partnered with Pat Patrick during Emerson Fittipaldi's 1989 CART championship campaign, before taking control of Patrick Racing in 1990 with sponsorship from Target, a rapidly growing discount store chain. Target/Chip Ganassi Racing earned Reynard's first Indy car win with driver Michael Andretti in the 1994 CART season opener, but Andretti returned to his former Indy car employer, Newman/Haas

Racing, at the end of the year when Nigel Mansell skipped back to F1. For '95, Ganassi fielded Reynard/Ford-Cosworths for Bryan Herta and Jimmy Vasser.

Herta (born May 23, 1970) won the 1993 Indy Lights championship and impressed in his first few races for A. J. Foyt's team in CART in '94 until he broke his pelvis in a big accident at Toronto. Another heavy crash on Carb Day at Indianapolis in '95, in which Herta sustained a concussion, also had a lasting effect on the young American.

Herta's struggles put Vasser in position to emerge as Ganassi's front runner. Born November 20, 1965, Vasser was a product of the American ladder system who excelled in Formula Atlantic. He impressed by driving Indy cars for smaller teams before landing with Ganassi when Chip acquired the assets of Jim Hayhoe's organization. Vasser outperformed Herta in '95, then put together a breakthrough '96 campaign in which he won four of the first five races—including the marquee U.S. 500 at Michigan that played out head-to-head with the Indianapolis 500 in the first year of the CART-IRL split—before holding off Andretti down the stretch to win the championship.

For 1996, Ganassi intended to switch to Firestone tires and Honda engines. But he was unhappy with Herta's performance in the second half of 1995. Ganassi had been one of the team owners Gorne had tried to sell on de Ferran when Gil was being shopped by Reynard, so at the season finale at Laguna Seca, Ganassi asked Gorne, "Do you have another de Ferran?"

Gorne replied: "I have someone even better than de Ferran—Alex Zanardi."

Ganassi said he had never heard of the Italian, but thanks to a bit of foresight on Gorne's part, Zanardi was already on the grounds at the scenic California road course. A meeting was hastily arranged, setting up a comparison test a few weeks later at Sebring International Raceway between Zanardi and Jeff Krosnoff, a thirty-one-year-old American who had been competing with some success in sports cars and Reynard Formula 3000 cars in Japan. Ganassi opted for Zanardi, while Krosnoff signed to drive a Toyota-powered Reynard for Arciero-Wells Racing in what would be the introductory season in the CART championship for both team and engine manufacturer.

BRYAN HERTA

"A. J. gave me my first shot, and he was just wonderful to me. Everybody pictures A. J. as this rough, gruff guy, and he can do that. He knows how to use that to his advantage. But he's also very warm, and I felt supported within the team. He was very nice to my family. The whole thing was all new to us and I had a great experience driving for A. J. When I got hurt and then had an offer to go to Ganassi the next year, that was probably one of my biggest mistakes—not staying another year with A. J. Ganassi were obviously a really good team, and it felt like a good step forward for me. So, I obviously jumped at that. But they needed somebody who could get in and deliver right away.

"I got the pole at Phoenix in '95, but I crashed at Indianapolis and had a massive concussion. For a long time after that, I wasn't right. But the biggest thing is that physically, I was still hurt from my crash at Toronto in 1994. That whole next year, I still had a substantial limp. I broke my pelvis in seven places and broke my femur, and I was back in an Indy car six months later. I wasn't fully healed. I could qualify well, but I really struggled with a lot of pain pushing the brake pedal, struggled to put enough force through my leg. It was really a year and a half before I felt I was in a place physically where I could drive the car again. But I had only done a few races in the sport, and I was afraid if I waited, if I didn't come back right away, I would disappear.

"I never shared the struggles I had; I just kind of kept it to myself. I was afraid of getting fired, so I didn't want to say, 'Guys, I'm struggling with this.' But if I had stayed with A. J., he would have understood. He'd been through it, and he would have been a lot more patient with me. But you learn as you go. At the point I drove for Chip, I think they had won only a couple Indy car races. It wasn't the massive juggernaut that they became yet. As a matter of fact, that was the first year they were running two cars, and Jimmy's was kind of a last-minute deal. They were still growing."

"Zanardi actually came as a referral from Malcolm Oastler [Reynard chief designer]," recalled Ganassi. "Mal told a story about when they went to Pau in Formula 3000. It was a place you couldn't test, there was no practice and then thirty-five minutes to qualify. Zanardi put the car on the pole, and he had never seen the place. Remember, qualifying was before practice so that was a tall order. Mal said that Zanardi impressed him time and time again in situations like that.

"When we met Zanardi, he was looking to redeem himself in the racing industry," Ganassi added. "We brought him over and we tested him on the same day that we tested Jeff Krosnoff. Honda didn't like Zanardi, to the point where they threatened to take our engines away. I'd be interested in what Robert Clarke had to say about that now."

Actually, Honda Performance Development (HPD) had already taken a shine to de Ferran. HPD regarded Gil's technical feedback so highly that it used him as its chief development driver from 1996 to '01. "We relied on him extensively," said Clarke, HPD's longtime president. "We found if you can tune an engine to Gil, it worked well for most drivers."

Those bold moves (the timely switch to Honda and Firestone and the "discovery" of Zanardi) produced a remarkable three-year run for Chip Ganassi Racing between 1996 and '98. Vasser won the '96 CART championship and U.S. 500, dominating the first half of the season before CART rookie Zanardi found his feet and won three times in the second half of the campaign to generally take over as Ganassi's front-running entry. In the final race of '96 at Laguna Seca Raceway, Zanardi hounded pole qualifier and leader Herta (who landed with Bobby Rahal's team following his single season with Ganassi), then made an incredible overtaking attempt at the famous Corkscrew sector on the last lap. Zanardi's car shot across the curbs and through the dirt in what looked like a desperate error, but he maintained control and emerged ahead to triumph over a crestfallen Herta. "The Pass" instantly became Indy car legend and lore.

In 1997, Zanardi won five times, including a three-race win streak in the summer, to easily top de Ferran and Vasser in the season standings. His first victory of the season came at Long Beach; after forcing de Ferran into making a mistake and crashing, Zanardi bested Mauricio

CHIP GANASSI

"In the early '90s, you had Carl Haas selling you Lolas, and you had Penske. Penske always had maybe one other team running their cars, which we did at one time. But you weren't going to get the latest and greatest from Carl, and you certainly weren't going to get the latest and greatest from Penske. You know, they used to take me on their airplanes to the owner's meetings, sell me cars and sell me parts. Then suddenly you start beating them, they don't invite you on their jets anymore.

"We were right on the cusp there of doing well, and I had an opportunity. I said 'Wait a minute, these Reynard guys understood aerodynamics and small formula cars'—they had done very well, were really dominating the small formula, F3, F3000. Everywhere they went, they won. It was kind of a natural thing for them to come to Indy cars. Reynard North America was my company, we were the North American distributor.

"It's hard to put into context what was going on in the industry at the time. If you look at CART in 1996, at the final race of the season at Laguna Seca where Vasser won the championship and Zanardi did 'The Pass,' you had three different chassis manufacturers, three drivers, and two brands of tires that could have won the championship. You had Penske with Al Jr., Mercedes, and Goodyear, Carl had Michael and Goodyear but with Lola and Ford, and we had Reynard, Honda, and Firestone. Just think of all the thousands and thousands of people—just in those companies—that had a vested interest in winning that race and winning that championship. Really spectacular. It was a little more complicated back then—it wasn't just 'get in your car and go.'

"Those days, '96 through 2000, our team was just on fire then. It was one sort of history-making event after another. They were really heady times for the series, for the team . . . Honda and Reynard were doing well, we seemed to be able to attract drivers, anybody we wanted. When you can have any driver in the paddock that you want, that's a big thing for a team, and a big change for us at the time. Vasser and Zanardi set the table for that."

Gugelmin to take a comfortable win. Overjoyed by his triumph, Zanardi stopped his car at the end of the Shoreline Drive straight at the entrance to Turn One and spun a series of celebratory donuts. It became a trademark spectacle that was often repeated over the next year and a half as the talented Italian continued to produce mind-boggling performances.

At the 1997 Cleveland Grand Prix, Zanardi led from the start, but was dropped to twenty-first place after a communication mix-up saw him enter closed pits. He drove back through the field, passing Herta and de Ferran in the closing laps. At Long Beach in 1998, Alex again fell to the bottom of the order, this time after an early collision. But he fought back and muscled by Herta and Dario Franchitti in dramatic late fashion to win.

In press conferences, Zanardi turned on the charm, mixing humility and braggadocio in equal measures in his thoughtful (and sometimes rambling) remarks. As Mario Andretti said, "He has charisma, the sharpest wit, extreme intelligence, and a gift of gab enjoyed especially by the media." Zanardi finally even won over Honda, which created a limited "Zanardi Edition" of the NSX sports car in his honor.

While Michael Andretti delivered the Ganassi organization its first win and Vasser its first championship, it was Zanardi who established Target/Chip Ganassi Racing as the juggernaut it remains today. "I could point back to 1995 and say we were already mature," Ganassi said. "We had the same people in '96 as we had in '94, but suddenly we were winning races. We just put the right guys in the car. It was the perfect storm at the time, and the rest is history."

In total, Zanardi won fifteen of his fifty-one starts from 1996 to '98, a level of domination that earned him something extremely rare for a driver in his early thirties: a second crack at Formula 1. For most of the '98 season it was an open secret that Alex would join Williams Grand Prix Engineering, the dominant F1 team of the '90s which as recently as 1997 had won the F1 World Championship with ex-CART star Jacques Villeneuve. For a man who felt he had unfinished business in F1, it looked like his time racing Indy cars had paid serious dividends. Zanardi took one last win at Surfers Paradise, Australia, besting Franchitti in a straight fight, then went out fighting tooth and nail with

JIMMY VASSER

"Zanardi wasn't unknown—we knew him for a spectacular crash at Spa in the Lotus F1. He had some pretty big shunts that sidelined him, but Rick Gorne and Adrian Reynard helped him with Chip and got him the test. Immediately you could see that he was special, but he had a lot to learn about IndyCar at the time and a lot of his focus at first was learning the ovals.

"Winning four of the first six races was the '96 championship for me. I struggled a bit in the middle of the year. I had a hard shunt in qualifying at Detroit, backed it into the wall in that fast lefthand sweeper by the fountain, with no tires there on the wall. It was a real stinger – I remember when I came to a stop, my right arm was doing circles in front of my helmet, but I couldn't control it. Then I got vertigo in the race. The last couple laps, I could barely get the car back to the pits.

"We tested at Mid-Ohio after Detroit, and again, I barely made it back to the pits. Luckily for me there was a two week break before Portland, because otherwise I would have missed a race or two with the vertigo. It was something I was still dealing with in the midseason. I struggled for pace and just wasn't myself. We really didn't have the concussion protocols that we have now. I'd lost midseason form, so my championship was kind of anchored by the start of the season.

"Then Zanardi went on to win the next two championships and pretty much destroyed myself. In '98, we were battling between the two of us, and I couldn't keep pace with him. I won two or three races that year, but he was just unbelievable. As a team, we went one-two in the championship, and that for me, is the greatest year in my racing career as a driver, for sure. And Alex and I, over the course of the three years that we raced together, developed one of the best friendships of a lifetime. We had the most fun. It was competitive, but truly, I was happy for him when he did well and won, and I felt the same from him to me when I did well. He was truly happy for me."

Vasser and Greg Moore in that memorable million-dollar 1998 season finale at Fontana.

Although he loved his three years with Ganassi competing in the CART Series and achieved more success than he could have ever dreamed of, Zanardi could not overcome his regret about not performing at the same level in F1.

"It was a hard decision to leave, because I had everything a driver could dream of with Target/Chip Ganassi Racing," he said. "I was with a team that loved me—each single member, not just Mr. Ganassi. Every time I walked in in the morning, they would make me feel like if they had a million options, I would still be their pick. That's a great motivating factor. The accomplishments we've achieved with this great team have been above every expectation by far. On the other hand, you could say, 'What more do you want?' You want to try to enter into a new challenge. That is what Formula One represents for me.

"My life is changing," he added. "Everything changes in life. I feel at peace with myself, because I know that I am leaving the team when nobody is angry. I feel, for me, departing, that I have paid my duty and now it's time, as everything changes in life, that it's time to try to do something else."

The outgoing champion rated Franchitti, Vasser, and Moore as the favorites to take over his crown.

"Jimmy is capable of winning even when people are not expecting him to win," Zanardi said. "He may not look very strong in the first part of the race, but then all of a sudden, he comes out. Greg, instead, wants to bring home always what he has in his mind prior to the event, which is to win the race. Sometimes in order to do that he leaves something on the table. But other times, not being happy, he does bring it home first. If he finds the right average, he will be a dangerous customer.

"Dario seems to be the right mixture between Jimmy and Greg: tremendous speed, and more than that, he's young too. Every race that goes by he seems to learn. He is already a star, but he will be even brighter next year, I'm sure. He just has to learn how to deal with the ovals better, especially the short ones."

George Dario Marino Franchitti was born May 19, 1973, in West Lothian, Scotland, just west of Edinburgh. His parents owned an ice cream shop, and his father George was an enthusiastic club racer. Dario was given a go-kart when he was three years old, and at age ten, he began competing in junior events at the West of Scotland Kart Club.

Franchitti showed enough promise in karting to graduate to small formula cars, and like de Ferran, he benefitted from the tutelage of fellow Scotsman (and three-time Formula 1 World Champion) Jackie Stewart. Driving for Paul Stewart Racing (PSR), Franchitti won the 1991 Formula Vauxhall Junior title at age seventeen and followed it up by claiming the Formula Vauxhall Lotus championship two years later.

After finishing fourth in the 1994 British Formula 3 series for PSR, Franchitti was out of money and lacking options to continue in F3 or step up to Formula 3000. Then he had a stroke of good fortune: He was recruited to a new Young Driver program being established by Mercedes-Benz, which assigned him to the D2 AMG-Mercedes team in the DTM (Deutsche Tourenwagen Meisterschaft, or German Touring Car Championship) and International Touring Car (ITC) championships. These series featured big factory budgets, high-tech, high-downforce cars, and an impressive group of seasoned drivers, including Keke Rosberg, Klaus Ludwig, Hans-Joachim Stuck, Nicola Larini, Alessandro Nannini, and Manuel Reuter.

Franchitti was teamed with German veteran Bernd Schneider, and he loved the experience. He won at Suzuka and finished fourth in the 1996 ITCC for Mercedes, but at the end of the year, he was twenty-three years old and again at a career crossroads. Once again Mercedes, this time through its engine building arm Ilmor Engineering, provided a career path in Indy cars.

"My DTM teammate Jan Magnussen had filled in for the Hogan-Penske team in CART when Emerson Fittipaldi got hurt in the summer of '96," Franchitti said. "He came back absolutely raving about the experience. Then Roger Penske came over to Stars & Cars, the Mercedes motorsport year-end banquet. We discussed me going over to the US and being Team Penske's test driver and doing some races. I just sat there listening, wide-eyed. I had another conversation at Stars & Cars with Paul Morgan from Ilmor. He asked what I was going to do after DTM, and I said, 'What I really want is to go to America.' He said, 'Whoa!

I might be able to help a bit there. Leave it with me.' Sure enough, he phones me in January '97 and says, 'I spoke to Carl Hogan, I've done the deal. You've got to go test for him. If Carl likes you, you're in.'"

Franchitti passed the audition and was signed to drive a Reynard/Mercedes for Hogan Racing. Hogan, who fielded racing teams in the SCCA Can-Am Challenge and Formula 5000 in the early 1970s, was running his own car independently for the first time in the CART series after splitting with recent partners Bobby Rahal and Roger Penske. Hogan Racing was a small, single-car team, but equipped with the increasingly important Firestone tires, the Reynard/Mercedes package was extremely competitive. Dario showed plenty of speed in '97, earning pole position at Toronto and often qualifying well, but he struggled to finish races. Still, Franchitti's performances in the Hogan car caught the eye of fellow team owner Barry Green.

A self-trained mechanic from western Australia who rose to the level of team manager in the Can-Am and CART championships, Green entered team ownership in partnership with Gerald Forsythe in 1993 to form a Canadian driver development program for Imperial Tobacco and its Player's brand. After a year grooming driver Jacques Villeneuve in CART's Formula Atlantic support championship, Forsythe-Green Racing graduated with Villeneuve to CART's PPG IndyCar World Series.

Green and Forsythe split after the 1994 season and Forsythe established his own Forsythe Racing outfit that would compete with the renamed Team Green. As part of a complicated business arrangement, Green maintained Villeneuve's contract and the Player's sponsorship for the 1995 CART season, with Forsythe taking over the Canadian driver development program to field Player's backed cars in Indy Lights for Greg Moore and Claude Bourbonnais. Villeneuve duly won the '95 Indianapolis 500 and CART championship and announced he would switch to Formula 1 to drive for Williams-Renault the following year. At the same time, twenty-year-old Moore absolutely dominated Indy Lights, the other top open-wheel feeder series to the CART championship.

The Player's sponsorship transferred in full to Forsythe to run Moore in CART in 1996, while Green fielded Raul Boesel with sponsorship from Brahma beer. Green then announced an ambitious program with Brown and Williamson Tobacco's Kool brand to groom American drivers for the CART series. Parker Johnstone was the chosen driver for 1997, but he had a poor season, and with no obvious quality American drivers available to replace him at year's end, the American development program was quietly dropped.

"Kool had done an incredible job entertaining hundreds of guests at every event, literally raising the game in sponsor experiences," said Green. "We had all the elements, but what we did not have was one of the best drivers. Dario impressed me and many other owners, and I felt like we would be back in the winner's circle when he agreed to join us."

Green's commitment to winning was further demonstrated when he convinced Kool to expand its sponsorship to a second car when Paul Tracy suddenly became available at the conclusion of the '97 season. Only twenty-eight years old, the Toronto native was already a six-year Indy car veteran boasting thirteen race wins for Team Penske and Newman/Haas Racing. But Tracy could be a loose cannon both on and off the track, which led to Roger Penske unexpectedly voiding the Canadian's contract shortly after the 1997 season ended.

While Tracy struggled all year to adapt to a Reynard/Honda on Firestone tires after years of driving Mercedes-powered Penskes on Goodyear, Franchitti finished on the podium at Long Beach in 1998 in his third race for Team Green. Following his breakthrough victory at Road America in August, he posted additional wins at Vancouver and Houston. Franchitti started from pole position five times and ended the year third in the CART standings behind the Ganassi duo of Zanardi and Vasser.

By the late '90s, the Canadian driver development program was really starting to bear fruit for Player's and Forsythe. Moore was born April 22, 1975, in Maple Ridge, then a town of about thirty thousand located on the eastern edge of greater Vancouver; his father, Ric, was a former sports car racer who operated a Chrysler/Plymouth dealership. Ric Moore hired a local mechanic named Steve Challis to prepare a Formula Ford car for Greg, and the fresh-faced kid was such a phenom that he was granted special dispensation to advance directly to Indy Lights in 1993 prior to his eighteenth birthday. Driving for a small team

PAUL TRACY

"Right after the Michigan race in the summer of 1997, I did a test at this little road course for three days in the Penske. Halfway through the second day, a Rahal truck rolled up and they unloaded a Reynard with a Mercedes motor into the tent. It took me literally five laps to go half a second quicker than I had done in two days of testing in the Penske. We were running Goodyears, and then at the end of the day, they had one set of Firestones that we threw on the car. By the end of the day, with thirty or forty laps on the Reynard, I was almost a second quicker than I had run in two days in the Penske car.

"After the Fontana race was over, I got called to Roger Penske's motorhome in the little boardroom that Roger had meetings in. It was me and a couple engineers, Teddy Mayer, and John Travis, the Penske designer. They're like, 'What do you think we should do next year?' I said, 'Well if you get that Reynard and Firestones with our engine program, that would be a home run.' I was just being honest and candid, maybe I wasn't politically all that smart, because I was only thinking about 'What do I need to do to win races?'

"About a week later, I get a call from my manager, who says, 'I got a call from Penske, and they want to meet us at some hotel in San Diego with a sponsor. Can you fly over here right now, on the next flight?' We both thought something didn't sound right about it. We get there, go into the hotel room, and there's no Roger. It was Teddy Mayer and one of Roger's lawyers. They handed me my walking papers. . . . That was two weeks after the season ended, and all the rides were gone. My manager pointed out that I had three years left on my contract, and they were like, 'Pound sand.' My manager threw out a threat of 'We'll sue you,' and they basically said, 'Good luck. Go ahead and try.' Which would probably have been a bad idea. I'm not that dumb!

"Within twenty-four hours I had a ride with Barry Green, but it was a huge financial haircut for me because they didn't have any budget for a second car. They made it happen through Honda and Kool, but it was probably a third of what I was getting paid by Penske. I think my anticipation was high to do well in '98. I thought it would be easy, but when I got in the car, it wasn't like anything I had ever driven before. I came from Penske, with a different car, different tires, and different engine. It just handled different, it acted different, the power delivery was different. It took me a long time to adapt. . . . I got more and more frustrated, and tried harder, and made mistakes."

organized by Ric Moore, Greg won three Lights races in 1994 before being drafted into the Player's program for '95. Challis was part of the package as Moore climbed the ladder, functioning as his race engineer.

"My dad was the team owner, from go-karts all the way through the end of 1994—team owner, manager, sponsor-finder, and pretty much the title sponsor in '93 and '94," Greg recalled to *Indy Car* magazine in 1998. "That was part of the growing up process. Once Player's came along in '95, it took a huge load off us. We were going into the '95 season as our own team, but there was still the question of 'Where are we going to find the money?' We were going to have to win every race, and kind of go race by race to go to the races off that prize money. That was our plan, but Jerry Forsythe and Player's came along, and we had that storybook season.

"For sure, [Ric] is still my manager," Moore added. "I think it's difficult for him because he's my manager, he's my dad, but he's also one of my best friends. I think it's difficult on him because you go to a race weekend, and say if I'm having a bad day, as a manager, he wants to jump all over my case and say, 'Why aren't you doing better?' and

DARIO FRANCHITTI

"In '97 with Hogan, there were a lot of bits that went well, but some fuckups too, whether it was the team or me. I was surprised I got interest. But by the start of '98, I realized with Barry's well-organized team with all those bits—the Firestones, the Honda engine, the Reynard chassis, the engineers—this could be good. At the time, I said we found all these ways not to win races. But starting with Road America, the wins came in a bit of a cascade after that from the midpoint of the season. Then it was going toe to toe with Zanardi.

"It's interesting, I felt over one lap I was probably quicker. But man, in a race, he was just unbelievable and that combination of him and the Ganassi guys was so hard to beat. End of '98, I knew he was going to F1, so at the last road or street course of the year at Surfers, I really wanted to beat him. I qualified on pole there, and he won the race. They beat us in the pits and Zanardi did Zanardi things, and they won the race."

'What are you going to do tomorrow to make improvements?' Then as a dad, he wants to say, 'That's okay, you'll do better tomorrow.' I think sometimes that's difficult for him."

Unlike most Indy car drivers, who move to Indianapolis, the location of their team shop, or to a warmer climate like Florida, Moore chose to maintain his residence in his hometown of Maple Ridge. And while he lived a jet-set lifestyle on the road with his driver buddies, Moore remained close with the peers he grew up with back in British Columbia.

"I first met Greg when we were sixteen or seventeen years old," recalled his friend Al Robbie. "I was refereeing hockey, and he was coaching his stepbrother James's hockey team. About three weeks later, I was out with the guys from my hockey team, and we stopped at a McDonald's or something. Greg was there, and Stu, the goalie on my hockey team, introduced me to him. A bunch of our guys went to school with him. We ended up hanging out all night, at the local arcade or something. From there, we just spent more and more time through the grade twelve graduation. We were friends from then on.

"In the Spring of 1993, Greg called and said, 'Hey, you guys wanna come by the house? We're going to fire up the Indy Lights car!'" Robbie continued. "Ric bought the Indy Lights car and Steve Challis and Kent Holden, who was previously one of Ric's mechanics, were working, putting the car together, basically in Ric's garage in the subdivision. They were large one-acre lots, and after they fired up the Lights car, people were driving up the driveway to see what it was. I'd never seen a race car up close before, and it was pretty crazy to see. It was around the start of '94 when I actually saw how everybody realized what his potential was and where things were going to go.

"We would often play pool at a local place called Zoo Cafe and we would always play for a toonie [a Canadian two-dollar coin]," he added. "The stakes got higher, to wherever who lost two out of three had to buy dinner—usually McDonald's or something. I said, 'Remember, once you make it to the big leagues, please don't change.' He goes, 'If I ever act like my head is getting too big, you're allowed to punch me.' That was the rule and the agreement. 'If it ever seems like I can't fit in my shoes, you have the green light to hit me with a punch in the face.' I never did. Greg was the same with the group he hung out with from Maple Ridge when he came back from a race. He was always very inclusive, always wanted to have the most people attend and have as much fun as they could."

Moore smashed most of the Indy Lights records his countryman Tracy set five years earlier during a crushing 1995 season that produced ten wins in twelve starts for Forsythe Racing. Greg's graduation to the CART series with Forsythe and Player's was a no-brainer, and he very nearly won his very first Indy car race at Homestead Miami Speedway in March of '96. Clearly the fastest man on the track, only a rookie mistake (Moore passed a car under caution and the penalty put him a lap behind) prevented the twenty-year-old from winning his Indy car debut. That immense skill and confidence on ovals was a sign of things to come. Jimmy Vasser shared his memory of Moore's very first race in the CART series.

"When I won at Homestead in '96, we were quick at that original track, always good there," Vasser said. "The race came to us. I got Gil de Ferran on a restart, and then winding the race down, I've got a reasonable lead. I'm looking in my mirrors and I see this light blue car coming. They said, 'Don't worry, that's Moore. He's a lap down.' A couple laps later, he blows by me on the outside of Turn Three. I thought, 'Jesus Christ!' and then he went off in the distance. Thank God he was a lap down. I thought, 'This guy's got some stones.' He really lived out there on the outside a lot."

Franchitti has his own recollection of Moore's remarkable breakout performance at Homestead 1996. "I used to sit with Norbert Haug [Mercedes-Benz motorsport director from 1990 to 2012] over a beer after DTM races," Dario recounted. "The DTM after-party would be kicking off, but if there was an Indy car race running somewhere, we would find a quiet place and watch it. That was my first exposure to Greg—Norbert would say, 'This kid is good, look at this!' I remember that first race at Homestead where it was like he was in a different lane than everybody else, or the track was a different shape for him. It was like, 'Holy shit, this guy is phenomenal!'

"At my first group test at Homestead in '97 where there were more than a couple cars, Greg was there," he continued. "I remember exactly where I was the first time I spoke to him. In the back of the Homestead paddock, there's the first of the right-hand hairpins on the infield road course. I was standing right there, and Greg was there. I was never one to walk up to somebody and say hello, but I felt I knew this guy. I thought he was such a great driver, so I went up and said hello, and he's like, 'Oh, hello!' And that was the start of this friendship."

Like Franchitti, it took Moore over a year to find his way to Victory Lane in an Indy car; for Greg, the first win came at the Milwaukee Mile in 1997 in his twenty-third start. Oddly enough, they both also won their very next race. Moore's second win came just a week later on Detroit's Belle Isle street course, when the leading PacWest Racing entries driven by Mauricio Gugelmin and Mark Blundell famously ran out of fuel on the final lap. But Moore finished only two of the final nine races down the stretch in 1997 and faded to ninth in the point standings.

Moore's '98 season started well with top six finishes in the first six events, including an audacious pass of Zanardi for the win at the Emerson Fittipaldi Speedway "roval" in Rio de Janeiro.

"He won Rio with a 'Zanardi-style move,' which really stung," wrote Zanardi in his memoir, *My Sweetest Victory*. "Greg moved into my slipstream. We came up to the corner, and he outbraked me on the outside—he certainly didn't lack courage—and came low looking for the only possible gap. I widened my line to avoid contact, he took advantage, and with only two laps left, I couldn't catch up. Greg took that race away from me. We were reaching the halfway point of the 1998 championship and Greg looked like my most dangerous opponent."

The rest of Moore's '98 campaign was blighted by issues with the problematic Mercedes-Benz IC108E engine, a tiny gem of a power plant that pushed the envelope of available Indy car technology too far. The Ilmor/Mercedes "E" engine's struggles created serious problems for several teams, but Moore's mastery of oval racing continued unabated, with a win in the first Handford Device race at Michigan Speedway later in the summer and second place in the million-dollar season finale at Fontana. His performances were often still electrifying, but by the end of 1998, Franchitti's rapid development had moved the Scotsman ahead of Moore as Indy car racing's next likely generational star.

But there was a wild card in the mix: Who would take over the Ganassi car for Alex Zanardi? Like so many other international road racers, Zanardi had arrived in the CART series virtually unknown in America, with little fanfare—just another failed Formula 1 wannabe. His performances with Target/Chip Ganassi Racing opened eyes and changed perceptions. In the space of three years, he had become a champion and a fan favorite in America, while also creating a path for his return to F1. Now he was departing a successful situation, leaving a prime open seat with what was, at the time, one of worldwide motorsport's hottest organizations. Could Chip Ganassi capture lightning in a bottle one more time with Zanardi's replacement?

Rookie Juan Pablo Montoya took Indy car racing by storm in 1999. *Michael Levitt*

CHAPTER 3

THE PUNK

Skip Barber was a record-setting SCCA road racing national champion in the 1960s who made a handful of Formula 1 starts in 1971 and '72. Three years later, he opened the Skip Barber Racing School and became renowned as a performance driving instructor and judge of young racing talent.

Barber reasoned that the best way to identify the best drivers was to pit them in equal equipment. From 1986 to 2003, the Barber Pro Series was one of the first forms of "spec" racing in America, featuring identical single-seat formula cars powered by modified Saab and later Dodge production car engines, all maintained and prepared by Skip Barber Racing. By the mid-90s, the Barber Pro Series established a solid reputation after launching successful racing careers for the likes of Robbie Buhl, Bryan Herta, and Kenny Bräck, who went on to star in Formula 3000 before landing with A. J. Foyt Racing in the Indy Racing League. Bräck, born in Sweden on March 21, 1966, restored respectability to Foyt's operation, winning three races and the IRL championship in 1998, followed by a win in the 1999 Indianapolis 500.

The 1994 Barber Pro Series was fought out between American Mark Hotchkis and a pair of Colombians: nineteen-year-old Juan Pablo Montoya and Diego Guzman, who in his third year in the series matched Hotchkis with three wins to claim the title. Guzman and Hotchkis advanced to Indy Lights the following season, but by the end of '98, both were effectively out of racing.

Montoya's architect father, Pablo, funded his son's successful karting career starting at age four and invested in a three-day course for Juan at the Skip Barber Racing School at Sonoma Raceway when he turned seventeen. Vic Elford, the great sports car racer, was a Barber School instructor, and he immediately singled out Montoya as a future star.

Montoya won his first Barber Pro start at Miami's Bicentennial Park and added another victory later in the year at Mid-Ohio Sports Car Course to wind up a close third in the standings. At that point, Juan Pablo decided "it was time to get serious." He landed on the radar of Jackie and Paul Stewart, who fielded him in Formula Vauxhall for Paul Stewart Racing following the path blazed by Gil de Ferran, Dario Franchitti, and Formula 1 star David Coulthard. After struggling initially, some tutelage from Jackie Stewart helped the young Colombian finish the season on an upswing with a pair of wins.

He graduated to the British Formula 3 series with Paul Stewart Racing, winning two races, and again finishing in the top five in the championship. That was enough to advance to Formula 3000 in 1997 with RSM Team Marko, co-owned by former racer Dr. Helmut Marko prior to his involvement with Red Bull Racing. Montoya won twice, finished second in the championship to Ricardo Zonta, and earned a testing role with the Williams F1 team. In 1998, now driving for David Sears's Super Nova Racing, Montoya won the F3000 championship with ease and, in his mind anyway, was ready to step up to Formula 1.

Unfortunately, there turned out to be no seats available for '99. Williams had decided to pair Alex Zanardi with Ralf Schumacher—the younger brother of then two-time F1 champion Michael Schumacher. The team's rationale was that it wanted a driver with recent F1 experience to offset Zanardi, who had been absent from that arena for five years. In addition, 1999 was a bridge season for Williams as BMW prepared to enter Formula 1 as an engine manufacturer in 2000, and the recruitment of Schumacher was strongly driven by his German nationality. In any case, Montoya was the odd man out and a plan was hatched to place him with Ganassi's Indy car team.

"When Zanardi wanted to go over to F1, Frank Williams and I struck up a relationship, and there was another guy called David Sears involved," Ganassi said. "David Sears had a Formula 3000 team, which when combined with my CART team and Frank's F1 team made for a nice little ladder. Montoya wasn't quite ready for Formula 1 yet, so he came over here."

Well, it's not quite that simple. Ganassi had to sell the notion of bringing on board a promising but rough-around-the-edges youngster to replace the cultured Zanardi to sponsor Target, to his team management, and perhaps most importantly, to Morris Nunn, the engineer widely credited with turning Zanardi into a star in the CART series. There was also the small matter of Tony Kanaan believing he already had a contract to drive the No. 4 car in 1999.

"Chip Ganassi hired me," Kanaan declared, many years later. "He bought my contract out from Steve Horne. Then he went to see Zanardi's first test at Williams, and Frank Williams convinced him to take Montoya for free. So, Chip comes back and basically says, 'Sorry, we can't do the deal.' But the contract was signed, so what am I going to do? It was my first year, I was young. We just undid the deal. Thank God Steve had not hired anyone, so I stayed with him. But in '99, Montoya was in the car I was supposed to be in."

Nunn had little enthusiasm for starting over with a raw rookie like Montoya who had no Indy car and almost zero oval racing experience. But then again, he hadn't been all that enamored by the idea of working with Zanardi at first, and they ended up having an almost telepathic relationship. Nunn also heaped praise on Ganassi team leader Jimmy Vasser.

"Jimmy is as good as anybody on the ovals, and when they get it right, also on the road courses," Nunn said. "I have never ever seen two drivers get along as well as Zanardi and Vasser did, and that was a huge part of the success of our team. They had fun together and were genuinely happy for each other's success. After Michigan last year, when Greg Moore pipped us, we really looked at that. Both guys wanted to win, because we didn't have any team orders for one or the other. In them fighting amongst themselves to win, Moore got an incredible draft and went by both of them. So, in Fontana, you saw what happened there. The two guys worked really well together. In his last race, Alex would have liked to win, but when he saw the situation, Alex helped Jimmy a little bit. When they made the last restart, Alex let Jimmy go and kind of kept Greg back a little bit. They just worked incredibly together.

"Now we've got Jimmy and Juan Pablo, and we're trying to do that the same," he added. "Jimmy has now signed a three-year deal, and we didn't want the old situation where the driver is financially sound and then he sits back a little bit. I told Jimmy I was looking for someone to keep him on his toes. He agreed with that. I said, 'We're going to get somebody to push you like crazy.'"

Ganassi convinced Nunn to make the trip to Europe to watch Montoya test at the Barcelona circuit in Spain by splurging for tickets to fly on Concorde. By the time they returned to America, Nunn had shelved thoughts of retirement and was ready to get to work.

"I watched the kid for a couple days, went all over the circuit, and I was astounded by his car control," Nunn marveled. "It was almost like his hands would move before the car would move, like the correction would come before anything happened. His reactions were so quick. Alex had won a lot of races and was a star in CART, but it didn't faze this kid at all. The other thing is he was quicker than Alex. He could get to the edge immediately and stay there. He was very consistent. When I got back home, I told the boys, 'This kid can win by Long Beach.'"

Not that Montoya was impressed with what had transpired. "When they told me they were going to go with Zanardi and Schumacher I couldn't believe it," he said. "The final insult was when they said, 'We're testing in Barcelona with Zanardi, and we want you to come and help him.' Of course, I was faster than Zanardi. And who should turn up at the Barcelona test but Chip Ganassi, with his engineer, Morris Nunn. I guess Frank had made some arrangement with Ganassi. I never really found out what the deal was, but in effect I was switched with Zanardi."

If anything, Nunn was even more impressed after guiding Montoya through his first Indy car test sessions in one of Ganassi's Reynard/Hondas. As the old adage goes, you can rein a fast driver in, but you can't teach a steady driver how to be fast. The team's biggest concern was Montoya's near total lack of experience on ovals. Contrary to the prevailing thought of the "Split" era, CART was increasing its emphasis on ovals in the late '90s, and the 1999 schedule featured nine ovals out of twenty total races.

"The kid is very young and very confident, and he definitely has all the speed you need," Nunn said. "Juan wants to drive fast every lap. He

CHIP GANASSI

"We went on the Concorde not necessarily to see Montoya, but to see Zanardi drive the Williams car at Catalunya. And, oh, by the way, Williams had this young kid who was really fast who they felt we should talk to. He was in the on-deck circle for Williams as their test driver. Frank didn't really have a spot for him, so he said, 'Why don't you take this guy Montoya? I'll keep him under contract, but you take him for a year or two and bring him along as a driver.'

"You just don't go from Skip Barber to being a race driver for Williams. There was no iRacing in those days, and no place else you could learn. There was no replacement for being in races and learning things like pit stops and points and how a car changes over a fuel run with more weight or less weight. All those things, you don't learn without doing them. I think Frank realized that Indy car racing was a good stop-off point if you had a driver you wanted to have in your stable long-term for Formula 1, but you really didn't have a place for them for a year or so. Indy car was a good place to do a couple semesters, if you will, to keep him sharp. And that's exactly what it turned out to be.

"Any new driver is a big risk, and Montoya was a bigger risk because he didn't have the maturity that Zanardi had at the time. So that was a bit of a risk and a bit of a learning process for both of us."

JUAN PABLO MONTOYA

"I was hoping I was going to be in Formula 1, but I wasn't sure. I do have to say I was disappointed I wasn't, because I felt I did a really good job as a test driver. I felt I was really competitive and everything. When the news came that I wasn't getting the seat, it was tough because they were getting two new drivers and I was their test driver, so I would have been one of the obvious choices. And I wasn't. I was pretty pissed off about it, to be honest. But when I got the chance with Ganassi, it was really good. It was all orchestrated by Frank Williams at the time. A lot of people didn't know that—I didn't even know that. It ended up working really well, and I made a lot of my career through Chip. That worked out pretty well."

isn't anywhere near as technical as Alex was. He reminds me a little bit of Michael Andretti. He just wants to go quick and stands on the gas and wants to enjoy his racing. I keep saying, 'Listen, you've got to feel the car,' but so far, he hasn't done anything wrong. He's done about ten days on the oval at Homestead, and on the last test he ended up as quick as Jimmy. The only question is whether he has the brains to put it all together and win. We won't know that until we've done a couple of races.

"We're putting no pressure on him at all," Nunn continued. "We keep trying to tell him there's absolutely no pressure on you on the ovals, we just want you to learn. The only pressure will come from himself. All race drivers put a lot of pressure on themselves. He'll be thinking he wants to win, and we all know how difficult ovals are. He's gone incredibly quick in all the testing so far, and touch wood, hasn't made any mistakes. But he seems to be lacking a little bit in the patience department. That's just the way he is. We played golf the other day and he doesn't even take a practice swing. He just walks up and cannons the ball."

Montoya's insouciance was present from his very first appearance on the CART scene. Tim Cindric, who in 1999 was team manager for Team Rahal, remembers an early test at Firebird Motorsport Park, a popular road course testing venue outside of Phoenix.

Cindric was born in Indianapolis on April 20, 1968. His father worked for esteemed Indy car engine builder Herb Porter, and Tim entered the racing industry soon after graduating from Rose Hulman Institute of Technology in Terre Haute, Indiana. He landed a job with Ohio-based Truesports as the production manager for that team's in-house chassis project, then followed his boss and mentor Scott Roembke when what was then known as Rahal-Hogan Racing took over the project in 1993. A year later, Cindric was offered the team manager role.

"I tried to turn down the job," Cindric related. "Are you sure you want me—four years out of school, twenty-five years old? But I told them I'd give it a shot. I worked with the competition side of it, and Scott Roembke basically dealt with the business side of it. He was general manager, and we both reported to Bobby. I was Bobby's race strategist from 1995 through 1998, then I transitioned over to Max Papis's car when he came on board and Scott was doing the strategy on Bryan Herta's car. We were two guys from Indiana, kind of living their dreams running a race team for one of the biggest names in motorsports. He grew up on the east side of Indy, I grew up on the west side; we were similar in age and certainly we were both big IU fans." Sadly, Roembke passed away in 2012 at the age of fifty-one.

Back in 1999, Cindric had little reason to pay attention to Montoya at that preseason Firebird test.

"I didn't even know his name or who he was," Cindric said. "That track was flat, and there was a lot of dirt if you got off track. He was testing Chip's car, and he would go through the dirt and kick up all the dust and shit every lap. All the other drivers were mad about it, right? Finally, we went down there and talked to him about it, and he didn't care at all. 'Hey, you gotta do what you gotta do. You should just be faster.' A total smart-ass. I thought, 'This kid is gonna be good, but wait until he gets to an oval.' But he showed everybody on the oval—that all carried over."

The young rookie radiated an aura of confidence, but he still found stepping into a 900-horsepower CART car at Homestead-Miami Speedway for his first oval test was an eye-opener.

"The car is like a bigger version of a Formula 3000 car," he recalled. "It just had more power, more grip, it just did everything better. It was good fun. I only did one Barber Dodge race on an oval at New Hampshire, and I remember how sketchy that was. The first oval test for Ganassi was good, and I was lucky because I had a big snap at the end of the test. I was getting really cocky, and the car stepped out and I was lucky not to crash, to be honest. That was an 'Oh shit!' moment."

Montoya had the advantage of taking over the departed champion's car, but there were plenty of other contenders for the FedEx Championship Series crown besides the obvious favorites in Vasser, Franchitti, Moore, de Ferran, and Paul Tracy. This was the height of the CART-IRL split, and CART still strongly held the upper hand entering 1999, with a total of twenty-seven entries. Manufacturer competition was strong, with teams choosing between five different chassis, four brands of engine, and two tire manufacturers. And the field of drivers was extremely compelling, from rookies like Montoya and 1998 Indy Lights champion Cristiano da Matta to seasoned veterans Michael Andretti and Al Unser Jr.

Brazilian Tony Kanaan (born December 31, 1974) overcame the emotional heartbreak of his father's death when he was thirteen and lived a hardscrabble existence in Italy trying to break into Formula 3. TK's big break came when he and another promising Brazilian named Hélio Castro-Neves (born May 10, 1975) won a shootout staged by Philip Morris's Latin American division to compete in Indy Lights for Tasman Racing in 1996. They moved to Columbus, Ohio, where they struggled with the cold winters and tried to learn English by watching country music videos on CMT.

Kanaan finished second to David Empringham in the 1996 Lights standings, then won the championship a year later, with Castroneves (he dropped the hyphen in mid-2000) the runner up. Both graduated to Indy cars in 1998; Kanaan remained in Steve Horne's Tasman organization and Castroneves earned a ride with Bettenhausen Motorsports. Hélio posted the best individual result with a second place at Milwaukee to Kanaan's pair of thirds, but Tony prevailed over the long haul as they finished one-two in the Rookie of the Year standings.

Both would be in new surroundings in 1999. Castroneves made a last-minute switch from the Bettenhausen team to Hogan Racing, displacing ex-F1 driver J. J. Lehto. Meanwhile, during the offseason, Horne sold his team to Gerald Forsythe, who changed the name to Forsythe Championship Racing with McDonald's sponsorship and a Honda engine. Forsythe retained Horne to run it as a separate satellite operation alongside his existing two-car Player's/Forsythe Mercedes team with drivers Moore and Patrick Carpentier. It was an important factor in Kanaan's development as a young Indy car driver.

"When Forsythe bought the team, I was a little bit conflicted: Was that good or bad?" Kanaan remarked. "We were a small husband-and-wife team with Steve and Christine [Horne], but it was functional. We got a great sponsor with McDonald's, which was a positive. But on the negative, the dynamic of the team changed. It was still the same people, but different management, so a little bit of adjustment there. The positive was it came with a little bit more budget. We didn't move shops or anything.

STEVE HORNE

"Tasman started in Indy Lights, and then in 1995, we stepped up to CART with Andre Ribeiro. He had a great season and won Honda's first Indy car race. That made us attractive as a team, because we had proven we could win. At the end of '95, I had a call from Philip Morris of Brazil saying that they wanted to create a program to develop Brazilian and South American drivers in Lights.

"Philip Morris selected the drivers, and we had a 'Gong Show' among eight candidates. I created a program where the drivers had equal time in the car in three stages and we evaluated them all. Hélio could speak a bit of English, but Tony hardly knew any. He was the reserved, quiet young man, hiding in the corner almost. Hélio was a bit more outgoing. He had been racing in British Formula 3, whereas Tony had been in Italy. Tony probably spoke Italian better than he spoke English.

"I don't remember what order they went out on the track, but it was like an instant flash of lightning when they both got in the car. You can always tell when a guy is hard on it straight away, regardless of what state the car is in. You can see it—this guy is good. Tony hopped in, and within three or four laps, he was on it. I thought, 'That's pretty promising,' and he set a respectable time.

"Then Hélio went out, and I could see he was right on it as well. What was interesting was after about five laps he came into the pits. I asked him what's the matter, and he wouldn't take his helmet off. He said he needed to get out of the car, and he went over into a corner. Tony went over to talk to him, and when Hélio took his helmet off, he was in tears. He was crying. What I didn't know was that the previous weekend, he'd had a big crash in the F3 car he was driving for Paul Stewart Racing. He had two cracked ribs, so he was in intense pain. He said to me, 'I've blown it.' I said, 'I don't think you have, actually. Let's see what you're like tomorrow. We'll have another go—don't think you're out of this.' I saw the times he did in five laps with pretty badly cracked ribs, and I thought, 'Shit, he's pretty good too.'

"They both rose immediately to the top of the ladder, and it was almost a foregone conclusion within about twenty laps who we were going to pick. The rest is kind of history."

"Jerry was a visionary; he was trying to grow his teams, and also the series. As a sponsor, McDonald's was huge. For me it was huge, because then Tony Kanaan is out there, right? That was a huge positive, especially when McDonald's started to activate a little bit. Bill Elliott was the McDonald's NASCAR guy, and they did a few things with me. It helped my brand grow. I didn't know it then, but it helped me out later in my career."

On paper, Castroneves's switch from Tony Bettenhausen's single-car operation to a similar, Mercedes-powered single-car effort for Carl Hogan looked like a lateral move. But Franchitti's impressive performances driving for Hogan in 1997 gave him the platform to advance his career with Team Green.

"Carl ended up firing J. J. Lehto because he wanted to race a new prototype for BMW, but Mercedes didn't want him to have anything to do with driving for BMW," Hélio recounted. "It all happened very late. I did a test at Sebring using J. J.'s seat with a lot of foam in it just so I could sit down. It was a last-minute scenario, but Carl liked me, and we ended up signing. Everything happened so suddenly, just a few weeks before the first race at Homestead."

The quiet Castroneves tended to keep to himself, usually sharing a hotel room on the road with his sister, Katucia, to whom he was very close. "Everyone has a different personality," he said. "I was trying to mingle with my team. I was trying to know my team and make my team feel I was part of them, and they were part of me. I was always thinking about that. I wanted to be with those guys to make sure they didn't think I was looking for something elsewhere, or the grass was greener over there. I was like, 'No, let's just get these guys as tight as we can.' That was my thing back then."

Kanaan, on the other hand, quickly integrated into a social crew that included Franchitti, Moore, and Massimiliano "Max" Papis (born October 3, 1969, in Como, Italy). Approaching his thirties, Papis was slightly older than the rest of what was starting to popularly be called CART's "Brat Pack," but he had not yet achieved the results of his off-track running mates while he and Arciero-Wells Racing (later rebranded Precision Preparation Inc., or PPI) struggled to develop the unreliable Toyota engine.

A starring performance in the 1996 Daytona 24 Hours sports car race boosted Papis's reputation after a generally fruitless partial 1995 F1 campaign. He landed in the CART series under the most unfortunate of circumstances as the replacement driver at Arciero-Wells after Jeff Krosnoff was killed during the 1996 Molson Indy Toronto. Two-plus years as the top driver for the struggling Toyota engine program was enough to convince retiring Indy car champion Bobby Rahal that Papis was the man to take over Team Rahal's Miller Lite–sponsored car. After lagging in the horsepower wars with Toyota, Max was highly motivated by the opportunity to race for a championship-caliber team using the proven Ford/Cosworth engine. His teammate would be Bryan Herta, who in his third season with Team Rahal had finally claimed his maiden Indy car win at Laguna Seca in late 1998. That win in a straight fight over Zanardi went some way toward putting to rest the ghost of 1996 and "The Pass."

"I was not looking to leave PPI," Papis said. "I was in Michigan for a driver appearance in 1998, and I started talking to Bobby. He was sitting on a couch. I asked him, 'Have you found a replacement?' He told me, 'No. Would you be available?' I said, 'As of now, no, but you never know.' I sat down with Cal Wells and told him what Rahal had offered me. I still had a year left on my contract. Surprisingly, Cal Wells told me, 'You should go, and take this opportunity.' He released me from the contract. I went in there with a lot of fire and a tremendous amount of desire, and I attacked from day one."

Adrian Fernandez, who listed his age as thirty-five, was set to anchor Patrick Racing, which stayed with Ford-Cosworth power but swapped its chassis from Reynard to Swift. Fernandez was a three-time winner in the CART series and a national hero in Mexico, backed by a powerful lineup of sponsors, including Quaker State and Tecate. His new teammate was Parnell Velko "PJ" Jones, the thirty-year-old son of American racing legend Parnelli Jones. PJ won five IMSA sports car races for Toyota and Dan Gurney's All American Racers (AAR) and was part of AAR's return to Indy car racing in 1996, but the problematic Toyota engine program made it difficult to judge his potential.

Another new Swift runner was Robby Gordon; after a three-year association with Walker Racing that produced a pair of race wins but ended in a messy fallout with Ford, Gordon was drafted into the Arciero-Wells effort alongside Papis in 1998. For '99, Gordon struck out on his own. He continued his association with Toyota as a full-time entrant in the CART series while also announcing plans to contest the IRL's Indianapolis 500.

"I want to have a choice, or at least an opinion, on the package we choose to win championships," Gordon said. "As a driver, you're just a shoe. You really don't have an opinion as to what you're going to get to drive, what tires you're going to use, or what chassis you're going to run. I've owned race car teams in the past and we've won off-road championships by just doing the basics and doing them right. I believe we can do the same thing in the CART series. I'm going to model this outfit on Barry Green's and Derrick Walker's. They've run very simple, very competitive operations.

"Nobody is as committed to becoming competitive as Toyota," he added. "If you look at when the Honda came alive, it was year four, and this is year four for Toyota. I think they'll give us a stable platform for the first half of the season, and I'm sure when they bring out the new engine it will be a race winner."

Della Penna Motorsports also moved to Toyota while staying loyal to Swift and driver Richie Hearn, the 1995 Formula Atlantic champion. Finally, Toyota's growing program also included an expanded Arciero-Wells effort featuring veteran Scott Pruett and '98 Indy Lights champion da Matta (born September 19, 1973), the latest Brazilian prospect looking to make a mark in Indy car racing. Da Matta enjoyed the quiet tutelage of his father, Toninho, a fourteen-time Brazilian Stock Car champion.

Michael Andretti continued to anchor Newman/Haas Racing, which remained with Swift and Ford for the third consecutive year. Christian Fittipaldi (born January 18, 1971), the nephew of former Formula 1 and Indy car champion Emerson Fittipaldi, was back on board as Andretti's teammate. Fittipaldi beat Alex Zanardi to the 1991 Formula 3000 championship, then switched from Formula 1 to the CART series with Walker Racing in 1995, finishing second at the Indianapolis 500. Four years into his American career, he was still in search of his first Indy car win.

CRISTIANO DA MATTA

"I didn't start racing very early because my dad thought I would miss out on the other things that come with being a kid because I would be at the racetrack all the time. He tried to keep things normal for me, and at the time, I was a little bit upset about that. But today, when I look back, I can see that I gained a lot by having a normal childhood.

"When I was maybe thirteen, Nelson Piquet won his third World Championship, and then Senna was at his best. When you looked at those guys and all they were accomplishing out of the country, it just made you want to do it more. You think you can do it too. Of course, once you get to the top level, you have to figure out how to do it your way. You're not going to drive like Piquet or Emerson . . . you're going to develop your own style.

"I got close to Formula 1, and I didn't like what I saw there. So, I decided to come over to America after racing for one year in Formula 3000. I enjoyed the way motor racing is in America a lot—especially when you compare CART to Formula 1."

It was difficult to assess where Andretti stood in the CART hierarchy in the later '90s. Prior to his ill-fated 1993 season with McLaren in Formula 1, he was absolutely dominant, despite winning just one championship in 1991. But after returning to Indy car racing in victorious fashion with Chip Ganassi Racing in 1994—"Michael was definitely the spark that lit the fire that still burns in this team today," says Chip Ganassi—Andretti's later '90s performances were sometimes strangely flat. He won five times in 1996 and could have won his second CART championship for Newman/Haas over Ganaasi's Vasser and Zanardi, who combined for seven wins. After the team's switch from Lola to Swift, Michael was victorious in the 1997 and '98 season openers at Homestead-Miami Speedway but winless elsewhere.

The biggest news out of the Newman/Haas camp was a shocking last-minute switch from Goodyear to Firestone tires. Firestone returned to Indy car racing in 1995 after a twenty-one-year absence; only bizarre circumstances denied a Firestone victory at the '95 Indy 500 (the last featuring CART teams and drivers pre-split), and by mid-1996, it was

MARIO ANDRETTI

"Firestone had a tremendous advantage over the field for about two years. That's when I fought really hard to get Newman/Haas on Firestones. I watched how Michael really struggled because of the tires. I remember he was alongside Zanardi at Mid-Ohio in '96. In those days, you had to start the race on the tires you qualified, and I was looking at Michael's tires. They were all grained, and then I looked at Zanardi's Firestones and thought, 'Oh man, the kid hasn't got a chance.'

"I said to Paul and Carl, 'Let's go to Nashville and talk to Firestone.' But Carl had a deal with Goodyear, an actual financial deal. Still, we went to Nashville and went to the top management there. Al Speyer, who was the head of racing, said, 'You know, we'd love to have you, no question,' especially with the relationship I used to have with Firestone. 'But to be honest with you, we gain more by beating you on the track with our competitor's tire than having you with our tires.' How can you argue with that?

"Paul, he was really on my side. The team had a deal with Goodyear, and we offered to pay for the Firestone tires. And they still didn't take up that offer! But I didn't give up, and finally I said to Paul and Carl, 'You owe it to Michael as a driver and you owe it to your sponsors to go after the best possible situation.' Finally, I harped enough that they switched to Firestone. You cannot make up that kind of difference on the performance of the car no matter how good you are. You need everything that you can get and put it together to be able to win."

MICHAEL ANDRETTI

"I don't know how many more races we could have won that we lost because of the tires. I was just tired of getting beat for all those years. Finally, I was able to convince them; it was a big fight. Carl turned down both Honda and Firestone twice. I was begging him, but he went for the money, and you see what happened. Chip wins four championships in a row. He had good people and there was real potential there, so I wasn't surprised. But what really put him on the map was that move. I think if Carl was around now, he would admit that was one of his biggest mistakes, turning them down. It was all about the size of a sticker on the engine cover."

clear that Goodyear was rapidly being left behind. Firestone won ten of sixteen races in 1996, thirteen of seventeen in '97, then Andretti claimed Goodyear's only win during the nineteen-race 1998 campaign in the opener at Homestead. And now Newman/Haas had switched to Firestone.

Michael ran his first test on Firestones on March 3, just eighteen days prior to the 1999 CART season opener at Homestead-Miami Speedway, yet he was convinced it was absolutely the right move. "The times were as quick as anyone has run at Homestead so far," he said. "This is definitely a step towards being a contender for winning the championship. I can't help wanting to win every race. We have some catching up to do, but by the looks of today, we are definitely on the right track."

Newman/Haas's eleventh-hour tire swap left Goodyear with just four entries on the grid, all single-car efforts: Gil de Ferran in the Walker Racing Reynard/Honda, Al Unser Jr. in a downsized Team Penske, Alex Barron in Dan Gurney's Eagle/Toyota, and rookie Shigeaki Hattori in the Bettenhausen Motorsports Reynard/Mercedes. De Ferran, who was already Honda's lead test driver, also bore the burden of Goodyear's development work heading into 1999.

"Just not having another couple cars on Goodyear does hurt our ability to win an event," admitted Stu Grant, general manager of Worldwide Racing for Goodyear. "By the same token, from a development standpoint, it's positive because it really focuses our effort with the few teams we have. Our objective is to demonstrate that we've got a product that's capable of winning races, can run consistent, can run up front with the objective of getting some competitive teams back to Goodyear in 2000 and beyond to give us a better chance of winning races."

The difficult challenge the Toyota engine program endured in getting up to speed in its first three years was well-known. Far more surprising was the competitive decline that Mercedes-Benz and engine building partner Ilmor had fallen into since winning the CART Manufacturer's Championship in 1997. Ilmor's 1998 IC108E engine set new standards for compact size and light weight, but it suffered frequent electrical glitches, offered poor drivability in road racing applications, and compiled an abysmal reliability record. Roger Penske, who owned

25 percent of Ilmor, had not seen his Indy car team win a race since May 1997, yet Mika Hakkinen had just won the '98 Formula 1 World Championship for Mercedes and Ilmor. There was a strong feeling among the Mercedes Indy car teams that the CART program was rapidly being pushed aside by F1.

Unser's slump was even longer than Penske's; his last race win came September 3, 1995, in Vancouver. Team Penske's new lead designer John Travis produced a beautiful car called the PC27 to take advantage of the tiny Mercedes "E" engine in 1998, but the combined shortcomings of the motor and Goodyear's increasingly uncompetitive tires masked the car's potential. For '99, Travis produced an aerodynamically updated "B" version of the PC27, but even before the season started there were already rumblings that Penske would acquire a Reynard or Lola chassis if Unser was off the pace.

The other team that the Mercedes/Ilmor woes severely affected was PacWest Racing. PacWest had steadily moved up the grid with a pair of ex-Formula 1 veterans in Mark Blundell and Mauricio Gugelmin, winning four races and leading the Mercedes effort in 1997. But in large part due to engine-related problems, the team's performance slipped badly in '98, with Gugelmin and Blundell finishing fourteenth and sixteenth in the standings. This was not only costly in terms of potential performance incentives, it also caused sponsors Motorola electronics and Hollywood cigarettes to start to lose confidence in the team and its drivers.

The full Mercedes lineup for '99 included Penske, the PacWest duo, two cars from Player's/Forsythe Racing for Moore and Carpentier (born August 13, 1971, he was the record-setting 1996 Formula Atlantic champion and another successful product of the Player's Canadian driver development program), plus the single Bettenhausen and Hogan entries. With Castroneves having departed in late January, Bettenhausen scrambled but announced plans to field a car for Hattori, a thirty-five-year-old Japanese rookie who was a race winner in Indy Lights, and more importantly, came with sponsorship for thirteen races from Epson Electronics.

Payton-Coyne Racing completed the field, set to campaign a 1997 Lola/Ford full time for Michel Jourdain Jr. The second-generation

Mexican racer was just twenty-two, but he had already started forty-five Indy car races. Tarso Marques, a Brazilian who ran a dozen Formula 1 races for the backmarker Minardi team in 1996 and '97 set some impressive testing times in Coyne's 1997 Reynard/Ford but could not raise the budget to secure the seat. So as usual, the second Coyne car would be driven by a rotating roster of drivers.

Led by Fernandez and Jourdain, who carried sponsorship from the food conglomerate Grupo Herdez, the Mexican influence on the CART series was steadily growing and within a few years would rival the Brazilian influx from earlier in the 1990s.

"The Houston race in 1998 was a big thing, and there were starting to be talks about CART going down to Monterrey," said Jourdain. "Houston was like racing in Mexico. Long Beach and Fontana were also quite big for the Latin American fans. Then in '99, you had Zanardi leaving, but Montoya was coming. The level of the teams and the drivers was like a small Formula 1 in the sense of development. You had Penske, Reynard, Lola, Eagle, and Swift. Four different engines, and there were updates every race for the big teams. The cars were so fast, and we were racing at amazing tracks. You had a lot of big, established names, like Michael, Little Al, and Bobby Rahal, but also a lot of young guys—Tony, Dario, Montoya, Hélio, Greg, Cristiano—and I was the youngest of them all. I feel very, very lucky."

Defending CART champion Zanardi may have departed for greener pastures in Formula 1, but CART still assembled a very stout field for the upcoming season. For the sanctioning group and most of its competitors, the outlook heading into 1999 was extremely optimistic.

1999 CART FEDEX CHAMPIONSHIP SERIES LINEUP

No.	Driver	Team	Chassis/Engine/Tire
2	Al Unser Jr.	Penske Racing	Penske/Mercedes/G
3	[No Full-Time Driver]	Penske Racing	Lola/Mercedes/G
4	Juan Pablo Montoya - R	Chip Ganassi Racing	Reynard/Honda/F
5	Gil de Ferran	Walker Racing	Reynard/Honda/G
6	Michael Andretti	Newman/Haas Racing	Swift/Ford/F
7	Max Papis	Team Rahal	Reynard/Ford/F
8	Bryan Herta	Team Rahal	Reynard/Ford/F
9	Hélio Castroneves	Hogan Racing	Lola/Mercedes/F
10	Richie Hearn	Della Penna Motorsports	Swift/Toyota/F
11	Christian Fittipaldi	Newman/Haas Racing	Swift/Ford/F
12	Jimmy Vasser	Chip Ganassi Racing	Reynard/Honda/F
16	Shigeaki Hattori - R	Bettenhausen Motorsports	Reynard/Mercedes/G
17	Mauricio Gugelmin	PacWest Racing	Reynard/Mercedes/F
18	Mark Blundell	PacWest Racing	Reynard/Mercedes/F
19	Michel Jourdain Jr.	Payton-Coyne Racing	Lola/Ford/F
20	P. J. Jones	Patrick Racing	Swift/Ford/F
22	Robby Gordon	Team Gordon	Reynard/Toyota/F
24	Scott Pruett	Arciero-Wells Racing	Reynard/Toyota/F
25	Cristiano da Matta - R	Arciero-Wells Racing	Reynard/Toyota/F
26	Paul Tracy	Team Green	Reynard/Honda/F
27	Dario Franchitti	Team Green	Reynard/Honda/F
33	Patrick Carpentier	Forsythe Racing	Reynard/Mercedes/F
34	Dennis Vitolo	Payton-Coyne Racing	Reynard/Ford/F
36	Alex Barron	All American Racers	Eagle/Toyota/G
40	Adrian Fernandez	Patrick Racing	Reynard/Ford/F
44	Tony Kanaan	Forsythe Championship	Reynard/Honda/F
64/71	[No Full-Time Driver]	Payton-Coyne Racing	Reynard/Ford/F
99	Greg Moore	Forsythe Racing	Reynard/Mercedes/F

*- R indicates a rookie driver

From pole position, Greg Moore leads the field at the start of the Marlboro Grand Prix of Miami at Homestead. *Michael Levitt*

CHAPTER 4

FINE IN '99

Ralph Sanchez and a small group of local political figures broke ground for Homestead Motorsports Complex on August 24, 1993. It was exactly one year after Hurricane Andrew, a Category 5 storm, destroyed sixty-three thousand houses and caused $27 billion in damage to the towns of Homestead and Florida City, about fifteen miles south of Miami off US 1 in an area known as the Gateway to the Florida Keys.

Sanchez was a Cuban immigrant who became a Miami property developer. He was also a keen amateur road racer who starting in 1983 served as the manager of the Miami Grand Prix in both IMSA sports car and CART Indy car guises. Another of Sanchez's notable accomplishments was luring two-time Formula 1 World Champion Emerson Fittipaldi out of retirement. He convinced Fittipaldi to make a one-off appearance in the inaugural IMSA Miami GP, and Emerson enjoyed the experience so much that he made a comeback to racing full time. Fittipaldi was responsible for bringing modern-day Marlboro sponsorship to Indy car racing, first with Patrick Racing, then Team Penske, and he had a very successful second career in America from 1984 to '96, highlighted by two Indianapolis 500 wins and the 1989 CART championship.

Sanchez believed that the construction of a new multipurpose racing facility, highlighted by a 1.5-mile rectangular oval that resembled a scaled-down version of the Indianapolis Motor Speedway, could lead the economic redevelopment of the shattered region. By 1996, what would become known as the "Pastel Palace" was ready to host the CART season opener, even if the Homestead/Florida City region wasn't. Only two area restaurants survived the hurricane; the Mutineer, a typically seedy Florida bar, and Richard Accursio's Capri, a classic old-school Italian joint that opened in 1958. On race weekends, the wood-paneled King Richard room at the Capri would be packed with racing people, patiently socializing while the hardworking staff tried to keep up with a rush from the new racetrack that they clearly did not anticipate. The Mutineer finally capsized in 2017, but the Capri remains in business, albeit under new ownership. No matter, because folks in the area for racing at what is now called Homestead-Miami Speedway can choose from all the usual national restaurant and hotel chains on a now fully redeveloped strip of US 1 that, palm trees aside, looks sadly like any other midsized American town.

The CART season opener at the new Homestead facility in March 1996 was the race in which Jimmy Vasser captured his first Indy car win, but Greg Moore stole the show with his dazzling comeback drive to seventh place. In the summer of 1997, the track was reconfigured from a mini-IMS into a true 1.5-mile oval with symmetrical 180-degree corners at each end, still maintaining a shallow 6-degree banking. This completely altered the character of the track, but Moore took to it right away. His 1998 pole speed of 217.541 miles per hour represented an increase of nearly 20 mph over Paul Tracy's '96 track record. Again, Moore was forced to fight back to the front in the race, this time after an air jack failed on his first pit stop. Despite having to run the last 114 laps on the same set of Firestone tires, he finished second to Michael Andretti by just 0.075 seconds. It was no surprise that Moore believed Homestead was the perfect place for the No. 99 car to kick off his '99 championship campaign. After the travails of 1998, the motto he coined with his father for the new season was "Fine in '99."

"Greg was unbelievable in those cars," marveled Dario Franchitti. "A modern Indy car, you can slide it around a little bit. There's a certain sort of yaw you can drive it in, where it's not too much of a problem. But the old CART cars, if they slid once and you didn't catch it, if you allowed it to snap again, it would bite you. And he could just hang that thing out there all day! He just drove the thing on the edge. I don't know of anybody else that did that. The move on Zanardi in Brazil was unbelievable. It was such an aggressive, assertive move. By that point his equipment wasn't the best and Mercedes was really starting to struggle. But he was making the best of it. When he snookered Jimmy and Zanardi . . . they were trying to play the team game, and he beat them both at Michigan. That was astounding. Not only was he a great driver, but he was as smart and crafty as they come."

Wanting to get the campaign off to a good start, several teams ran private tests at Homestead in the lead up to the race. But the Player's/Forsythe team elected to focus on road and street course testing, reasoning that it was the Mercedes engine's weak point in 1998 while their oval form had been solid over the past three years. When the entire CART field gathered for the first time February 3 and 4 for the annual "Spring Training" media days and open test, the Player's team's confidence was not misplaced as Patrick Carpentier and Moore posted the top speeds, ahead of Jimmy Vasser and Gil de Ferran. It was the first time in four years of Spring Training at Homestead that Vasser was not fastest.

"This gives us a lot of confidence," said Carpentier, whose dominant performance in winning the 1996 Formula Atlantic Championship earned him an Indy car ride with Bettenhausen Motorsports in 1997 and the opportunity to join an expanded two-car Players/Forsythe CART team in '98. "It's a big help to stick with the same team and the same guys."

"We decided that rather than come here and use some of our allotted test days, why not come here and use Spring Training for what it is for?" added Moore. "If you can't find out what a car wants in seven hours on the racetrack, there's something wrong. It was a good couple of days for the team, and I think we rattled a few cages among some of the people who had already tested here three or four days. The list of people that are competitive and able to win races is just massive, but the most important thing is to be consistent over the entire season. I certainly expect us to be race-winning contenders pretty much everywhere we go."

In the lead up to the season opener, Wally Dallenbach was generating headlines like never before. In early March, Dallenbach made his intention to retire public, and CART created an eight-member search committee for his replacement. But the biggest reason the outgoing

PATRICK CARPENTIER

"It was tough. I came in as a rookie after winning everything in Formula Atlantic, and I thought I was going to be up front all the time in [CART]. I was amazed at the speed difference between an Atlantic car and an Indy car at that time. We had almost a thousand horsepower. It took me years to get used to that power and handling and everything it had. It was a beast, actually. We had no help—no traction control, and the pace was incredible. Fernando Alonso recently said he doesn't think he could last today if the pace was wide open all the time. Back then, we had more pit stops, and it was crazy fast. The race pace was basically very similar to the qualifying pace. When you won a race, you deserved it.

"Greg was very, very fast. He was relentless every lap, whether it was yellow, whether it was going into the pits or out of the pits, he didn't miss one thing. He reminds me a bit of Max Verstappen on that side. He was the most talented and complete driver I've had as a teammate. Paul was fast, but not complete like Greg was. Tag [Alex Tagliani] was fast on and off, but not complete. Greg was definitely to me the high bar to measure with."

CART chief steward was in the news was his decision to suspend Paul Tracy for the season opener after a series of incidents the hard-charging driver was involved in throughout a '98 campaign that had all the drama of a soap opera.

Tracy was put on probation then fined $20,000 following accidents in Detroit and Portland. Then in Houston, he got into a televised scuffle with team boss Barry Green after crashing while trying to pass teammate Dario Franchitti for the lead. One race later, Tracy was racing aggressively when he got together with Michael Andretti, who claimed that Paul was blocking and weaving. And in the million-dollar season finale, PT had the lead when he spun and crashed approaching the restart with just five laps to go. It was an ignominious final act to an ego-deflating first year with Team Green.

The one-race suspension was tough on Tracy, who was the first driver to be excluded from an event for disciplinary reasons in the twenty-year

PAUL TRACY

"Wally was tough on me; he wasn't easy. But I probably deserved it. I did like to beat and bang. I would bump guys and put my nose into their tire and cut tires and things like that. The suspension was like an accumulation of things, almost like a point system. I kept having issues with guys and it culminated in Surfers with Michael and I getting into it with each other. I don't even think that was so much my fault. I was trying to pass Michael, and he kept fading over and over on me on the straightaway. I had my nose to his back wheel and was trying to pass him and he kept coming over and coming over. I just held my ground. We touched and my front wing cut his tire. He went off through the grass and I kept going. It wasn't even a crash, but Michael went crazy over it, he went nuts over the thing. He kind of flexed his muscles over it, and they sat me out for the first race. Could I have lifted out? Yeah, I could have lifted out. And he could have not kept moving over. I thought it was a little unjust, but it was the culmination of a lot of situations. They wanted to send a message."

history of CART. "I've crashed cars, I've had accidents, and I always admit to my mistakes," he said. "Sometimes it's gone pretty equal, but I always get painted as the bad guy. The frustrating thing is that Wally is not tough on some guys, and overly tough on others. And it's not right to pull somebody out of a race at the start of the season." Raul Boesel drove the No. 26 car at Homestead.

Shigeaki Hattori had a rough Spring Training, and his fortunes did not improve when the CART circus returned to Homestead six weeks later for the Marlboro Grand Prix of Miami. Hattori, whose sponsorship budget from Epson office equipment was the deciding factor that put him in the Bettenhausen seat vacated by Hélio Castroneves, crashed on his twelfth lap at Spring Training and wrote off a new Reynard/Mercedes. Hattori then sustained a concussion when he smashed up another $400,000 chassis less than an hour into the first practice session of the race weekend.

Meanwhile, Moore started off his championship challenge by securing his second consecutive Homestead pole. His 24.914-second,

217.035-mph lap was 0.998 mph up on outside front row starter Adrian Fernandez. "I could see on my dash that I was a little short on the first lap, so I decided to go in a little harder in Turn One," Moore said. "Then it understeered, and I had to lift. I thought that was it, but I got back on the throttle pretty quickly, and the car stuck through Three and Four. I was little surprised that we did it but happy, because you always want to get the pole."

Spooked by the Swift chassis in preseason oval testing, Patrick Racing prepared 1998 Reynards for Adrian Fernandez and P. J. Jones. Fernandez rewarded their effort by planting his car on the front row. "The Swift pushes all the time on ovals, and we couldn't jeopardize our chances for the championship," said Fernandez. "Since we unloaded the Reynard, it's been good." Robby Gordon also parked his Swift and acquired a pair of '98 Reynards.

Carpentier backed up his Spring Training form by qualifying third, while Castroneves provided a shock by running fourth fastest in Hogan Racing's Lola/Mercedes. But the biggest surprise in qualifying was the performance of rookie Cristiano da Matta, who put the Arciero-Wells Reynard/Toyota sixth on the grid after finding more than 4 mph over his best practice speed. "To say I am happy right now is just not enough," da Matta smiled.

ADRIAN FERNANDEZ

"I was a little mad at Pat Patrick and wanted to make sure we didn't repeat what happened at Tasman in 1997 with the Lola chassis. I was not happy we were changing to Swift, especially since we were doing so well with Reynard. And we were also changing drivers. We were testing with the Swift, and it was just not competitive. I said to Pat Patrick, 'We're going slower than the previous car, the Reynard, and the car doesn't feel right.' At the third test, we came with a Reynard on the back of the trailer in case things didn't improve with the Swift. And that's what we did. The test was not going well with the Swift, and on the last day of testing before the season, we got the '98 Reynard out. Within the first lap, I already felt the car was so much better. I did four or five laps which were the fastest of all the winter testing . . . boom, boom, boom."

Gil de Ferran's Honda engine exploded into a ball of fire in Turn Two of his first qualifying lap, pitching the Walker Racing Reynard into a spin and a 58-g impact with the wall. "My elbow and ribs are a little sore," he said with a grimace. "I'm disappointed I'm going to have to start at the back because I really felt the car was hooked up and thought that perhaps I could have a run at the pole."

Moore took control of the race from the start on a pleasant eighty-degree day. He settled his Homestead score by leading ninety-six of 150 laps (including the final thirty-seven) for his fifth career Indy car victory, jumping to the top of the PPG Cup standings with the maximum of twenty-two points. He won by 1.11 seconds over Andretti, whose first run on Firestones earned some redemption for the struggling Swift chassis program.

Michael was upset with himself for stalling the car exiting his final pit stop, convinced it cost him a third consecutive Homestead win. "It was a stupid mistake," he said. "I gave up my track position to Greg. But I don't think we would have been on the podium without the Firestones. It was a bold move but a good one. We still have a lot to learn about the tires, so we have room to improve."

The race came down to pit strategy. Most of the leaders pitted for the second time under yellow on lap eighty-five, and Team Green elected to bring Franchitti in for a third stop on lap 114, again under yellow, dropping him to eighth. Dario moved through the field quickly but ran out of laps after reaching third place. It was the Scotsman's first podium finish in sixteen oval race starts. "I feel confident about driving on an oval," he said. "We've found something in the setup that works."

A low-on-fuel Vasser lost out on a podium finish when he was passed by Franchitti with four laps remaining, followed in a career-best fifth place by Papis in his Team Rahal debut. De Ferran turned in a storming drive from the back to earn sixth place, while Carpentier rallied from a pit lane penalty to take seventh.

But the story of the day was Moore finally breaking through at a track where he had produced so many remarkable memories during the first three years of his career. The Homestead win was Moore's seventh podium result in the last nine oval races, and four of his five CART victories had come on oval tracks.

"I wouldn't say we were dominant; we had the lucky breaks," Moore observed. "Many, many times I've had the dominant car and not had the breaks. I think Dario probably had the best car, but he was playing it a bit conservative, and we knew we could make it to the end. We had a pretty eventful day. We changed the car quite a lot—dramatically for us. We usually don't change the car that much on an oval. At the beginning, the car was extremely loose. But we made it better and better. We made tons of changes to tire pressures and wing angles. We were fast at the end when we needed to be.

"For the last stint, the car was quite good," he added. "I was very confident that once I had a decent lead over Michael, I had a good shot at winning the race. It all goes down to the boys. They're the ones who told me to stay out when Dario came in. My fuel light came on down the back straight of the white flag lap, but I knew I had enough to make it to the finish. I was really skeptical, but that shows how good the Mercedes engine is on fuel."

Drivers are rarely happy about third-place finishes, but it was Franchitti's most competitive and complete performance to date on an oval. It didn't hurt matters that his pal Moore was the winner.

"We took the decision early in that race rather than trying to eke out the fuel, to take a safe strategy," Dario reflected. "I felt my car was a rocket ship that day. That was the first time that I felt really good on an oval, but we took that safe strategy. That was another party, that night in Miami—Greg organized another whaler of a party! My God, that was a good one . . ."

As a twenty-year-old rookie in 1996, Moore's performance at Homestead—highlighted by several spectacular outside passes as he fought back from his penalty—immediately marked him as a future star. Three years later, after winning in 1999, he looked back on the marker he laid down that day with amusement.

"In '96, I was nuts when I made all those passes around the outside," he laughed. "I think I took way more chances in '96 than I did this year. We really worked on the car a lot. In '96, I think I really grabbed the car by the scruff of the neck and drove around whatever problems we had. Today we improved the car as the race wore on and at the end, we were the fastest. I think that really is a sign of maturity, not only on my part, but on the part of the team. We've proved that we can win races on the ovals. Now we have to go out and show that we can run with these guys on the road courses and the street courses."

Moore's performances in the early stages of his Indy car career quickly earned the admiration of Neil Micklewright, vice president of operations for Player/Forsythe Racing. But Micklewright was convinced that even after three full seasons, his twenty-three-year-old driver was still learning.

"I think he is just now beginning to realize that he is as good as he is," Micklewright said. "He has such an abundance of natural talent that it didn't always occur to him in the same way it wouldn't to a virtuoso piano player . . . that, 'OK, I can do this.' I don't think it occurred to him until maybe the end of last year that maybe everybody can't do this. I think he has perhaps gained more respect for himself and his own abilities, and that he is trying more concertedly to channel those abilities to gain the maximum benefit."

The win at Homestead, when Moore drove a calm and collected race in which he perfectly executed a fuel strategy, confirmed Micklewright's confidence about the No. 99 car making a championship run in '99.

"I think that Greg's drive today was probably the most mature drive that I've seen from him," Micklewright remarked. "It shows what he's learned over the past few seasons. He's definitely a much better driver now. He's still just as aggressive, but he really used his head.

"Greg's a real joy to work with," he continued. "He's one of the boys. We have very good camaraderie between both the drivers on our team and all the personnel. It's a very nice little family. We all know what we're trying to achieve, and we work at it together. Greg is so competitive that running fifth or sixth is something that's very hard for him to deal with. If anything, it's been all or nothing. He made the commitment this year that every point is valuable. He's just going to be consistent and keep on going, and hopefully we'll be able to get past the lulls in the season that we've endured in the past."

Montoya qualified on the outside of the fourth row for the first oval race of his career. He struggled in the first stint with oversteer, then fell a lap down after a lengthy first pit stop in which he knocked over crew chief Butch Davis and stalled the engine. With the car handling more to his liking in the latter stages, Montoya finished tenth.

"I'm happy," he said. "We had some problems since the beginning of the race. The car was very loose in the first run. I was like five seconds off the pace and couldn't even drive the car. I was just asking, 'Please, I want to come in because this is dangerous!' But the team did a great job after that to make the car quite good and at the end, we were very quick, I think."

Fernandez left Homestead disappointed after dropping out when an oil leak pitched his car into a crash, heavily damaging the '98 Reynard. But he could at least look forward to competing in the next race at Twin Ring Motegi, unlike Japanese rookie Naoki Hattori and Al Unser Jr. They were involved in a first-lap crash at Homestead and faced the prospect of missing multiple races.

Naoki Hattori, no relation to Shigeaki, had impressed by qualifying twelfth for his CART debut in a hastily arranged second Reynard/Honda for Walker Racing. But he appeared to lose control in Turn Two, spun out toward the wall, and collected Unser, who was attempting an outside pass in his Penske/Mercedes. Both drivers were extricated from their crashed machines by the CART Safety Team and flown by helicopter to Jackson Memorial Hospital in Miami. Hattori sustained a badly fractured large bone in his lower left leg, on which Dr. James Hutson performed surgery the same evening. He was expected to be sidelined for four to six months. Unser suffered a fracture of his right ankle and a ligament tear of his left knee.

"When the car stopped, my legs were on top of each other," Unser said. "When I went to untangle them, I could feel my right foot was mush and I couldn't control it." Unser was flown Sunday night to Indianapolis, where Dr. Terry Trammell performed surgery at Methodist Hospital the following day. "It will be four to six weeks before Al can get back in a race car, and we will need to build a carbon fiber brace for the ankle, which will allow him to push the pedal," Trammell stated. "It will be eight to twelve weeks before he can walk and put weight on the right ankle." They targeted the race at Nazareth Speedway in eight weeks for his return to racing.

This was the worst possible way the season could have started for Unser. It was an open secret that Al Jr. was struggling in his personal life. His wife, Shelley left him in early 1996 after eighteen years of marriage; they reconciled before splitting for good late in the '98 season. Then on February 5, 1999, Al and Shelley's youngest daughter Cody contracted transverse myelitis, a rare autoimmune condition that left her paralyzed below the waist at age twelve.

"My little girl's sickness devastated me this winter and spring," Unser said. "I felt really sad, laid up in the hospital wondering 'What's going to happen next?' My personal life has been in turmoil for three or four years, and now my daughter's illness. I was very fortunate to have the good fortunes that I had when I was younger. I guess what goes around comes around."

Unser was under considerable pressure from Roger Penske to clean up his life and return to race-winning form. Depressed by the prospect of missing at least two races, Al Jr. sought solace in alcohol, marijuana, and pain medications. Meanwhile, with his driver out of action for the short-term, Penske finally understood he needed to make some hard decisions about his increasingly uncompetitive Indy car team and started by acquiring a new Lola chassis.

"We obviously have to determine where we are with the chassis," Penske said. "If we choose to run the Lola, it will be a business decision we have to make. No sentiment. We've given our car every opportunity. You never know what are the specifics that make you two-tenths quicker or slower unless you have some kind of baseline."

Asked why they chose a Lola over a Reynard or Swift, Penske replied: "We contacted Reynard, and it was going to be twelve weeks before there was a car. Swift didn't have the capacity to get us a car. Lola had a car available that Tony Bettenhausen hadn't taken. It was simple availability. I wanted to get some answers now rather than later. The trigger was that I looked at the schedule and looked where we were, and I didn't want to wait another eight races. There's a window here of three weeks between races. We could test it, and if it's good, we could use it right away. Even if we decided to use it, it could take a couple races just to get it up to speed."

MARLBORO GRAND PRIX OF MIAMI

Homestead-Miami Speedway — March 21, 1999 – 150 laps

1. Greg Moore
2. Michael Andretti
3. Dario Franchitti
4. Jimmy Vasser
5. Max Papis

CHAMPIONSHIP STANDINGS AFTER 1 OF 20 RACES

1.	Moore	22
2.	Andretti	16
3.	Franchitti	14
4.	Vasser	12
5.	Papis	10

Dario Franchitti signs autographs for Japanese fans at Twin Ring Motegi.
Kazuki Saito

CHAPTER 5

RUFFLING FEATHERS

Carl Haas was eccentric, intensely private, and almost always a soft-spoken man. But he was shouting and screaming and generally causing a ruckus in Pit Lane at Twin Ring Motegi on April 8, 1999.

The subject of Haas's wrath was Juan Pablo Montoya. The brash young rookie had just been involved in—directly caused, in Haas's mind—a jarring crash with Michael Andretti during practice for round two of the 1999 CART championship, and Newman/Haas Racing's lead driver was steaming. So too was his boss when he stormed down to the Chip Ganassi Racing garage to confront Montoya, or anybody else who got in his way.

Montoya's first line of defense was his race engineer, Morris Nunn, along with Ganassi himself, who soon got into a heated argument with Haas. After a bit of foul language and gesticulation, Haas grabbed the enormous cigar that is perennially clenched in his jaw, threw it at the ground, and he started slapping at Ganassi's chest. A crewman intervened and Montoya, upon seeing the commotion, quickly emerged from the garage and tried to calm things down. "There's no problem," Ganassi said a few hours later. "We both just got a bit hot at the time."

A few minutes earlier, a similarly heated argument had gone down between Montoya and Andretti. The drivers blamed each other, but CART Chief Steward Wally Dallenbach put the onus on Montoya, whom he fined $5,000 and put on probation. "Had to be done," Dallenbach said. "That could have been avoided."

"I'm not sure what disappoints me more—the move he pulled, or the way he handled the situation afterward," fumed Andretti. "He laughed at me in the hospital and said it was my fault. He thought it was funny. That's the mentality you're dealing with. I told Wally if he drives like that at Michigan, he'll kill somebody. I hope he changes his attitude."

Target/Ganassi Racing issued a bland statement in which Montoya took responsibility for the incident. But behind the scenes, he was more candid. "He tried to intimidate me," Juan insisted. "I catch him on the back straight, I'm going alongside, and he turns in like I'm not there. I locked up the fronts trying not to hit him. So, on the front straight I get in his draft. As I start to pass him, he turns left. I don't lift off, so we crash."

They both played nice for the television camera when interviewed by ESPN's Gary Gerould. "He apologized, and we go on," Andretti said. "He just has to learn he can't use his race car as a weapon out there, and that's what he did." Responded Montoya: "Yeah, yeah, it's perfect. I don't see why side by side we cannot race each other."

All of this happened halfway around the world from America, but news was starting to travel at a much faster rate as the internet era unfolded. CART had invested heavily at the start of 1999 in a partnership with Quokka Sports to create a state-of-the-art website, featuring newfangled innovations like live audio and video streaming. The Ganassi/Haas bust-up was captured on camera by the Quokka crew, and it immediately provided the fancy new CART.com website with video footage that would have been instant viral gold had YouTube and social media been around back then.

Located two hours north of Tokyo in the Tochigi prefecture, Twin Ring Motegi looked like something out of the future compared to most racetracks back home in the USA. Created by Honda and christened on August 1, 1997, Motegi was envisioned as a state-of-the-art motorsports complex highlighted by a 1.549-mile oval and a 2.983-mile road course built to FIA standard. The site was also home to the Honda Collection Hall, a 100,000-square-foot shrine to Honda's history in manufacturing and racing cars and motorcycles, along with several other fan-friendly activities that made the facility a car or motorcycle enthusiast's dream even when there was no racing taking place. Honda

MICHAEL ANDRETTI

"That was unbelievable. It was just practice. We were coming out to do a long run, and then, bam! I came out of the pits with a full load of fuel, and in those days, that was forty gallons. It was a big difference. I went into Turn Three, and I had to brake early because I had full tanks. He thought I short braked him or whatever, and in the middle of the front straightaway, he just turned right into me. It was a big hit—it hurt. Then in the medical facility we were ready to go at it. They held us back. Carl and Chip had at it, and I think Chip grabbed Carl's cigar and threw it.

"I said, 'We've got to sit down and talk, Juan, because we don't drive like that over here—especially on an oval.' I told him, 'First of all, I would never do anything like that on purpose. I was just coming out of the pits. You should have seen me coming out of the pits. And we just don't do this. It's not road racing. It hurts when you hit the wall. You've got to have respect.' So anyway, we sat down and talked about it, shook hands, and I think that day we both gained respect, then we respected each other from then on. I remember in that race we went wheel to wheel a lot and raced clean. The rest of the time we raced together, we had great races, like at Michigan in 2000."

JUAN PABLO MONTOYA

"I remember I was doing a qualifying run, and he was doing a race run. I caught him on the back straight and went to pass him and he turned down on me like I wasn't there. I remember I locked the tires up, and he went so deep to try to block me he actually got on the gray and everything. I was pissed! When I came off the corner, I got a run on him, and I was really angry. When I went to pass him, he moved just a little bit. I don't know whether it was to piss me off or what. But as soon as he moved, I fucking lost it. I'm like, I could go straight, all the way down there, and I can turn in down there. Before there, I don't need to turn. I just went straight, and he turned into me. I knew how far I could actually go before I needed to turn and make the corner, and he either needed to lift or turn into me. That was my approach.

"In a way, it created really good respect for each other. I learned he wasn't going to move, and he learned I wasn't going to move, you know what I mean? We learned the hard way that neither of us was going to give up."

even built a five-star, 135-room hotel on site for competitors featuring Italian, Chinese, and traditional Japanese restaurants. Chip Ganassi and Carl Haas settled their brief beef over cocktails at the Motegi hotel bar.

The fact that Twin Ring Motegi exists at all is a remarkable feat. Honda literally took the top off a mountain to carve out a natural

CHIP GANASSI

"I don't think it was anything purposeful. It just so happened that's the way it was, one of those things. I guess Michael was on the outside of Juan, kind of wheel to wheel with him, and Juan just kept his foot in it and carried him down into Turn One and they both crashed. Juan wasn't going to give up, and they ended up both crashing. It was unfortunate.

"I don't think Juan had any remorse. I mean, I guess he was sad that he crashed, but he wasn't going to back down. That was an early sign, one of Juan's signature moves. He just didn't back down, whether it was Michael Andretti or Michael Schumacher. People just moved over for Schumacher, and Juan didn't do that. You were going to have to work to get around him. Juan was going to stake his claim, and he wasn't going to back down from those things. That was one of his trademarks—he didn't back down for anybody."

JIMMY VASSER

"What I remember the most is Chip and Carl, the two of them face to face. I think a cigar maybe hit the ground. There was a little bit of tension there. But that kind of showed Montoya's fabric or his makeup. He wanted to show a top guy on a top team—Michael Andretti, one of the greatest who's ever run in the sport—that he wasn't going to take any shit on the track. Kind of like the new kid in school picking a fight with the bully in the schoolyard. One thing you can say about Montoya, he was never intimidated, as far as I could tell, in any situation throughout his whole career. Like he did in Formula 1 with Michael Schumacher. I don't know if that was him naturally, or how his dad raised him to be, perhaps, when he was younger."

amphitheater-like bowl that provides spectators with a view unmatched at any other oval venue. But the shifting of land didn't come at an ecological cost; Honda folklore has it that when trucks came down off the mountain, they were washed off over a huge grate, and the residue was recycled back into the new landscape. Since the days of Soichiro Honda himself, racing was always a key part of Honda's corporate philosophy for improving products and developing people, but the construction of Twin Ring Motegi represented Honda giving something back to the sport that has contributed so much to its history. Sadly, the oval track was damaged in the 2011 Tohoku earthquake and subsequent tsunami that devastated Japan and has not been used for racing since.

The drama of Montoya's first visit to Japan continued in qualifying. He drifted high when exiting Turn Four on his second lap and pancaked the wall, but he was able to complete the lap to secure fifteenth on the grid. Andretti, nursing a sore neck and back, lined up fifth. Up front, Gil de Ferran claimed his first career pole on an oval; he was joined on the front row by Mauricio Gugelmin in the PacWest Reynard/Mercedes, representing Big Mo's best qualifying effort since he earned pole position with a closed-course record 240.942-mph average for the 1997 season finale at California Speedway.

"Goodyear has taken a lot of criticism the last few years, so this pole has a very sweet taste," de Ferran said. "It also feels really good to get the pole here for Honda."

When footage of the Haas/Ganassi contretemps was aired at the start of ESPN's tape-delayed Motegi broadcast, viewers could see that the bickering team owners were wearing heavy parkas. The cold temperatures no doubt contributed to de Ferran's spin as the field exited Turn Four to take the green flag. Nobody hit the Walker Reynard and Gil kept the Honda engine running, so he reassumed his position at the front of the field for a restart. This time, he got away cleanly and led the first twenty-five laps before his car's handling started to fade. By the time he pitted on lap thirty-eight, he had dropped to fifth.

Gugelmin passed de Ferran for the lead and maintained it until he stopped on lap forty-seven, and it looked like things were finally starting to turn around for the Brazilian and the PacWest team after a frustrating 1998 season. But Gugelmin locked a rear brake as he pulled into his pit box; the car slewed sideways and lightly mowed down a couple crew members. Uninjured, they jumped back up and got their man back on the track, but the chaotic stop and resultant penalty put Gugelmin a lap down.

That elevated Adrian Fernandez into the lead. Fernandez, Patrick Racing, and Ford-Cosworth had rained on Honda's parade at Motegi in 1998, winning the race the Japanese manufacturer most wanted to win. They were about to spoil the home team's party again. With his '98 Reynard damaged in a crash during the season opener at Homestead and still unconvinced the Swift 010.c would be competitive on ovals, Fernandez and Patrick Racing opted to field an updated 1997 Reynard they nicknamed "Frankenstein" for Fernandez in Japan. The two-year-old chassis was clearly still on the pace, because Fernandez qualified fourth fastest and led 153 of the final 155 laps. But it was no easy victory because he had to fight off stern challenges from Andretti, Montoya, and Greg Moore.

Montoya cut quickly through the field from the eighth row and by the seventy-fifth lap he had caught up to his new BFF, Andretti. Anyone expecting fireworks was left disappointed when Montoya made a clean pass for second place on lap eighty. He whittled away at Fernandez's three-second lead, but before he had the chance to attack, the No. 4 Target car slowed, out of fuel. The miscalculation left Montoya several laps down in thirteenth place at the finish.

Moore took over second place during an exchange of pit stops under caution on lap 143 of 201 while Montoya was towed in. As the laps wound down, it was increasingly obvious that Fernandez and Moore were attempting to stretch their fuel to the finish. Andretti passed Moore for second place with fifteen laps to go and got within 0.8 seconds of Fernandez. But Michael pitted for fuel five laps later, and his hopes of winning stalled with his Ford-Cosworth engine, the product of a broken first gear. That left him fifth at the flag.

While Andretti was fuming in the pits, Papis spun at the pit entry, bringing out a full-course caution. When the pits opened, all the front-runners other than Fernandez stopped for a splash and go. That set up the scenario of Fernandez, running on fumes, trying to hold off Moore, with ten lapped cars between them.

ADRIAN FERNANDEZ

"Before the Homestead race, everybody had their new cars, and then after I got in my '98 Reynard at the last minute, I was very fast with my old car. We were very strong in practice but in the race we had an oil leak, and that got me into the wall very hard. It was enough to damage the chassis. We didn't have another '98 chassis, so they got out Scott Pruett's '97 Reynard chassis. For Japan, it was a '97 tub, which was pretty much the same as the '98 tub, and basically, we put parts from the '98 and '99 car on it, a combination of the three of them. That's how the Frankenstein car started. The car was very strong in Japan, and I was running at the front. I was right there with a '97 car when everybody else was in brand new cars. The owners at that time said, 'What the fuck? This is not right. We're buying all these expensive cars, which at the time cost like half a million dollars. Why are we spending this kind of money for chassis that are not better?' They pretty much stopped making new chassis every year, and that change basically came because of my crash at Homestead and winning Japan in an old car. . . .

"When I joined Patrick Racing at the start of 1998, they turned me into a monster. I am a slim person—my bones are thin. Even though I worked really hard on my fitness and cut out a lot of my endurance training because I had to maintain the muscles, I couldn't really be competitive with guys like Mansell, Montoya, Zanardi, and Tracy, who were muscular. Basically, I had a handicap in qualifying. My engineer John Ward and the team started working really hard on saving fuel and tires and being as competitive as we could be. In those days, we were the best at all of that. No one could compete with us in terms of fuel. . . . My strength couldn't match them over six qualifying laps, but my fuel saving and endurance was among the best.

"I didn't get into Indy cars until I was thirty years old. When I went to Europe in the early '90s, I didn't want to lose the opportunity because of my age. I took advantage of the fact that I looked young. When I later won with my own team at Portland in 2003, I told everybody, 'Well, actually, I'm not thirty-eight, I'm forty.' By that time, I wanted people to know that I was not that young. I was fighting with the younger guys, and I was a lot older than people thought. I was like the Alonso guy in those days. Even before I became an owner, I was always doing everything myself, selling sponsorships. I didn't have any managers."

Moore had the benefit of fuel, but he did not take on new tires. Perhaps as a result, Moore made little ground on Fernandez before he spun 180 degrees exiting Turn Four without hitting the wall on the 199th of 201 laps. Moore somehow controlled his car as it rolled backwards across the start/finish line and down the straight for nearly half a mile. "Instead of standing on the brakes and hitting the wall, I kept my foot in it and spun around," he said. "I found reverse, and it was like doing a burnout the wrong way. At least we were able to finish the race."

It was a remarkable sight, and the resulting caution allowed a relieved Fernandez to feather-foot it across the line to win over de Ferran, with Chrisian Fittipaldi third. Despite completing the last two laps on shredded Firestone tires, Moore was classified fourth, the last car on the lead lap.

"It was so close!" Fernandez exclaimed after his car ran dry on the cool down lap and had to be towed in. "The last two laps, I was half-throttle on the straights, and I just saw the fuel number getting closer to the end. I thought we were not going to make it. I'm sorry we had that yellow, but we were strong all day, all weekend. Montoya was pretty strong at one stage, and we were saving so much fuel. We had the car, but I told the guys, 'If you want me to keep him behind, I'm going to need some help.' But everything went good for us. It's another dream come true."

Fernandez may have been the winner on the track in Japan, but it was Montoya who made the biggest statement. Not only did he stand his ground to Andretti's "intimidation," he defied skeptics by making it to the finish of the first two oval races of his career with his car and his reputation undamaged.

"I learned a lot, but I'm disappointed because we had a winning car today," he remarked. "The way we performed today, I think we are going to be winning races very soon."

In fact, it took just a week.

Taking advantage of time zones, the twenty-fifth annual Toyota Grand Prix of Long Beach was scheduled just eight days after the race at Motegi. First staged in 1975 for Formula 5000 cars, the Long Beach Grand Prix was run as a Formula 1 race between 1976 and '83 until promoter Chris Pook realized he could no longer afford F1's rapidly rising sanction fees. The event was transformed into an Indy car race in 1984

FIRESTONE FIREHAWK 500

Twin Ring Motegi — April 10, 1999 – 201 laps

1. Adrian Fernandez
2. Gil de Ferran
3. Christian Fittipaldi
4. Greg Moore
5. Michael Andretti

CHAMPIONSHIP STANDINGS AFTER 2 OF 20 RACES

1.	Moore	34
2.	Andretti	26
3.	De Ferran	25
4.	Fernandez	21
5.	Fittipaldi	18

and continued growing into the '90s. Mario Andretti regards his F1 win at Long Beach in 1977 as one of the most memorable in his career; he won the LBGP three more times as an Indy car racer. Al Unser Jr. usurped Mario as "King of the Beach," winning six times between 1988 and '95, memorably punting Mario out of the lead to triumph in '89. Outside of the Indianapolis 500, Long Beach was considered Indy car racing's biggest and most prestigious event, and it was a key element in CART's growth.

Not that any of that history or tradition meant anything to Montoya. Just one week after ruffling feathers in that controversial incident with Andretti in Japan, Juan Pablo earned his first CART victory with a confident drive on the Long Beach streets. He qualified fifth and won by 2.805 seconds over Dario Franchitti (who ran in the midfield at Motegi before dropping out with a broken suspension just before half-distance), with Bryan Herta third.

"This weekend it finally all came together for us," said Montoya. "The car was perfect. Now I'm just going to try to keep on winning."

Montoya's chief competition came from second-year star Tony Kanaan, who earned his first Indy car pole in the Forsythe Championship Racing Reynard/Honda. After briefly losing the lead to third-placed qualifier Herta at the first turn, Kanaan led laps two through forty-five before he succumbed to pressure from Montoya and ran into a tire barrier in Turn Six.

The leaders had made their first pit stops during a full-course yellow for an incident between Tarso Marques (subbing for Al Unser Jr. at Team Penske) and Scott Pruett. On the lap thirty-one restart, Montoya made an aggressive pass on Franchitti for second place and immediately began piling pressure on Kanaan. The lead pair was pulling steadily away from Franchitti when Kanaan crashed.

"I made a mistake," admitted a tearful Kanaan. "The track was breaking up and I just ran offline a little bit and lost it. Sometimes you learn the hard way."

The memories remained vivid for Kanaan some twenty-five years later. "I had a bet with my mechanics if I got the pole, they would give me their watches," he said. "Obviously, I gave them back to them, but they lost the bet. I remember on Saturday night after I got the pole that Mario Andretti came to my table to congratulate me. It was only my second year in the series, so you kind of think you're becoming a big deal. That was pretty cool. Then I made a mistake and ended up hitting the wall when Montoya was running second, and that's how he got his first win, in the car I was going to drive. Pretty costly mistake."

After Kanaan's exit, the leaders again pitted under yellow on lap forty-seven. Montoya resumed a lead he would not relinquish. He controlled the race until the end, building leads as large as ten seconds only to see them evaporate to full-course yellows. Franchitti, who started on the outside of the front row, was never able to seriously challenge for the race win despite running well all weekend.

"I tried to take it easy over the last ten laps," Montoya said. "In the beginning, I pushed pretty hard. It was quite a tough race, but we worked pretty hard with Morris and Jimmy throughout the weekend. Bryan was the hardest guy to get past. It's a shame for Tony, because he had a good car, and we were running about the same pace.

"What happened in Japan, we kind of just let it go by," he added. "You take steps in your career all the time, and this is another step. I think this is the best win I've had."

Franchitti did not appear too disappointed with second place. "I gave it everything I had, but we didn't have the car to win today," he observed. "We were just lacking a little bit compared to Juan and Tony. Still, it was good points, we'll take it and move on to Nazareth." Herta expressed a similar sentiment. "We had a fourth- or fifth-place car in terms of speed, and we got the maximum result out of it."

Behind the podium finishers, Fernandez drove a steady race to earn fourth place in what turned out to be his only start in a Swift. The Swifts of fifth- and seventh-placed Newman/Haas Racing teammates Christian Fittipaldi and Michael Andretti were split by Gil de Ferran, who was by far the most competitive Goodyear runner of the weekend.

"I'm feeling pretty confident," Montoya said. "We've done a lot of testing on the ovals, and I was disappointed in my race at Homestead. In Japan, we were close to winning. I've tested at Nazareth, and I don't think we will be too far off the pace. We're ready to win more races, and then maybe we can think about the championship. Right now, I just want to enjoy this moment."

Chip Ganassi expressed quiet satisfaction that his latest discovery had found Victory Lane so quickly. Since the start of 1996, Target/Chip Ganassi Racing had won twenty-four of fifty-five races, and despite running a rookie driver, it did not appear the winning was about to stop anytime soon.

"We have high expectations as a team," said the team owner. "We like to think we have a pretty good group of engineers and guys screwing the car together. You don't want to put pressure on the driver, but when you steer the car with No. 4 on the side, you know you have big shoes to fill.

"I think we let him down in the first couple races," Ganassi added. "We had some mechanical and mental errors. We wanted to get back to our trademark of cars running and running. I knew he had the talent to drive like he did today, but I didn't know he had the mental toughness to put those things behind him. You don't see that very often in a young driver, and that's what has impressed me. I guess a short memory is good."

TOYOTA GRAND PRIX OF LONG BEACH

Long Beach street course — April 18, 1999 – 85 laps

1. Juan Pablo Montoya
2. Dario Franchitti
3. Bryan Herta
4. Adrian Fernandez
5. Christian Fittipaldi

CHAMPIONSHIP STANDINGS AFTER 3 OF 20 RACES

1.	Moore	39
2.	Fernandez	33
	De Ferran	
3.	Andretti	32
4.	Franchitti	30
5.	Fittipaldi	28

Juan Pablo Montoya qualified third on the Emerson Fittipaldi Speedway "roval" but took the lead into the first corner. *Paul Webb*

CHAPTER 6

WINGING IT

The next stop for the FedEx Championship Series was Nazareth Speedway, a tight bullring that spread three distinctly different corners over just 0.946 miles. Mario Andretti's family settled in Nazareth, a Pennsylvania borough of around 6,000 residents located in the Lehigh Valley some eighty miles from New York City, when they emigrated to America in 1955. He never left. The Nazareth site, about three miles from the Andretti family home, featured a pair of dirt ovals prior to being reconfigured into its paved tri-oval configuration by a group led by Roger Penske in 1987.

Patrick Carpentier set the Nazareth lap record in 1997 at 186.896 miles per hour, but that mark was set using large, maximum-downforce front and rear wings typically utilized at road and street courses. For 1999, CART had mandated low downforce "speedway" wings for all ovals less than two miles in length. This was not so much an issue at 1.5-mile "intermediate" tracks like Homestead and Motegi, but prerace testing at Nazareth in low-downforce trim raised considerable concern about the potential quality of the show.

"My first impression was that it was going to be really tough, but I got used to it," commented PacWest Racing's Mauricio Gugelmin, who was unofficially quickest in testing with a 20.08-second clocking, well off Carpentier's benchmark of 18.419. "You really have to drive the car more, and the biggest problem is braking into Turn Three, where it's easy to lock the rear brakes. I did some long runs and was able to do consistent 20.8s on my own, but it gets pretty dramatic in traffic. When you get to within two or three car lengths of the car in front of you, there's just no grip. It felt like I was riding my son's bicycle at 200 miles per hour."

Gugelmin's opinion carried weight. Born April 20, 1963, Gugelmin followed in the wheel tracks of his fellow Brazilian Ayrton Senna to England to race Formula Fords and start up the open-wheel ladder to Formula 1. They became great friends, and as Senna worked through the F1 ranks with Toleman and Lotus to McLaren, he shared his home with Gugelmin and his wife, Stella. Mauricio raced four years in F1 and achieved his only F1 podium finish in the 1989 Brazilian Grand Prix.

"Stella and I basically lived with him when I was in Formula 3 and Formula 3000, from when he was just getting into F1 with Toleman, up to '87," Mauricio recalled. "That's when the English government kindly asked him to leave England or pay taxes. And he chose to leave in a hurry. We shared all the expenses, but he didn't charge me any rent, which was good. And there was always a nice Mercedes or Renault or whatever he was driving at the time."

Discouraged by his prospects in F1, Gugelmin took most of the 1993 season off before running a handful of exploratory CART races. For '94, he put together a last-minute deal to run a second entry for Chip Ganassi Racing in Reynard's first season of Indy car racing, much to the displeasure of Ganassi's lead driver, Michael Andretti. Within a few races, Andretti softened his stance when he realized the value Gugelmin brought in terms of engineering prowess and car setup.

PacWest Racing owner Bruce McCaw appreciated Gugelmin as much for his quality as a human being as his racing talent. Mauricio anchored the PacWest team for seven years, but it was fellow ex-F1 driver Mark Blundell who claimed PacWest's first win at Portland in 1997. Gugelmin won later that year at Vancouver and concluded the campaign by running the first 240-mph laps in Indy car racing history at California Speedway, reaching 242.333 mph in practice.

By the late '90s, Gugelmin was regarded as one of CART's most proficient oval drivers and he was elected president of the Championship Drivers Association following the '99 season. His comments about the suitability of speedway wings for the Nazareth bullring were echoed by Team Green's Paul Tracy, who had a minor accident which ended his first of two scheduled test days early.

"I'm not a big fan of the new wing configuration," stated Tracy, whose best time was a 20.92 over the course of 168 laps. "I was doing 80 mph maximum when I crashed. There's no grip, no security, and the window of controllability is virtually nothing. Under these conditions, it takes fifteen laps just to get your tires up to temperature."

CART had struggled for several years with the challenge of controlling speeds on short ovals as the intensifying battle between engine manufacturers led to rapid increases in power and drivability. Another factor was Firestone's reentry to the sport in 1995 and the resultant battle for tire supremacy with Goodyear. CART's decision to mandate an ultra-low downforce aerodynamic setup as a means of slowing the cars on short ovals achieved its aim, but it created processional racing and a lot of unhappy drivers. The aerodynamic changes reduced the amount of downforce by around 2,000 pounds, or roughly 30 to 40 percent.

"The 1990s brought a string of technical caps on aero performance," said Mark Handford, an aerodynamicist and designer for Lola and later Swift. Handford designed the unusual "Handford Device" rear wing that had transformed CART's superspeedway races in 1998 into thrilling, slipstreaming affairs.

"All were aimed at countering wind tunnel developments, ever-increasing power outputs, and the effects of the Goodyear/Firestone tire war. From a constructor's point of view, this was frustrating. Neither the engine manufacturers nor the tire companies were willing to make regressive developments to contain performance. The entire burden of pegging back performance therefore fell onto the shoulders of the chassis constructors, specifically the aerodynamicists."

In the lead-up to the Nazareth race, several drivers stated they believed their input was not taken seriously when the decision to switch to the small wings for the bullrings was made. Kirk Russell, CART's vice president of competition, refuted that.

"The rules committee has been working on this for a long time," Russell said. "We had an owner meeting at Motegi, and the consensus that came out of that meeting was that we needed to stay with the [low downforce] package that was implemented last November. Every time we reduce downforce, we know that the way the race is run and the predictability of the cars is going to change. I think what the drivers are telling you is that the comfort level they are used to and the speeds that they are used to are not what they're experiencing here."

After two days of practice and qualifying, most of the drivers predicted a follow-the-leader race. "I don't think that we should be at this track with the level of downforce we have and nine hundred horsepower," said Blundell. "That's not a criticism of Nazareth. It's a great little track, and Penske has done a wonderful job upgrading it. But this show should be somewhere else."

"It depends on what kind of entertainment you want to see," added championship leader Greg Moore. "If you want to watch some carnage, it will be entertaining. The pace car may lead more laps than the leader. I think there will be zero opportunity for passing."

Some drivers, however, maintained a more even keel. "It's the same for everyone," said Michael Andretti. "If anything, it's better than I expected. It definitely puts the driver back into the picture."

"I think most of the experienced drivers, or at least 80 percent of them, can get used to it," predicted Juan Montoya, whose pole lap of 19.600 seconds (173.755 mph) was more than a second off Carpentier's track record from a year earlier. "Even running in traffic. I mean, I never ran with the big wings here, but there's a limit to what the car can do, and you just have to find that limit."

Some observers suggested that drivers with less experience found it easier to adapt to the new regulations. "I think it makes it harder for guys like Al [Unser Jr.], Michael [Andretti], Jimmy [Vasser], and me, because we knew what a good car feels like around here," said 1994 and '97 Nazareth winner Tracy. "It's like learning the track all over again, trying to forget the old habits."

The unacknowledged elephant in the room was the Indy Racing League. IRL cars featured much less power and barn door wings that created more downforce than the CART cars of the era. With all that downforce, they were a lot easier to drive, and that produced closer racing on all lengths of ovals. To date, CART's efforts to spice up the show had failed. The conundrum of balancing power, aerodynamic grip, tire traction, and mechanical grip has still not been solved more than twenty-five years later.

"That's the problem we're facing," Gugelmin admitted. "I agree you have to reduce downforce, but you have to look at power and tire grip as well. If you take away horsepower, you're flat out all the way around. If you take away downforce, you're sliding everywhere. Look at the IRL . . . they have big wings and lots of grip, and that makes the drivers overconfident. You have to find a happy medium. I would like to see us take two hundred horsepower away, then crank the wings back on. Then you will have three-abreast racing again, which is what short oval racing should be all about.

"Until we get it right, there are going to be a few problems," he concluded. "The race at Nazareth is going to be interesting. I think it's going to be nearly impossible to pass, and there will be some guys in the wall. Qualifying will be at a premium, but within a few laps, you're going to be lapping people, and that's going to be a real challenge."

Gugelmin's prediction proved right on the mark, though there were only two accidents in the race—neither of which could be blamed on the smaller wings. Shigeaki Hattori didn't even make it to the race; his competition license was suspended by CART Chief Steward Wally Dallenbach after Hattori's fourth major crash of the 1999 season halted the first practice. Hattori lost it in Turn Three and pounded the wall just eleven minutes into the Friday morning session. Before crashing, "The Shigenator" was over four seconds off the pace on a twenty-second lap.

"He's a nice kid and I want to give him every chance, but I've got to take care of him and the guys around him," said Dallenbach. "Four crashes in three and a half races is not acceptable."

"I was fighting the car all the way around the track," said Hattori, who left the circuit with a dejected look and a swollen hand (a legacy of yet another crash at Long Beach) on Saturday afternoon. "I found this low downforce wing package makes the car very unstable to drive. I feel very bad for the team because I know they are working very hard for me. We just need more experience."

Any questions about whether fellow CART rookie Montoya could put together a run for the PPG Cup title were emphatically answered in the race as the twenty-three-year-old Colombian cruised to a 5.103-second victory in the Bosch Spark Plug Grand Prix. A strong run by P. J. Jones in the Patrick Racing Visteon Swift/Ford resulted in second place—Jones's best career finish in CART competition. Tracy was third for Team Green, marking his first podium finish since he won at Gateway International Raceway in May 1997.

It was a happy and lighthearted podium as the burly Jones and Tracy picked up the more compact Montoya and pretended to pitch him into a mosh pit.

Starting from the pole, Montoya led 210 of the 225 laps at Nazareth, but he had to fight off a fierce challenge from the Hogan Racing Lola/Mercedes of Hélio Castroneves. The twenty-three-year-old Brazilian passed Montoya on track for the lead on two occasions, but quick work by the Target crew put the Colombian back in front both times.

Montoya led from the start, but he was hounded by Castroneves until lap thirty-nine, when Hélio got a run exiting Turn Two and passed Montoya on the outside of Three. But ten laps later, the yellow came out for Al Unser Jr.'s crash, and Montoya retook the lead in the pits. Castroneves continued to stalk Montoya, and he seized another chance on lap 145. Blundell was coming out of the pits from a routine stop, and he and Alex Barron unwittingly balked Montoya. It set off a wild chain of events. Castroneves dived under Montoya in Turn Two, and the two cars touched. After Montoya caught a big wiggle between Two and Three, Jones passed both Montoya and Castroneves on the inside of Turn One, only to spin on the exit. Again, the yellow came out, and again, Montoya emerged from the pits in the lead. Despite the spin, Jones managed to maintain third place.

"We had quite a good car," Montoya said. "At one point I got a couple of cars between Hélio and me, and I could see that he was having trouble getting by them. I was really pushing hard, but we were pretty equally matched. The Target team did a great job. The guys deserved this more than me. Two times I went into the pits second and came out first."

Castroneves lost second place to Jones on a lap 154 restart, then spun exiting Turn Three without hitting anything on lap 170. Just after the next restart, Castroneves (now three laps down) crashed hard in Turn Three, fortunately without injury. It was a poor reward after an excellent weekend.

The second-place finish was a much-needed boost for Jones, whose seat at Patrick Racing was already under threat. After years of toil with

JUAN PABLO MONTOYA

"Hélio was very good on the short ovals, a guy you always wanted to beat. To be honest, until I was his teammate at Penske [starting in 2014], I never really liked him. We actually raced for the same team in England, Paul Stewart Racing. He was racing Formula 3, I was in Formula Vauxhall, and he said to me, 'You're an amateur driver and I'm a professional since I race in Formula 3.' When I got to race IndyCar against him, I just wanted to kick his ass as badly as I could. You think his personality is fake, but when you get to know him, that's just him."

All American Racers developing Toyota's engine, the move to Patrick was supposed to be the opportunity for the thirty-year-old Jones to show his talent. Instead, Patrick struggled with its switch to the Swift chassis and Jones was left to carry that bag while teammate Adrian Fernandez won the Japan race in a Reynard.

"I'm honestly glad I'm in the Swift, but I'd be happier if Adrian was in the car too," Jones said. "It's almost like I'm a real experienced rookie. It's not like I was driving around at the back of the pack and not learning anything. I did learn how to drive these cars and set them up. But I've been working with a new team, new tires, a different engine, and different chassis every week. It took me a little while to get comfortable, and I think we're getting there.

"I needed this result," he admitted. "It's really important for both me and the team."

His bosses didn't sound convinced, seemingly forgetting Jones's pedigree as a two-time champion in the IMSA Camel GT sports car championship. "PJ and I have had some come-to-Jesus talks about his driving style," owner U. E. "Pat" Patrick told *Autoweek*. "He tries to drive these cars like he did sprint cars. You have to drive these cars with more finesse. He's capable, and he's absolutely totally brave, but unfortunately, the days of Gordon Johncock are gone. You can't carry the car anymore. He's trying hard to adapt, I know he is, and nothing could make me happier than to see him succeed. The kid has talent, if we can just get it out of him. He's like a child who is a good student, but you can't get him to do his homework."

Team manager Jim McGee delivered a similar message, noting specifically that Jones would need to improve his qualifying performances.

"You can't win a race from sixteenth place, no matter how hard you drive," McGee said. "He has to have patience—we have to have patience. In the old days, the guy who drove the hardest would be the winner. Today, there are lots of guys who drive too hard. There has to be balance. You've got to be smarter—it's the thinker who wins. PJ will succeed if he learns from his mistakes—like Nazareth, for example. But first he's got to recognize them."

Behind Jones and Tracy, Cristiano da Matta scored Toyota's best Indy car result to date with a fine drive to fourth place, ahead of Fernandez and Michael Andretti. "We did everything right during the race," da Matta said. "The guys had amazing pit stops, and they really pushed me out front. I have to give them a lot of credit for giving me a good car and helping me get so far up in the field. This is a great day for Toyota, and I'm really proud to be a part of it."

Montoya's success thrust his teammate Jimmy Vasser's struggles into the spotlight. At Nazareth, where one year earlier he had led Alex Zanardi in a Ganassi one-two finish, Vasser qualified and finished eleventh. His only top five of the season had come in the opener at Homestead.

Montoya became the first CART rookie to post multiple wins in a season since Nigel Mansell. He also took over the PPG Cup lead by two

JUAN PABLO MONTOYA

"It was really good to have Jimmy as a teammate. He made a big impact on my oval career. He really helped me and guided me. It's funny, because I won a lot of races on the ovals and it looked like at the end that I could beat him pretty easily on the ovals, but I think if I hadn't had Jimmy as a teammate I probably would have struggled. I remember when we used to go test, and on lap three, Jimmy was on pace, and it took me to like lap nine. I was just building up and building up and just really respecting it. I was really lucky as well to have Morris Nunn as an engineer that first year, because he really guided me through what I needed to do."

JIMMY VASSER

"Zanardi's departure going to Williams was kind of like, 'Thank God! Can't get any worse than that from a teammate!' But then lo and behold, you get this young guy coming in and, Jesus, I've got my hands full with another of the best guys on the planet. You've got to just accept that you're having a lousy year, especially when you're getting your ass kicked by your teammate. You've just got to deal with it, really. Take it one race at a time. Sometimes there's character building in life. It's not always podiums and champagne.

"Montoya was just phenomenal from the get-go. It didn't take long. He won at Long Beach pretty early on. He was quick on ovals, quick on all disciplines, he conquered it. He was a different driver than Zanardi, who was the last to leave the trailer with the engineers at the track. He was more of an engineering-minded driver, where Juan would just kind of speak his piece to Morris Nunn and bugger off. 'Just fix it, whatever you do is fine with me.'

"Winning early at Long Beach and picking up the short ovals like he did . . . it was really spectacular to watch. But being a teammate, I wasn't over the moon about it. The team would say, 'Hey JV, can you do the first test day at St. Louis and make sure the car's good?' Then Montoya runs the second day, and by the tenth lap, he's on the pace or faster, never having seen short ovals. He did things on those tracks that were never really seen before, or after.

"You look at his speed traces and say, 'Man, I think you want to keep it more secure than that.' I tried to tell him, but he's like, 'Eh, it's okay, Vasser, it's okay.' Maybe it was the younger generation; I kind of bridged from the Mario and A. J. generation. I raced with those guys, and I learned that you want to keep a little comfortable understeer in the car. That could be because the tires weren't as good for the previous generation, and you'd get more degradation from the rears. You really had to build a lot of understeer in to protect the rear. The younger guys coming in were driving a much more neutral car and keeping it on the edge because the tire could take it. If you came from a previous era, maybe you didn't trust that the tire could take it. You kept a little more friendly understeer, but it wasn't as quick."

CHIP GANASSI

"I will say this: Vasser handled it like the champion he was and is. On the one hand, he complained that he went from having Zanardi as a teammate to getting Montoya, but I think it made him a better driver having those teammates. He had to push. There were several examples of where Jimmy had great days going and probably two or three wins didn't happen because of one thing or another, through no fault of his."

points over Fernandez, while Moore and Andretti fell five points back in third.

He was nonplussed by comparisons to Mansell's 1993 run to the CART title as a first-year driver in the championship. "Mansell is Mansell; I'm Montoya," he shrugged.

Despite his youth and lack of Indy car racing experience, Montoya was now consistently showing that he could be the type of thinking driver capable of winning races on any kind of track, and maybe even a championship. He was quickly winning over his detractors, both within his team and from outside. Race engineer Morris Nunn was at the top of that list. Nunn, who joined the Ganassi organization in 1992, enjoyed an eclectic career that started as a driver in the late '60s and took him into team ownership in Formula 1 a few years later. He moved to America as a race engineer in the mid-80s and had been contemplating retirement for the last few years. Nunn's attitude was rejuvenated by his time alongside Zanardi, and Montoya took it to another level.

"I've been absolutely astounded," Nunn revealed. "He's so quick, it's scary. At first you think he's a little arrogant, but I really don't think that's the case. He's full of confidence, and as I get to know him, at twenty-three, his mind is just on winning and driving. All else doesn't matter. So far, I can't fault him. He's championship material. His feedback is good. Alex got more involved with the car; he wanted to know everything. This kid just tells you what the car is doing and says, 'Fix it for me please—I'll go quicker.' If you ask him to find a way to get a little better fuel mileage by shifting a little early or whatever, he figures it out. He does it right off. So, he's A-plus across the board, and it makes my job easy. He's got a career ahead of him brighter than anybody I know."

Even Michael Andretti was impressed. "He's been driving well, maybe a little over his head," Andretti said. "He hasn't felt the wall yet, so most guys, when they're his age, with his experience, drive like that. Then when they get that BANG, they figure, 'Maybe we don't need to push that hard.'

"But he's been doing a good job," Andretti continued. "He's been handling himself very well in the races. We had our problems, but after we talked, I haven't had a problem racing against him since. He's won two races, and in a lot of ways, he's been a surprise. He's done a lot better, I think, than a lot of us expected. Get a couple years under him, and he's going to be very difficult. In a lot of ways, he seems to be a little bit better than Zanardi. In the races he's won, he hasn't put a wheel wrong, where Alex had a way of putting a wheel wrong and recovering."

Years later, Montoya expressed his admiration for Andretti. "From that time, for me, honestly Dario and Michael were the best," he said. "Greg was really good, but for me, he had his days. His good days were really, really good. But the off days were off as well. Dario was more consistent, but when Michael had everything lined up for him—fuck, the dude was hard to beat. He was so good, and I remember he would come and say how he had us covered and was going to kick our ass a couple times. I would go, 'Nah!' just to piss him off. I grew up playing mental games and being an asshole, and I was very good at it."

Despite both having shit-stirring personalities, there was never any controversy between Montoya and Tracy and the Canadian still has a great deal of respect for his younger rival.

"Montoya and I got along great," PT reflected. "You would think that we wouldn't have gotten along, because we're very similar to each other—both very aggressive, we don't back down. But he and I actually got along really well on and off the racetrack. We raced each other super hard, but I don't think we ever got into any major conflicts on the track. We seemed to like each other off the track, and as a driver, he's one of the best there is in anything. You can put him in any situation, and he'll drive the wheels off that car. He's one of those guys that can do that."

One constituency in the Indy car community that Montoya failed to win over was the media. Not much of a talker, Juan Pablo was perceived by many of the beat writers as aloof, arrogant, and sometimes downright rude thanks to the brevity of his answers in press conferences and even one-on-one interviews.

"I'm not a guy who speaks a lot of words," Montoya offered. "I want to make it as simple and easy as possible. That's the way I do it. If anyone asks me something, it's just 'yes' or 'no.' That's it. You don't have to go and tell all your history since you were born.

"Some people like to talk. I don't," he added. "I prefer to do the job and don't talk. You're not going to go quicker if you talk a lot. You've got to do what you've got to do. I wasn't hired to go and speak in front of the press for an hour. I was hired to do my job—to go out there and go as quick as I can and try to win as many races and championships as I can."

I once told Juan that a couple of the media regulars referred to him as "The Punk."

"Why would they call me a punk?" he smiled. "That's pretty good. I like that. No, honestly, it's good. To be honest, you can't expect everybody to love you. I'm not here to make friends and meet a lot of lovely people. I'm here to win. One thing Chip told me that actually really works is, 'You don't go to the track to make friends. You bring the friends with you.'"

Four races into the 1999 season, Montoya had already established himself as a threat to win the CART championship. He was riding a wave of confidence, far, far ahead of where anyone had expected him to be.

BOSCH SPARK PLUG GRAND PRIX

Nazareth Speedway — May 2, 1999 – 225 laps

1. Juan Pablo Montoya
2. P. J. Jones
3. Paul Tracy
4. Cristiano da Matta
5. Adrian Fernandez

CHAMPIONSHIP STANDINGS AFTER 4 OF 20 RACES

1.	Montoya	45
2.	Fernandez	43
3.	Moore	40
	Andretti	
4.	Franchitti	35
5.	Fittipaldi	34

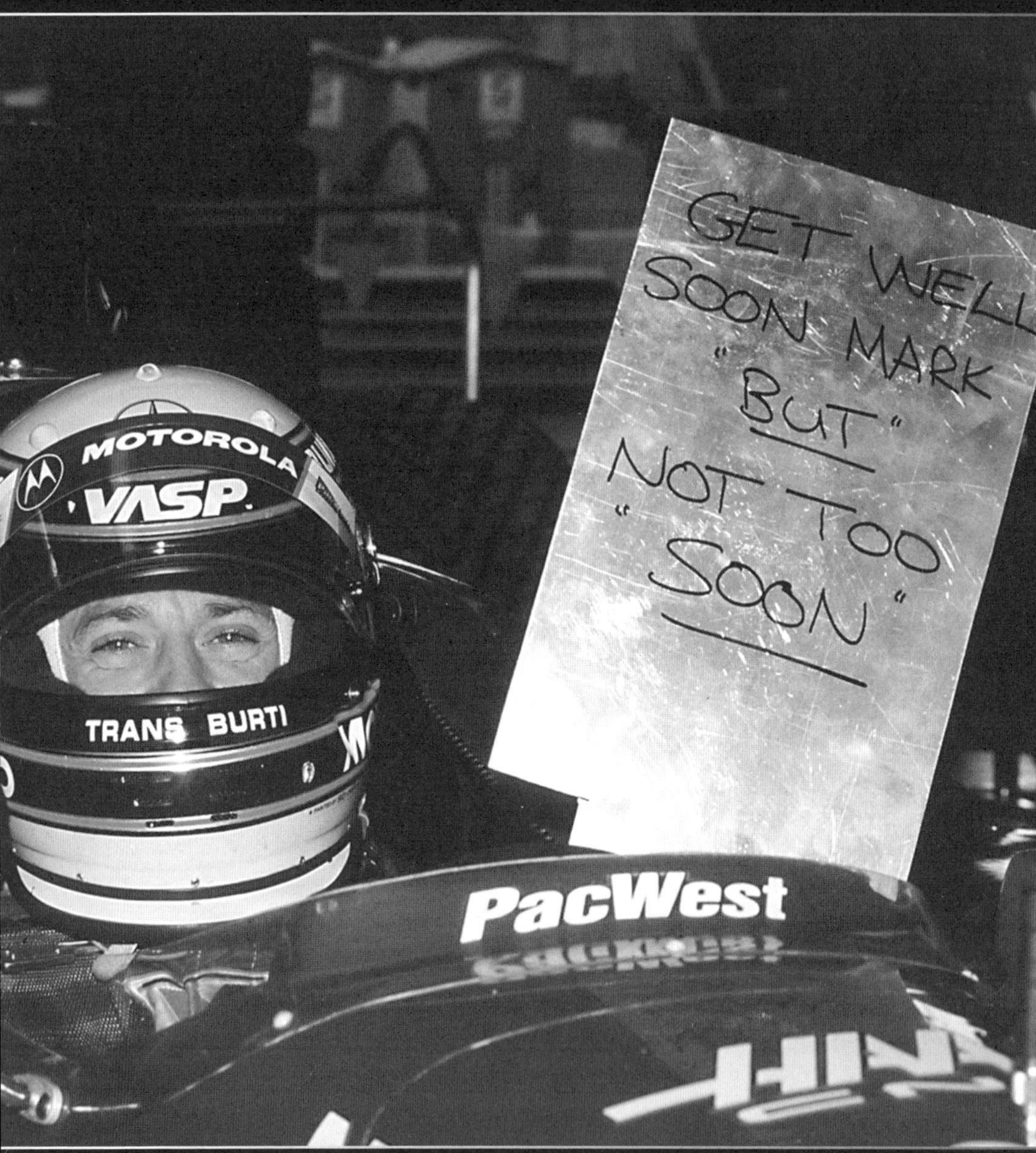

"Supersub" Roberto Moreno took over the No. 18 PacWest car for nine races midseason when regular driver Mark Blundell was injured in a test crash. *Dan R. Boyd*

CHAPTER 7

THE MONTH OF MAY

For more than one hundred years, the month of May has been synonymous with the Indianapolis 500. But that wasn't the case for CART's teams and drivers starting in 1996. Tension that had been simmering for decades between the Indianapolis Motor Speedway and participating teams boiled over and recently installed IMS President Tony George created a whole new racing series that included the Indy 500. As leverage, George reserved 75 percent of the grid for every Indy Racing League event for IRL points leaders, meaning more than two dozen CART entrants would be fighting for eight places in the thirty-three-car Indianapolis field unless they joined George's upstart series.

It was an audacious grab for power, and CART's reaction was to say, "Thanks, but no thanks." CART leased Michigan Speedway from Roger Penske and staged its own five-hundred-mile race on the last Sunday in May, the traditional Indianapolis 500 date. May 26, 1996, was arguably the strangest and saddest day in the long history of Indy car racing; shortly before Buddy Lazier crossed Indy's famous Yard of Bricks to win the first IRL-sanctioned Indianapolis 500, half of the twenty-seven-car CART field crashed at Michigan before even taking the green flag for the inaugural U.S. 500. When Jimmy Vasser took the win in his backup car four hours later and quipped "Who needs milk?" it was rendered virtually meaningless by the unrelenting focus on the humiliating start-line wreck.

By 1999, the IRL wasn't showing significant growth. But it also clearly was not going away; old grudges die hard, and the Hulman-

George family war chest ran far deeper than the $100 million CART had raised through its 1998 stock offering. Both series publicly proclaimed they were charting a course of independence. But behind the scenes, George and CART CEO Andrew Craig met several times in late 1998 and early '99 to discuss a potential "merger of equals." The talks went nowhere, but George went public in May 1999 to air his theory that CART leaked word of the negotiations to try to boost its stock price. Coincidentally, the CART share price peaked in the summer of 1999, prior to the start of a precipitous decline. The CART share price was already a hot topic, because as soon as a one-year no-sell requirement was lifted, several team owners—including Barry Green, Pat Patrick, and most notably, Roger Penske—sold large quantities of the 800,000 shares of CART stock they received as franchise owners in CART's initial public offering.

Fred Nation was the executive vice president of communications for the Indianapolis Motor Speedway in that era. A Terre Haute native, Nation served as press director for Senator Birch Bayh and later for Indiana Governor Evan Bayh, and his experience in state and national politics helped him start to repair the Speedway's antagonistic relationship with the media and the CART community.

"I didn't have a motorsports background, though growing up in Terre Haute, where Tony Hulman owned the newspaper and the television station, it wasn't much different than Indianapolis in terms of 500 coverage in the 1950s and '60s," Nation said. "It was a big learning curve, but what I had going for me was having been a journalist myself and having spent the last eight years in the Indianapolis media market as the press secretary/executive assistant for governor Evan Bayh's administration. I had a pretty good idea how to treat reporters and what reporters wanted, and that was what I brought to IMS.

"At that time, the Speedway was still pretty insular, still operating on a 'need-to-know' basis," he observed. "I worked hard to provide more access to print media and television stations especially during May. They were very grateful for that, and that helped our coverage at a time when there were a lot of stresses and difficulties due to the CART-IRL split. The politics of racing and the regular kind of politics have a lot of similarities and a lot of differences. I did notice that in that era the politics of racing were more vicious than the politics of the statehouse."

The '99 Indianapolis 500 included one full-time CART team. Robby Gordon, the son of off-road racer "Baja" Bob Gordon, started out like his father by dominating SCORE International desert competition in the late '80s. He began racing SCCA Trans Am and IMSA GTO sports cars and developed a work relationship with Ford that took him into Indy cars for a partial season with Chip Ganassi Racing in 1992. Gordon then drove for A. J. Foyt in '93, earning the Foyt team's first podium finishes since A. J. himself finished second at Milwaukee in 1982. A three-year stint with Walker Racing produced two CART race wins but ended with Gordon burning his bridges to Ford after loudly complaining too many times about engine unreliability.

Gordon sat out the '97 season but landed with the Arciero-Wells team for '98, and he produced some of Toyota's best performances to date. Gordon then secured his own Toyota engine deal to field a car in 1999 under the Team Gordon banner, with sponsorship from John Menard and his chain of Midwestern home improvement stores. Menard owned a racing team that was a frontrunner in the IRL, winning the 1997 series championship with future NASCAR star Tony Stewart. He was hopeful that his dual effort would have a positive effect on the Indy car split.

"I felt for some time that probably it might help get the two sides together somewhat if someone would run a program in both CART and the IRL, just to show people that it can be done," Menard said. "It's a decent business opportunity to accomplish some goals for my company and some of my racing goals as well, so it all came together pretty nicely. We're going to get some exposure for our stores in the Midwest, where our stores are located with our CART program, and the IRL program has some advantages too.

"I love open-wheel racing, and I'm trying to do all I can to try to make the sport work better—not for one side or the other, but for both sides," he added. "CART and the IRL have more in common than they do separating them. I don't know if they will ever totally get back together again, but it would sure be nice if we could come up with some kind of working relationship so that we could do things to better the sport as a whole. Rising water lifts all boats. Somewhere along the line, I think we can come to some kind of accommodation. As tempers cool and people start reflecting on the business aspect of the sport, perhaps it will just gradually come."

Gordon nearly stole the show at Indy. He qualified fourth, ran near the front all day, and took the lead on lap 171 of two hundred, trying to stretch his fuel the last thirty-six laps. He almost made it. Gordon's car sputtered as he approached the white flag, allowing Kenny Bräck to lead the final two tours to take the win for Foyt's team. Gordon was credited with fourth place.

Meanwhile, CART decided after just one year that it was pointless to try to go head-to-head on Indianapolis 500 race day with a copycat version of the Indianapolis 500. In 1999, it took full advantage of the open month of May to schedule three races. Nazareth took place on Sunday, May 2, followed on Saturday the fifteenth by an event in Rio de Janeiro, Brazil, then Saturday the twenty-ninth at Gateway International Raceway in western Illinois, just outside St. Louis. That would allow Gordon to attempt a Gateway/Indy "double," racing CART on Saturday and IRL on Sunday, May 30.

As it turned out, two drivers ended up doing the double. Mark Blundell was one of eleven CART drivers testing at Gateway on May 4, two days after the Nazareth race, when his PacWest Racing Reynard/Mercedes crashed heavily on the final run of the day. Entering Turn Three, Blundell attempted to shift down one gear, but the car's sequential gearbox dropped two gears instead. That caused the rear wheels to lock and instantly pitched the car into a spin and a hard backward impact with the wall. It was a worrying return of a problem for Reynard that had triggered big crashes in 1998 for Greg Moore at Motegi and Mauricio Gugelmin at Nazareth.

Blundell suffered light bruising to his brain and was battling some fluid buildup in his lower spine, but the initial diagnosis was that he was fundamentally uninjured. "It was a big accident, but the chassis stood up very well and the seat and the headrest did the job," said PacWest Technical Director Allen McDonald. "Mark is a bit stiff and sore, but he's in good spirits considering what he's been through."

Perhaps the most difficult part about an accident with injury that takes a driver out of the car is the mental aspect. While focusing on physical rehabilitation, they are put in the position of having to watch another driver behind the wheel of 'their' car. In a performance-related business where your last report card is your last race result, that can be a nerve-racking experience.

"The crash was not easy to go with," Blundell said. "I don't think it was the fault of the team or anything. It was one of those scenarios when you dropped into a forced neutral when I was in the middle of a downshift for a quick corner at St. Louis on the oval. It went into neutral and before I knew it, it decided to drop itself into the lower gear and locked up and put me in backwards at 175, I think. That was costly to me physically. I had some neck injuries and back injuries and so forth. It was a hard hit."

For the short-term, PacWest turned to veteran Brazilian Roberto Moreno—remember him? The guy who drove two 1991 Formula 1 races for Jordan between Michael Schumacher and Alex Zanardi was tabbed to drive the No. 18 car for the race in Rio, and potentially beyond, while Blundell was out of action. For his part, Blundell knew what it was like to be a substitute driver, having stepped in to complete the 1995 season for McLaren in Formula 1 when the team parted ways with Nigel Mansell a quarter of the way into the campaign.

"I think the Moreno situation was acceptable," said Blundell. "I'm old enough and big enough to understand that the team has to continue, and they needed someone in the car. But I think what happens as well, because someone else goes in there—and I don't think it matters who it would be—all of a sudden, maybe there's a fresh approach or a fresh way of looking at things. You're no longer part and parcel of the everyday scenario and things may take a different slant. Don't get me wrong, I'm quite confident in my abilities, I'm quite confident in what I achieved and what was achievable. That's only achievable when the whole package is working towards the same aim.

"It's very easy to blame the drivers for many things if things are not going right, and it's an easy switch just to take one out and plug another one in. It's something you get used to in your career. And that was just one of those situations where things didn't work out and it started to become a process of lack of confidence in the relationship."

ROBERTO MORENO

"The 'Supersub' thing actually started back in 1981, when I finished my full-time ride with Van Diemen in Formula Ford 2000 but didn't have enough money to do a full Formula 3 season. I replaced a driver in Kees van de Grint's team and won my first F3 race in my third start as a substitute driver. Then for a few years, I was traveling between Japan, Europe, and the US, and instead of having a steady competitive ride, I ended up doing bits and pieces everywhere. It's funny that I finally got a full-time ride in IndyCar in 2000, and my first race in CART was back in 1984.

"I was always with low-budget teams that had a hard time to even qualify. When Sandro Nannini got hurt in a helicopter accident in October 1990, the break with Benetton changed my career all over again. I was very lucky to get that break because I hadn't shown anything in Formula 1 up to that point. I was very glad to have that opportunity. But Michael Schumacher spoiled that. Benetton wanted him in the team, and when it came to kicking Nelson Piquet, a three-time World Champion out the door, or Moreno . . . I was much cheaper. They paid me off, but that hurt my image.

"I tried racing touring cars, but I didn't like it at all because all my life, everything I learned, was about Formula cars. I took the challenge to develop the Forti Corse Formula 1 car in 1995, but I knew I wanted to come back to the States. By then, I realized that if I wanted to go back to CART, I'd have to find a sponsor. We raised enough money to just get by for the '96 season with Dale Coyne. It was a very limited budget team, but I thought it would be better for me to be around this scene and learn the racetracks, to get credibility. Unfortunately, I think people saw me as a back-of-the-grid runner, and I had a very hard time getting credibility in CART. It wasn't until Christian Fittipaldi got hurt in '97 and I did some races as a substitute for Newman/Haas that people realized what I could do with one of the top Indy car teams. It was my first good break, but it still wasn't enough to build me up. But I've only seen happiness in my career."

The well-travelled Moreno had already signed to compete in the Indianapolis 500 for Truscelli Racing, so he joined Gordon in hoping for favorable weather on the May 29/30 Gateway/Indianapolis weekend. But first up was a trip to his homeland for the GP Telemar Rio 400 at Emerson Fittipaldi Speedway.

Emerson Fittipaldi's role in both blazing an international trail for Brazilian drivers and shaping modern Indy car racing cannot be overstated. The son of an automotive journalist and broadcaster, Fittipaldi was a phenom out of Sao Paulo who left home to race in England in 1969. He made such an instant impact in Formula Ford and Formula 3 that he made his Formula 1 debut for Team Lotus in the British Grand Prix on July 18, 1970. He won his fourth F1 start in the 1970 United States Grand Prix at Watkins Glen, and by the end of 1972, he was Formula 1's youngest-ever World Champion at age twenty-five.

Fittipaldi switched F1 teams from Lotus to McLaren in 1974 and won a second World Championship. But after finishing second to Niki Lauda in 1975, Emerson made the shocking decision to leave McLaren for a native team formed by his brother, Wilson (Christian Fittipaldi's father), with lucrative sponsorship from Copersucar, the Brazilian national sugar and alcohol fuel cooperative. He managed just one podium finish in five years of driving for Fittipaldi Automotive, and two more years struggling to keep the team financially afloat left him broke and disillusioned about racing.

The call from Ralph Sanchez to compete in the 1984 Miami Grand Prix IMSA sports car race reignited Fittipaldi's passion for competition. Buoyed by setting pole position at Miami, Emerson made his CART debut a couple months later at the first Long Beach Grand Prix staged for Indy cars. He finished fifth in an unsponsored pink car, ran the Indy 500 as a thirty-seven-year-old rookie, and by the end of the year parlayed it into a full-time ride with Patrick Racing. Fittipaldi relocated to Miami and enjoyed a highly successful second career in America, winning the 1989 CART championship and twenty-two Indy car races, including the 1989 and '93 Indianapolis 500.

Fittipaldi brought Philip Morris and Marlboro into Indy car racing in 1985 as a sponsor with Patrick Racing and later Team Penske, and Emerson's experience and success in America created a career path outside of F1 for aspiring South American racers. Moreno, Gugelmin, Raul Boesel, Gil de Ferran, and Andre Ribeiro all made the switch from pursuing F1 to Indy cars even before Fittipaldi helped create the Marlboro Latin America program that brought Tony Kanaan and Hélio Castroneves into the CART series.

Emerson reflects warmly on his days racing Indy cars, which could have started earlier than they did. "In September 1974, I drove Johnny Rutherford's Indy 500 winner at Indianapolis," he said. "I drove two days and went quite fast. My style of driving allowed me to adapt very quickly to high-speed corners. Johnny was very good to me, and A. J. Foyt was there as well. They took me around and showed me the track. The car had big wings, lots of downforce, and a lot of power—about a thousand horsepower. I liked the car very much, but the car was very fragile. At that time, if you crashed at Indianapolis, the car disintegrated. They wanted to make a white car called Texaco Star for the '75 Indy 500, but I decided not to race it.

"I would have loved to drive Indianapolis, because I remember when I was a teenager, they had an auto club in São Paulo that made a documentary about Indianapolis, from the 1950s or '60s—beautiful coverage of Tony Bettenhausen and the Unsers. The club sponsored a car called the Bardahl Special. So, I always had an attraction to Indianapolis, and when Jim Clark won in '65, for me it was a big thing in Brazil. I fell in love with Indianapolis, because the atmosphere is fantastic. I thought one day I should participate there. In 1970, I asked my teammate Jochen Rindt about it, and he said, 'Oh, it's a shit place—I'll never go back!' But Jack Brabham liked it.

"In '84, the car I tested was much stronger, with a carbon-fiber monocoque. And I loved Indianapolis—I liked the ambience, and I knew Roger Penske well, from Formula 1. Then Jim McGee of Patrick Racing called me to replace Chip Ganassi (a heavy crash at Michigan Speedway essentially ended Ganassi's driving career), and guess what? My engineer was Morris Nunn! I had a fantastic relationship with Mo, he was incredible at setting up the car. We competed against each other in England in '69, and now we were working together.

"I was driving a car sponsored by 7-Eleven, but I went to Park Avenue to Philip Morris, because most of my friends from Formula

1 were working back in New York. I asked the guys, 'What aren't you in Indy car? Can you imagine being at the Indy 500, on ABC, at the Number One race in America?' They said, 'Well, Emerson, we have the cowboy image, the Marlboro man.' So, they made the Marlboro International team and sponsored myself and Al Unser Jr. and Danny Sullivan. After one year, they had so much coverage on TV, they said, 'Yes, we will come into Indy car,' and then Pat Patrick had the full Marlboro sponsorship like McLaren. Racing in America was one of the happiest times of my career."

With interest led by Fittipaldi, Indy car racing was extremely popular in Brazil by the mid-90s, with at least half a dozen full-time Brazilian drivers. "Our generation was lucky—there was a particularly good amount of Brazilian drivers in that generation," remarked Kanaan. "It was helped by Emerson coming to America, then you had Andre, then you had Gil. And then IndyCar in Brazil was huge—we were getting the sponsorships, and Philip Morris was putting in a lot of money. Look at the Indy Lights program we had . . . Philip Morris was paying for me and Hélio and Andre and Gualter Salles. Hollywood did a huge program with Mauricio Gugelmin—he was a big name. We were helping each other because we kept elevating IndyCar in Brazil. We had just lost Ayrton Senna a few years before that, and Brazil was seeking another national hero in racing."

The next logical step was a CART-sanctioned race in Brazil. A 1.864-mile, four corner quadrilateral was created using the Jacarepaguá road course in Rio de Janeiro that hosted the Brazilian GP F1 race from 1983 to '89; Indy car legend Rick Mears instantly dubbed it a "roval," but appropriately, its official name was Emerson Fittipaldi Speedway.

Ribeiro, who had taken Honda's first Indy car victory at New Hampshire Motor Speedway in 1995 for Tasman Motorsports, won the first Rio 400 in 1996 and sent the Brazilian crowd home ecstatic. But he shockingly retired from driving at the end of the 1998 season at the age of thirty-two after spending the last year of his career with Penske Racing. That dovetailed with Roger Penske's desire to cut back to a single full-time entry. "I have been discussing my future a lot with Roger," Ribeiro said. "A lot of business opportunities were coming from Brazil, and we felt this was a good moment to pursue them."

Emerson Fittipaldi Speedway was also notable for its experimentation with padded walls starting in 1997, an important step in the evolution of soft wall technology that ultimately resulted in the development of the SAFER Barrier system that was successfully introduced at Indianapolis in 2002. It was Mark Blundell's crash due to brake failure during the 1996 Rio race that motivated the Brazilian promoters to begin seriously exploring the notion of a soft wall.

Brazilian drivers desperately wanted to perform well in their homeland; in addition to Ribeiro's triumphant win in '96, Gugelmin claimed his first Indy car pole at Rio in '97. In 1999, it was Christian Fittipaldi's turn to shine, as he also broke through for his first career pole in the Newman/Haas Swift/Ford. "As a Brazilian, I have only one chance to do well at home," he said.

Having triumphed on the Long Beach street course and a more traditional oval at Nazareth, the uniquely challenging Rio "roval" did nothing to slow Juan Pablo Montoya's momentum. From third on the grid, he seized the lead from pole-sitter Fittipaldi before the first turn and proceeded to lead ninety-three of 108 laps to win by 1.736 seconds over Dario Franchitti, with Fittipaldi taking third.

Montoya only dropped out of the lead during pit stop exchanges, though Al Unser Jr. led ten laps toward the end of the race, running a different fuel strategy that ultimately netted him twelfth place. It was Montoya's third consecutive victory, and it left the rest of the field wondering if the lead Ganassi car could ever be beaten.

"Chip said to take it easy at the start, but I thought I had a chance and just went for it," Montoya said. "After that, it got pretty close. We were all running at the same pace, and after the second pit stop, it got a bit exciting."

It certainly got a bit exciting for Franchitti, who had a huge moment when he got up into the marbles trying to pass Montoya. "He braked really late, and we came close to tangling," Montoya said. But Dario held on and ultimately prevailed for second after trading the position with Fittipaldi several times during the race.

Max Papis and Tony Kanaan rounded out the top five, while Vasser and Michael Andretti were the race's first two retirements. Moore, the dramatic winner in Brazil in 1998, was a disappointed eighth. "It was a frustrating day; we just didn't have it," he said.

In truth, all of Montoya's opposition had to be dejected after the young rookie claimed his third consecutive race. "I was expecting to win some races when I came in this series, but three in a row? No!" he said. "So far it's been great."

GP TELEMAR RIO 200

Emerson Fittipaldi Speedway — May 15, 1999 – 108 laps

1. Juan Pablo Montoya
2. Dario Franchitti
3. Christian Fittipaldi
4. Max Papis
5. Tony Kanaan

CHAMPIONSHIP STANDINGS AFTER 5 OF 20 RACES

1.	Montoya	66
2.	Franchitti	51
3.	Fittipaldi	49
4.	Moore	45
5.	Fernandez	43

Any grumbling about how an unknown rookie was dominating the FedEx Championship Series was at least temporarily quieted two weeks later when Michael Andretti fought back for the old guard and injected the FedEx Championship Series with some name-brand recognition on Memorial Day weekend. He scored a well-judged victory by 0.329 seconds over Hélio Castroneves in the Motorola 300 at Gateway International Raceway, his first win since the 1998 CART season opener at Homestead.

Backing off from the confrontational, same-day approach it employed with the 1996 U.S. 500 at Michigan Speedway, CART for the third year in a row elected to run its Memorial holiday event on the Saturday of Indy 500 weekend. The chosen venue was Gateway, which featured a drag strip and an oblong 1.25-mile oval built for $25 million by Chris Pook and the Grand Prix Association of Long Beach Inc. on an existing racetrack site a few miles east of St. Louis in Madison, Illinois. Gateway was briefly shut down in 2010 before being acquired by a private group led by Curtis Francois. All these years later, the facility—now known as World Wide Technology Raceway—remains sparse and undeveloped, and it's still located in an unattractive industrial area across from a truck stop and a landfill. The less said about Gateway, the better.

The 1999 Gateway race started slowly but brought the crowd of fifty thousand to its feet for the final thirty laps as Andretti dueled with Castroneves and a charging Franchitti to the checkered flag. Michael moved up quickly from eleventh on the grid and assumed the lead on lap 110 of 236 after the field made their second round of pit stops under green flag conditions. Running an alternate fuel strategy, the Newman/Haas team vaulted Andretti from fifth to first by not changing tires on his last pit stop. The thirty-eighth win of Andretti's career moved him up to third in the PPG Cup standings, four points behind Franchitti and eight back of championship leader Montoya.

"I've got to give a lot of credit to Firestone, because we took a real gamble by not changing tires at the last stop," Andretti said. "The Firestones were incredible—they just kept going and going. The team called a perfect race. When they brought me in early [under yellow] for the next-to-last stop, I questioned them, but they told me that we would need less fuel at the final stop and gain track position, and that's what happened."

Castroneves was on Andretti's rear wing for the final thirty laps, but he could never find a way past. "After the last pit stop [when he came out in sixth place], I just had to focus on passing the guys in front of me," Hélio said. "My car was so good; I was just taking chances everywhere. When I caught Michael, I was braking very late into Turn One, but he was very good exiting Turns Two and Four. I saw his car moving around in the rear, so I told myself to be patient, and wait till we caught the backmarkers, but he passed them perfectly. He's an excellent driver who knows how to win."

Midway through his second season racing Indy cars, it was starting to become clear that Castroneves was an exceptionally talented oval driver. It's fair to say he was overshadowed by CART's other twenty-something drivers like Moore, Montoya, and Franchitti at this stage of his career.

"I remember my first podium with Hogan," Hélio recalled. "I was battling at St. Louis, which was my team owner Carl Hogan's home race, with Michael Andretti. Ah, I couldn't believe it . . . I was racing for the lead with Michael Andretti in front of me—this is crazy! I remember when I got on the podium, I thought, 'This is a dream come true!' I had Michael here and Dario there and I thought, 'Dang! I'm part of the club.' That was actually a great moment in my life.

"Michael, Al Junior . . . those are the iconic drivers you watch when you are growing up," he added. "Then all of a sudden I'm battling with them, racing them. It was super special just to be on the same track with them. Bob Rahal too. It's intimidating—for me, it at least was—and it was really cool to be sharing the track with these legends. Very special to be racing those guys."

Franchitti had an eventful day, capped by a huge sideways moment when he was punted by Team Green teammate Paul Tracy on lap 158. Running second, Tracy had been trying, perhaps too hard, to keep Montoya from regaining the lead lap. Montoya, who had lost his lap when he ran out of fuel entering the pits on lap 104, muscled past Tracy in Turn One, causing Paul to lose momentum heading toward Turn Three. Franchitti looked to have made a clean move to the inside, but the two Kool cars touched, and Tracy slid backwards into the wall. "That was as sideways as I've ever been in a car without hitting something solid," Franchitti said. It was the second controversial clash between the Green teammates in the last eight CART events.

"I certainly didn't want it to happen, but when you have the inside line and you're level with somebody, if you back off, then you have to ask yourself why you're doing this. There comes a point when you know there's a move on, and when there's not a move on," Dario added. "There was definitely a move on there. But I understand why Paul is not happy."

Years later, Dario added: "PT and I had that St. Louis crash, but we never had a problem. We always would sort that stuff out straight away. He was great—I enjoyed PT as a teammate. We still occasionally talk about these times."

Behind the podium finishers, Moreno gave the Motorola brass something to cheer about in their home race as he brought PacWest's Reynard/Mercedes home fourth. It was the struggling team's best result of the season. "The PacWest team did an excellent job—I really have no words to say how great they were today," said Moreno. "They called the

MARIO ANDRETTI

"Quite honestly, I drove against him and everything else, and I don't know if I ever drove against anyone that was as fierce as Michael was in his day. I think his record shows he was winning races by totally winning. It cost him at times, obviously. There were races he could have made an extra pit stop and still won, but you try to get him to save fuel, and there was no freaking way. His strength was balls out, balls to the wall. A lot of these guys who were calling strategy for him were not reading that at all. I know the guy was on the same racetrack as me, in a lot of the same equipment, so I know what the hell he was capable of.

"I think Michael was probably already thinking ahead in 1999. You know, I had always had a tough time coming to terms with that because in my entire career as a driver, I never really looked over my shoulder and said, 'Oh I want to be an owner like Penske,' or be like anyone else. I never had that interest, but I think Michael did look at his future beyond driving. Whatever team he was driving for, when he thought his performances were fading, he just looked at the business side of it. You can see that he's done very well there. But that was his ambition. Michael said that he was always afraid of losing; it was not that he was going for the win, in a sense. You know what I mean? It was put in those terms.

"As soon as he officially stepped out of the cockpit, you could see he was a totally different man. Michael was so incredibly intense throughout his career that I could see that he could not deal with a really, really long career. I mean, he had a long career, but nothing like some of us did, because he could not let go of his focus during the weekend. I think it took its toll. Now in this different role, he is still involved in the sport he loves but wearing a different hat. He really relishes that."

BRYAN HERTA

"It's interesting, Michael became one of my closest friends among the driver group in the mid-to-late '90s. When he came back from F1 and he drove for Ganassi, I think he helped convince Chip to put me in the car the next year. I talked a lot with him about the team at that time and he was very open and helpful with me. We became really good friends; we vacationed and did a lot of stuff together. He gave me a call when he needed somebody when Dario got hurt in 2003. It was only supposed to be three races, but it turned into this whole second career that I never really expected. It was an amazing time. Then he gave me the opportunity to sort of spearhead the launch of the Acura LMP2 program, which was a really great car and a fun time in my life.

"But then he fired me midseason, which really upset me at the time. I didn't handle it well; I was mad, I was hurt. But time heals all wounds, and he was the one who saved me when I lost the sponsor at the end of 2015 and didn't know how I was going to continue. I had already been left short by sponsors in 2015, and I had a lot of debt from that year. I had a contract with a sponsor that was going to be the primary the next year and they pulled out. I couldn't see a way forward and he was the guy I called, just for advice.

"He said he wanted to run a fourth car and had this kid, Alexander Rossi. I still had some sponsors, but I didn't have the equipment and people. He said maybe we could find a way to do something together. I got on a red-eye to Indianapolis that night and by ten o'clock the next morning, we had basically blocked out a deal to go racing together in 2016. He saved our team. They took every single one of our employees to continue and some of them are still there today. He kept us together and he put the logos on the car and allowed me to keep the sponsorship money I had for that year. That's how I paid off the debt that I had. He became the most important person in my life kind of overnight because he helped me solve all these big problems I didn't know how to solve. It's been a great partnership. I've enjoyed it and I think it's worked out well for them."

strategy exactly right. The car was fantastic all day long, and I'm just so happy."

Moreno failed to finish the Indianapolis 500 the following day, dropping out with gearbox issues; Robby Gordon crashed on the tenth lap to finish dead last at Gateway prior to his close call with victory at Indy.

CART championship leader Montoya started on pole position at Gateway and was running third when he ran out of fuel. He fought back to regain the lead lap, eventually finishing eleventh. "I'm disappointed," he said. "We finished in the points, but not really where we should be. Everybody has bad luck sometimes, and today it was me."

With embarrassing memories of 1996 still fresh, the CART community was relieved to get through the month of May without any gaffes at the time of year when the eyes of the motorsport world are traditionally focused on Indianapolis and Indy car racing. In fact, it had been a hell of a month, with Montoya's emerging dominance brought back to earth by Andretti's timely victory at Gateway.

"It's great to win again—it's been too long," Michael said. "This really brings us back into the hunt for the championship. We needed a shot in the arm, and this will really pump up the team.

"We've had some good races, and we could have won at Homestead and Motegi," he added. "But today absolutely everything went perfect. Now we're heading to one of my favorite tracks at Milwaukee, and we should run well there. We're still learning about the Firestones on the road courses, so hopefully we'll be in a good position when we get to Portland in a few weeks."

MOTOROLA 300

Gateway International Raceway — May 29, 1999 – 236 laps

1. Michael Andretti
2. Hélio Castroneves
3. Dario Franchitti
4. Roberto Moreno
5. Max Papis

CHAMPIONSHIP STANDINGS AFTER 6 OF 20 RACES

1.	Montoya	69
2.	Franchitti	65
3.	Andretti	61
4.	Moore	53
	Fittipaldi	
5.	Fernandez	43

Paul Newman was a dedicated supporter of CART during the Indy car "split." *Michael Levitt*

CHAPTER 8

INTO SUMMER

"Everyone goes to Milwaukee after Indianapolis." So said Paul Newman's character Frank Capua in the 1969 movie *Winning*, which costarred Newman's real-life wife, Joanne Woodward, as his on-screen wife, Elora. Robert Wagner completed the love triangle as Luther Erding, the teammate and rival racer who disrupted Capua's marriage as much as his relationship with team owner Leo Crawford. *Winning* wasn't a critical or box-office hit, but it sparked a love of auto racing in Newman that he carried for the rest of his life. As a driver, he won multiple SCCA National Championships and several Trans-Am races, finished second overall in the 1979 Le Mans 24 Hours, and shared in a class victory (third overall) in the 1995 Daytona 24 Hours. Newman was seventy years old at the time.

Newman was also the co-owner of Newman/Haas Racing, a staunch supporter of CART, and perhaps the most vocal critic of Tony George and the IRL. "The tradition of road racing in this country runs deep, it runs powerfully, and it runs loyally," Newman told me in a 2004 interview for *RACER* magazine. "I would much rather go watch a good road race with sixty thousand or seventy thousand people in the crowd than to stand around where there are more people in the pits than there are in the stands."

He didn't hold back on his disdain for George, and the damage Newman believed George caused by starting the IRL. I once asked him if there was any hope, sooner or later, of everyone working in the same direction for American open-wheel racing.

"Well, you saw what happened when there was a change of regime in Iraq," he responded. "I don't know if the president would be prepared to send in the National Guard to attack Indianapolis, but who knows? If Tony George were $200 million less rich, this whole thing might come together very quickly.

"At least our fans are honestly come by and loyal," he added. "With all the crap and the backbiting that the fans have heard, the people that have remained the most loyal, the most patient, and the most forgiving are those people sitting out in the stands. They are the ones who are really to be applauded—and in the final analysis, those are the ones that we should pay the most attention to and should honor. I mean, Jesus, they should have divorced us a long time ago."

Like the fictional Frank Capua after his victory in the big screen 1968 Indianapolis 500, Newman went to Milwaukee on the first weekend of June 1999. But he had traveled there after watching his driver Michael Andretti win the Motorola 300 at Gateway International Raceway outside St. Louis, not from the 83rd running of the Indy 500. Like every track on the pre-split Indy car schedule except Phoenix Raceway and New Hampshire International Speedway (and obviously Indianapolis), the Milwaukee Mile remained loyal to CART. In fact, Newman/Haas Racing co-owner Carl Haas was the Milwaukee promoter, as he was for many years for Indy car races at Road America, the bucolic road course an hour and change north near the town of Elkhart Lake.

The Mile boasts a history of auto racing dating to 1903—six years before construction started on the Indianapolis Motor Speedway and eight years prior to the first Indianapolis 500. Originally a horse racing track about six miles west of downtown Milwaukee, in what became known as the city of West Allis, the land was eventually transformed into the permanent site for the Wisconsin State Fair. The dirt oval was paved in 1954, and by then, the tradition of running a Championship car race at Milwaukee the week after the Indianapolis 500 was long established.

Milwaukee may have kept its traditional early June date, but it no longer enjoyed the box office benefit of being able to promote the new Indy 500 winner. For 1999, Haas invested in a round of improvements

HÉLIO CASTRONEVES

"The pole at Milwaukee was also something very special that year. I remember when I did the pole on the first lap, they never told me on the radio if I had the pole or not. Then I almost stuffed it in the wall, and they're like, 'You've already got the pole, just finish the lap!' I'm like, 'Guys, I wish somebody had told me that!'

"For me, 1999 was an interesting season. I learned so much, so much, that year. It was so incredible to learn from each individual driver. Robby Gordon was doing these incredible restarts, going from twentieth to tenth, and I think Tony Kanaan learned from that later.

"The Lola was a car that nobody believed in, and the Mercedes engine wasn't on its prime. We found some areas to improve that made the Lola really good. The interesting thing is that Penske switched to Lola because their '99 season wasn't the best. We still ended up beating the crap out of them! It's really funny that we were able to surpass that, but it shows that my group was incredible.

"My engineer, Andy Borme, went with me to Penske the next year and that was a big part of my success, because he was really able to accommodate what I like. Matt Swan, who today works at Meyer Shank Racing, he was my crew chief back then. So, I had an amazing group of guys, incredible people pushing wherever we could. And of course, Carl was incredible, putting in his own money and pushing it as far as he could. I became a really good friend of the whole Hogan family. It was a dream team with what we had. It reminded me a lot of my dad's stock car team, and that's probably why we were able to do so well."

---

to the famous oval, which included new walls, fencing, and an increase in seating capacity. But the crowd appeared down from recent years and was generously estimated at thirty-five thousand. CART's television ratings had been decreasing since the start of the split, and in 1999, attendance at a few events started to slip noticeably, mainly at oval tracks.

Unlike most ovals, Milwaukee continued to draw a strong crowd for qualifying. Hélio Castroneves, who had been consistently the fastest oval track driver in the FedEx Championship Series in 1999, finally put it all together over one lap when it counted to claim pole position for the Miller 225. Castroneves had missed out on claiming his first career pole by one-thousandth of a second at Nazareth Speedway, but he appeared to have plenty in hand at Milwaukee. The last man to run made it worth the wait for an audience of around fifteen thousand by turning the only sub-twenty-two-second lap of the afternoon.

With the cars using low-downforce speedway wings for the first time at Milwaukee, speeds were down by more than fifteen miles per hour. Another factor in the mix for qualifying was the sweltering heat, which approached ninety degrees on the thermometer.

Jimmy Vasser qualified his Ganassi Reynard/Honda on the front row for the first time in 1999. "It's really the first time this year we've had a trouble-free weekend," commented the Californian. "There has always been some little problem or technical glitch that has held us back. We're also working more with [engineer] Morris Nunn and that's really helped. He's got a lot of knowledge and talent and we're starting to tap into that a little bit on the No. 12 side."

Greg Moore qualified third, while Dario Franchitti improved from seventeenth fastest in practice to line up on the outside of the second row, just ahead of Juan Pablo Montoya. Montoya never looked happy with his car throughout practice and had several tense moments as his car pushed out of the groove into Turn One.

Reporters were already eager to create a rivalry between Montoya and Franchitti, the two men at the top of the championship points table. "The thing is, I like Juan," Franchitti said. "We have a good laugh at the track. It's a situation where he knows I want to beat him, and he wants to beat me, but at the same time, we get along well. When we get out there and race, it's going to be no holds barred, but it will be done in a good way."

Paul Tracy was fastest in Friday practice and second behind Castroneves on Saturday morning, but he faded to sixth on the grid. Like several others, including P. J. Jones, Tracy had a lurid moment on his qualifying run as his Team Green Reynard/Honda fought for grip in the midday heat. PT was one of several drivers who suggested that with the cars sliding more with the small wings, tire wear could be the deciding factor in the race.

Instead, Tracy used superior fuel saving to score a tactical victory, ending over two years of frustration. Tracy managed to stretch his final fuel load 102 laps while leaders Montoya, Vasser, and Gil de Ferran all pitted near the end for a splash of methanol. Aided by a couple of late-race yellows for harmless spins by Roberto Moreno and Jones, Tracy cruised to the flag 5.88 seconds ahead of Moore (who also did not stop) and Gil de Ferran.

Pole man Castroneves led the first fifteen laps until his Mercedes engine acted up. Tracy started sixth but emerged in the lead on lap sixty-six after the first round of pit stops. He held the point for forty laps before relinquishing it to a charging Vasser, who ran at the front until the second round of stops on lap 124. That set up the key to Tracy's victory. Early in what turned out to be an eighty-four-lap stretch of green-flag racing, Team Green engineer Tony Cicale advised his driver over the radio to conserve fuel.

"Tony said to run in sixth gear all the way around," Tracy said. "I was lifting on the straights and coasting into the turns. We came out of the pits in fifth place, and I ran pretty lean but was still able to keep up with Gil. We could still do the times, but the fuel mileage from the Honda was the difference."

Montoya took the lead during that second round of stops. He and Target/Ganassi teammate Vasser then commenced a tight duel over a full stint, until Montoya came in for a splash of fuel on lap 209. When the yellow flew just one lap later, Vasser and de Ferran came in for fuel, while Tracy and Moore stayed out. They were aided by an additional three laps of yellow when Jones spun in Turn Four while approaching the restart.

"My fuel light came on with five laps to go," Tracy said. "When that happens, you usually run out within a lap or two, so I can't believe it." It was his fourteenth career Indy car win, and the fiftieth in the CART series for Firestone since it returned to the sport in 1995. Goodyear had claimed twenty-six victories in that time frame, but fifteen of those wins came in '95 while Firestone was still underrepresented and getting up to speed.

"Last year was really tough for me," Tracy added, paying tribute to the role Cicale played in helping him rebuild his confidence. "When you go from rock bottom, you kind of feel you can't get any lower and pick yourself up. Each weekend, we've been building, trying to build one block at a time. Two years is a long time. You keep scratching your head. You're doing everything right, you make the right decisions on the car, you get yourself into position, and it falls apart. It's very frustrating. It seemed like every time I picked myself back up, another boulder would fall on me. To get that win again is almost as tough as the first one."

Years later, Tracy still recognizes how important his 1999 win at Milwaukee was. "It was good to break through," he said. "Milwaukee was a great track for me, one of my favorite ovals. I think I won four times there. I didn't win there when I was with Penske, but I ran up front, and I won in '95 with Newman/Haas. Wins in '93, '94, and '95 came pretty frequently for me, and then I had three in a row in '97, but then came that kind of lean period all the way through '98 to when I finally got that win at Milwaukee in '99. That was a big monkey off my back."

Vasser forced his way by Montoya for fifth on the final lap, but Montoya and original fourth-place finisher Patrick Carpentier were penalized a lap by CART after the finish for passing under the yellow, dropping them to ninth and tenth respectively. Ganassi Racing managing director Tom Anderson blamed himself for denying Vasser the opportunity to win at Milwaukee for the second year in a row. "We had enough fuel to finish, but I made the call to bring Jimmy in," Anderson said. "I cost him the race."

Michael Andretti's hopes of maintaining momentum after his win at Gateway went unfulfilled. Andretti slashed his way from eleventh on the grid to first in just fifty laps, culminated by an amazing sequence of four passes on laps forty-eight to fifty that moved him into the lead. But disaster struck during his first pit stop. Despite having the clutch depressed, Andretti's Swift/Ford crept forward after it was dropped from the jacks. Michael misunderstood a "No! No! No!" message on his radio as "Go! Go! Go!" and accelerated away with the fuel and vent hoses still attached, and vent man Ty Manseau was run over by the car's left-rear wheel. It was a scary looking incident but Manseau, who was wearing a helmet, suffered only superficial injuries and was released from the infield care center the same day.

"When the tire inched toward my helmet, I closed my eyes and thought, 'Let's get this over with,'" Manseau said. "I knew the tire was on my helmet when I felt my head jostle. Then everything got still. Instinctively, I put my hands over my head. Then I opened my eyes, and everything was black. And I thought, 'Oh, I'm dead.' Then I heard cars, and I saw a little light. That's when I realized my helmet had been turned 90 degrees. I turned it back and didn't feel any pain, so I felt my hand and feet and they were fine too."

Andretti finished the race in fifteenth place; CART immediately mandated a 50-mph Pit Lane speed limit (down from 60 mph) and the use of helmets by all over-the-wall pit crew personnel beginning with the next race at Portland International Raceway. Dave Stephens, a crew member for Gil de Ferran and Walker Racing, had sustained a concussion at Gateway in a pit incident while he was wearing a helmet, and the mandatory helmet rule was already scheduled to go into effect at Cleveland, one week after Portland.

MILLER LITE 225

The Milwaukee Mile —June 6, 1999 – 225 laps

1. Paul Tracy
2. Greg Moore
3. Gil de Ferran
4. Jimmy Vasser
5. Adrian Fernandez

CHAMPIONSHIP STANDINGS AFTER 7 OF 20 RACES

1.	Montoya	73
2.	Franchitti	71
3.	Moore	69
4.	Andretti	61
	Fittipaldi	
5.	Fernandez	53

Most people think of Indianapolis and Milwaukee when it comes to ancient American racing history. But the Portland area can be included in that conversation. An open-wheel race was held on a 14.6-mile course of paved and dirt city streets and country roads on June 12, 1909. The seven-lap, 102.2-mile contest was won by Bert Dingley in a Keats Auto Company Chalmers-Detroit 40 at an average speed of 58 mph.

Like the Indianapolis 500 from 1911 to 1955, the first Portland race was sanctioned by the American Automobile Association. It was part of the Portland Rose Festival, a tradition revived with an event called the Rose Cup sports car races when Portland International Raceway (PIR) was created in 1961 out of streets and country roads in an area called West Delta Park, north of downtown and near the Washington state border.

PacWest Racing always threw a good party at Portland, the closest race to Bruce McCaw's Seattle-area home, especially when the event coincided with his birthday. That didn't occur in 1999, and McCaw also didn't have much to celebrate about his team's recent performance either as the Mercedes-Benz engine program continued to struggle. But he was delighted to be named the 1999 Motorsportsman of the Year by the Cascade Pacific Council of the Boy Scouts of America. McCaw received the award at the tenth annual Motorsports Breakfast sanctioned by the Portland Rose Festival, a function attended by around 1,200 people.

"It's a real pleasure to receive this honor," McCaw stated. "Over thirty years ago, I drove in my first race here long before the Festival Turn, or even the chicane. In that car [an Austin Bugeye Sprite], the straightaway went on forever. I still love to drive here when I participate in vintage races."

Fuel strategy races can be exciting, and they often earn plaudits for the successful team and the pilot in the cockpit. The inaugural CART event at PIR in 1986 saw Mario Andretti snatch victory from his son when Michael ran out of fuel coming out of the last corner on the last lap. On Father's Day, no less! But they sometimes leave a sour taste for a segment of the audience that wants to see flat-out action from green flag to checkered. That's what they got at Portland in 1999, and it was as satisfying for winning driver Gil de Ferran as it was for the fans.

Montoya took pole and was happy to be back in a road racing environment. "I was expecting to be quick here because it's a road course," he said. "I think the drivers' level is a bit harder on the road courses than the ovals. I actually enjoy the ovals a lot, but I'd prefer to see more of a mixture. You get six ovals in a row, then a few road courses, then an oval. It's hard to get used to driving on a road course again."

Castroneves earned the first front row starting spot on a road course for a Lola since 1996, while de Ferran was quietly confident after qualifying P3. "I think Goodyear made some tremendous gains from last year," he related. "We worked very hard before the second phase of the championship started. We came here twice to select a tire for here and Cleveland and to set a tone for the rest of the road courses. The consistency is to me is really an unknown—ask me tomorrow! But I'm very confident about the performance."

Castroneves muscled into the lead at the start, and he and Montoya gapped the field until they made their first pit stop on lap thirty. Almost immediately, Castroneves suffered yet another Mercedes-Benz engine failure. "What can I say? The car was strong enough to win the race," he said.

Montoya led until he spun on lap fifty-one in the final corner accelerating for a restart. Amazingly, he lost only one place to de Ferran, and he quickly repassed the Brazilian, only for another caution to fly a few laps later when P. J. Jones spun and stalled. The leaders all pitted, and a slow stop dropped Montoya to third behind de Ferran and Tracy. Thirty-eight laps remained to the finish, and with track position, Walker Racing owner/strategist Derrick Walker decided to go on the offensive and committed de Ferran to a flat-out, three-stop strategy rather than trying to save fuel and complete the ninety-eight-lap race on the two stops already made. It was reminiscent of the strategy that Ferrari sensationally used to help Michael Schumacher score a famous victory in the 1998 Hungarian Grand Prix.

De Ferran did his part, running a series of fast laps that gave him a big enough margin to make a splash-and-go pit stop on lap ninety. Meanwhile, Montoya was driving an uncharacteristically conservative, fuel-saving race, allowing de Ferran to emerge with an eight-second advantage. He cruised to the finish with a 4.393-second margin of victory over Montoya, who showed remarkable discipline but did not enjoy being put on a fuel economy run.

"It's a hard thing to go down the straight at part throttle," he said. "I was using half-throttle on the straights and fifth gear in most of the corners. We've tried it [the fuel strategy game] both ways in the last two races, and it didn't work out for us either time. That's the way it goes sometimes. It's no fun to drive like that."

Franchitti, who was very unhappy after qualifying twelfth with mismatched rear tires, drove a forceful race to third place and his fifth podium finish of the season. "After the disaster in qualifying, I'll take third place," he said. "We're still in the championship hunt."

The hard-fought victory shook monkeys off the backs of de Ferran, Walker, and especially The Goodyear Tire and Rubber Company. It was the first FedEx Championship Series race win for de Ferran since Cleveland in July 1996 (forty-nine starts), the first for Goodyear since Homestead '98 (thirty-five starts), and the first for Walker since Robby Gordon won at Detroit in '95.

The driver nicknamed "Professor" had come close to winning at Portland before, most notably in 1997 when Mark Blundell stole the win at the line for PacWest by 0.027 seconds in what remains the closest road racing finish in Indy-style racing's history. De Ferran also finished second at Portland 1996.

"It's a great feeling—fantastic!" de Ferran exclaimed. "The team called a perfect strategy. Early in the last stint, I wasn't saving enough fuel, so five or six laps in, Derrick called me on the radio and said, 'Let's go for it—try to build a gap.' I knew we needed a gap of at least twenty seconds, and by the time I stopped, it had grown to twenty-six seconds. I still wasn't positive it was enough until I came out and they told me 'Plus eight.' Juan still had to conserve fuel, so I knew we were good to the finish."

But the biggest story coming out of Portland was the much-needed victory for Goodyear against what had turned into a relentless Firestone onslaught. Rumors were already starting to circulate that Goodyear's time in the CART series was approaching the end.

"We like to think that this isn't a tire war, because in a war, you have a winner and a loser," said Firestone racing director Al Speyer. "An ultimate victory, if it means one company is getting out, is not the preferred result. I'm still surprised we've done as well as we have. Our realistic expectation was to come to a level where we'd be head-to-head, battling on an equal basis."

BUDWEISER / G. I. JOE'S 200

Portland International Raceway — June 20, 1999 – 98 laps

1. Gil de Ferran
2. Juan Pablo Montoya
3. Dario Franchitti
4. Adrian Fernandez
5. Paul Tracy

CHAMPIONSHIP STANDINGS AFTER 8 OF 20 RACES

1. Montoya 90
2. Franchitti 85
3. de Ferran 71
4. Moore 69
5. Fernandez 65

Just seven days later, the FedEx Championship Series was back in action some 2,500 miles away on arguably the most unique track on the calendar. Since 1982, CART staged a race on a fast and bumpy 2.106-mile circuit consisting of runways at Cleveland's Burke Lakefront Airport on the shore of Lake Erie, next to the Rock and Roll Hall of Fame. Traditionally held near the fourth of July holiday, the Cleveland Grand Prix was often a steamy, physically taxing race that occasionally tossed up a surprise result.

Not so in 1999, as Montoya claimed his fourth pole of the season on what he called his "new favorite track" then controlled the race from start to finish for victory number four. The Colombian rookie led seventy-six of ninety laps on the one-off airport course in a race that ended ten laps short of the scheduled one-hundred-lap distance under CART's two-hour time limit rule.

Montoya led under green flag conditions until his first pit stop on lap thirty-one. At that point, the light drizzle that had been spitting for several laps soon turned into full-fledged rain. After several drivers crashed, notably Vasser and Tony Kanaan, the yellow came out on lap thirty-five and Montoya emerged in the lead after re-pitting for rain tires.

The field ran sixteen laps behind the pace car while standing water was removed from the course before the race resumed with Montoya leading de Ferran, Tracy, and Andretti, who had fought back from fifteenth place after incurring a penalty for speeding in the pits. Montoya sped out to a four-second advantage, but the Goodyear rains became the preferred tire as the track dried and de Ferran overtook Montoya for the lead on lap fifty-eight. Gil still ran first after he and Montoya made routine pit stops to change back to slick tires under the green four laps later.

But Firestone tires soon reasserted their superiority. Following a lap sixty-four to sixty-seven caution for Adrian Fernandez's Turn Eight wreck, it took Montoya just one hot lap on the rapidly drying track to pass de Ferran. He cruised to a 10.604-second margin of victory.

"My race went quite well," Montoya commented. "When it was really wet, the car was really good. But as the track dried, the car didn't work so well on the wet tires. The same thing happened to me in qualifying at Portland."

De Ferran also reported his car was very quick on Goodyear's latest rain tire. "But after the full course yellow, I couldn't get the tires up to temperature quick enough," he said. "I tried hard to keep Juan under pressure, but it was all I could do the keep the gap from growing any faster. Second is a good result for us in terms of the championship, but I have to admit we're a little disappointed."

Andretti and Tracy staged a hectic battle for the final rostrum spot throughout most of the race with plenty of passing for position. Michael eventually claimed the honor after an eventful run. His Ford/Cosworth engine died briefly late in the race, but he coaxed it back to life and made it to the finish. "Considering all we went through today, I'm happy with third," Andretti said. "When it was wet out there it was like ice."

It was a bad day for championship contenders Franchitti (broken throttle cable), Moore (blown header), and Fernandez (crash). Their misfortunes allowed Montoya to open a twenty-five-point lead over de Ferran in the battle for the PPG Cup, with Franchitti another two points behind. Dario's misery was compounded by the inclement weather.

"Cleveland was weird, something strange like a throttle linkage broke," he noted. "How the hell does that happen? I remember it rained, and I had to sit there in the rain because I'd pulled to the wrong side of the circuit. I got soaked, and I was so pissed off. At that point in the season, that was a pain in the ass. I knew I had to get on with it if I was going to contend for the championship, I really did. I knew podiums weren't going to cut it. Monty was really finding his stride."

Al Unser Jr. finished fifth at Cleveland, his best result since Penske Racing switched to a Lola chassis as Indy car racing's most successful team tried to claw its way back to relevance. Junior hadn't been competitive since he returned at Nazareth after missing just two races. It didn't help matters that Penske was comparison testing two different chassis mid-season while occasionally fielding rookie Tarso Marques in a second car and making plans to utilize other drivers. The striking but difficult-to-set-up-and-maintain Penske PC27B was shelved following the race in Brazil, even though it was clear to most outside observers not contracted to Goodyear, Mercedes-Benz, or Ilmor that the chassis was the least of Team Penske's problems. At Cleveland, the favorable performance of Goodyear's rain tires helped Unser deliver a morale-boosting performance in the team's Lola-Mercedes.

"We found a good race setup and the car stayed with me all day long," Unser stated. "If you don't have the right combination, even Ayrton Senna couldn't do anything about it. That's what has happened to me for a couple years. I had a good time out there today except during the downpour when I couldn't see out of my visor. We just need to focus on qualifying better."

Al Junior's appearance was a major talking point at Cleveland; he showed up with a shaved head. Given the rampant rumors that swirled around his personal life, it wasn't too difficult to deduce that he was trying to avoid or circumvent some form of drug testing. Many years later, he revealed that was exactly why he broke out the clippers. Team Penske was on the verge of major changes, and after keeping his party-heavy lifestyle hidden for many years, Unser was finally starting to realize that his racing career—and indeed his overall well-being—was in serious jeopardy.

MEDIC DRUG GRAND PRIX OF CLEVELAND

Burke Lakefront Airport — June 27, 1999 – 90 laps

1. Juan Pablo Montoya
2. Gil de Ferran
3. Michael Andretti
4. Paul Tracy
5. Al Unser Jr.

CHAMPIONSHIP STANDINGS AFTER 9 OF 20 RACES

1.	Montoya	112
2.	de Ferran	87
3.	Franchitti	85
4.	Andretti	78
5.	Moore	69

Greg Moore and Hélio Castroneves share a moment on the pit wall. *Michael Levitt*

CHAPTER 9

ELKHART LAKE TO LAKE SHORE BOULEVARD

Being born with a famous name doesn't automatically pave the road to a successful racing career. Just ask Bobby Unser Jr. or Jeff Andretti.

As detailed in chapter 5, the name Fittipaldi represents racing royalty in Brazil. Wilson, the family patriarch, was often called his country's version of beloved British Formula 1 announcer Murray Walker. The Fittipaldi boys, Wilson Jr. and Emerson, grew up to be Formula 1 drivers—a two-time World Champion, in Emerson's case. Wilson Jr. founded the Fittipaldi Automotive F1 team that constructed and fielded cars from 1975 to '82.

In 1991, Wilson Jr.'s son Christian narrowly edged Alex Zanardi for the FIA Formula 3000 championship. The final round took place at the Nogaro circuit in France, and Fittipaldi, then twenty, beat Zanardi in a straight fight to win the race and the title. That accomplishment earned him three seasons in F1 with backmarker teams Minardi and Footwork, with a trio of fourth-place finishes as his best results. Fittipaldi then made the switch to Indy cars; he ran the 1995 CART season for Walker Racing, highlighted by a second-place finish at Indianapolis in the last pre-split Indy 500.

Christian appeared to land his big break when he was signed by Newman/Haas Racing to partner Michael Andretti in 1996. He almost won at Detroit, but a late-race mistake allowed Andretti to slip past. Later the same season at Road America, he was out front when his engine blew with four laps remaining. Fittipaldi's 1997 season was truncated by six races after he broke his leg in a nasty wreck early in the season at Surfers Paradise, Australia; "Supersub" Roberto Moreno took his place. He missed another race in '98 due to a concussion sustained in a testing accident and ended the year with just half of Andretti's points tally. People were questioning whether his performances were living up to the Fittipaldi name.

Christian's star-crossed story is part of why his victory in the 1999 Texaco/Havoline 200 at Road America was so popular. It came in his seventieth career Indy car start, and it came at the expense of Juan Pablo Montoya, who parked his Ganassi Reynard/Honda with a broken gearbox while leading with six laps remaining. Fittipaldi led Andretti home in a one-two finish for Newman/Haas Racing in front of an announced crowd of seventy-five thousand, making it a lucrative day for Carl Haas as both team owner and race promoter.

Fittipaldi may have taken the longest victory lap in CART history when he celebrated his win. But after almost five years of trying, he was entitled.

"I have been waiting for this day for quite some time," he explained. "To be honest, it does go through your mind that you're never going to win. You just try to be strong and put that to the side. This is even sweeter because in 1996 I had a nice race here with Michael before my car stopped four laps from the end. But that's racing. Sometimes you need a little bit of luck. The same way Michael was a little lucky three years ago I was a little lucky here today. I guess things turned around a little for me today."

Haas was delighted for his driver. "He has more talent than people give him credit for," said the longtime entrant. "He has been on the verge all season and I am just so happy for him. What a great race for the fans, and with Michael finishing second, it only makes this better. You can't ask for much more. I am walking on clouds right now."

Four miles in length, a lap at Road America is the longest track Indy cars compete on by a wide margin. In 1999, the race length was extended from fifty to fifty-five laps to discourage fuel-saving strategies. The event had been decided in 1982 and 1989 by the lead driver running out of fuel on the final lap.

"Too many times the outcome here was dictated primarily by which team got the best fuel mileage," said Jim Haynes, president of Road

America. "By lengthening the race slightly, we have made this a three-stop race for everyone, which allows more teams to be racing full-bore at the finish. That means more exciting racing."

"You won't have guys running their engines almost a hundred horsepower down out there just trying to make the end of the race," added Andretti, who ran out of fuel on the final lap to lose the '89 Road America race to Danny Sullivan.

Like virtually every other driver, Greg Moore adored Road America, located in the heart of Wisconsin's Kettle Moraine region. "Of all the tracks we race on, I would say it's the purest of all road courses," he said. "You know, four miles long, the Carousel, the Kink . . . extremely challenging. But not only is that track challenging because of those two turns, but there's also some slow turns—Turn Three, Turn Four, and the last turn coming onto the main straight. You'll see the track will change in the middle of the race. Turn One and Two might be slippery early on but might pick up grip as the race goes on. Then down in the valley, maybe some dew comes in or some mist comes in and it changes the track down there. You've got to be on your toes no matter where you are on that circuit. It's almost a two-minute lap, and it changes from lap to lap. Setup-wise, it's a real challenge because you've got to change so many things. Fuel strategy is a concern anywhere you go, but at that race, because the track is so long, you're going to use two or three gallons per lap. You've got to be right on with your fuel strategy. But racing-wise, it really is a ton of fun."

The drivers also had a lot of fun off the track at Road America, and the party celebrating Dario Franchitti's first Indy car race win has gained mythical status among racing fans. Siebkens Resort was never known for luxurious accommodations or amenities. Instead, the quaint hundred-year-old inn and tavern at the center of the village of Elkhart Lake became famous as a watering hole for the racing fraternity. Just a five-minute drive through rolling countryside from Road America, Siebkens is where racers have congregated for decades to celebrate or commiserate over beers and bratwursts.

Franchitti and Moore awoke the morning of August 17, 1998, on opposite ends of the lawn outside the sprawling Osthoff hotel after what Dario dryly called "a big party." Moore organized the bacchanalia that took over Siebkens and eventually ended with the two key protagonists passed out on the grass under the stars. "We don't need to go into the details of that night," said Max Papis, another notable party participant along with Tony Kanaan. "It's too compromising."

The wild impromptu celebration not only exploded the myth that drivers in the modern era were joyless automatons focused on car setup or physical training twenty-four hours a day, it cemented a growing friendship among a group of talented twenty-somethings who were living a dream life as Indy car drivers.

In 1999, Friday's action started with an accident that looked far scarier from the outside than it apparently was for driver Patrick Carpentier. Approaching Turn One at nearly 200 miles per hour, Carpentier lost control of his Player's/Forsythe Reynard/Mercedes under braking. After sliding sideways into the gravel run-off area, the car was pitched into a series of barrel rolls—five by most counts, but six according to the driver.

"I hit the gravel sideways," Carpentier recalled. "At 200 mph, there's not much you can do once it goes sideways, just lock the brakes. It spun the car in the air and the only thing I saw was sky, gravel, sky, gravel—six times. When I watched it on a TV screen, I didn't realize it was such a big hit. We came into the weekend saying we need to hop our game up a little bit to stay with Montoya. That's what we did, but I guess we'll have to bring it down a touch."

Carpentier had several spectacular accidents during his career, including a backwards flip over a retaining fence at Laguna Seca in 2000. But he always escaped serious injury.

"CART was doing the right stuff before the split," Patrick said. "The medical team they had back then was way, way ahead of its time. Trammell and Olvey were miracle doctors. I've stayed at Terry Trammell's house a couple times. He would always bring drivers to his house when they got injured. He had a racing simulator in his basement with some weights on the steering wheel. When I fractured my wrist in 2001 just before the race that was cancelled at Texas because we were going too fast, he did surgery and put me in his basement on that machine. I could have raced in Texas less than two weeks later."

At Road America in 1999, Andretti took pole position with a lap of one minute, 40.206 seconds, working out to an average speed of 145.428

DARIO FRANCHITTI

"By '98, we were great pals. Tony, Max, myself, Greg. Thick as thieves, did all these crazy travels together. Ric, Greg's dad, was getting really worried that we were becoming such good pals that on track maybe we were a bit too friendly. Then Ric saw a couple races and realized it was alright. . . .

"Greg said, 'When you win your first race, I am taking you out for a big night.' Mark Webber was at that race, Bernd Schneider was there, and Gerhard Ungar . . . Greg and I had dinner at the Siebkens restaurant, which I'd never been in before. Then we went to the bar, and it was just lots and lots of Jägermeister. I've only drunk Jägermeister once in the twenty-six years since. It will do that to you. I vaguely remember walking back to the hotel and meeting a friendly Elkhart Lake policeman who helped us in the right direction. The next morning, we were discovered at opposite ends of the Osthoff lawn, both passed out.

"My plan when I won my first Indy car race was always to fly home on the Concorde. I was excited about that. Instead, I have all these pictures of trying to get to the Chicago airport and having to stop. It was a very messy event, and I missed the Concorde. Then I missed a couple more flights trying to get home. But that gives you an idea of the relationship between the drivers and that ability to be friends.

"Greg was sort of the one who led the charge. On the track, we could kick ass, but then off the track, we were going to have a lot of fun. We all bought into that, and we were very, very lucky. . . I used to go around and hang out with Greg and Steve Challis at his bus, and Max would come over. We always had a blast around at his bus. As they say in Irish, the craic was great, but the food was terrible . . . He'd say, 'Hey, you guys wanna stay for dinner? I'm making pasta!' Max and I were like, 'Sure.' And out would come this instant Kraft macaroni and cheese. That was Greg's idea of pasta. So, it was great, apart from the food. I think those two years, '98 and '99, were some of the happiest times of my life.

"Some people have got 'it,' and you can't really explain what it is, but [Greg] had 'it.' That drew people to him out of the car. Then you put him in the car, and you watch what he did with it—especially in the early days when he had those funny, goofy glasses. You'd see this guy get out and you'd say, 'He just did that?' He was such a magnetic personality. I used to say Greg taught me to be more extrovert and I taught him to think a bit more, so our personalities complemented each other. We just had a shit-ton of fun."

mph around four miles and fourteen corners. A year later, Franchitti set the track record at 1:39.866, a mark that is yet to broken.

The pole-winning experience left Michael buzzing with adrenaline. "When it comes down to the last lap like that, you say, 'This is it,' and you go for it," he related. "You just have to close your eyes, suck it up, hold your breath, and go for it. You brake very late, and you try to carry a lot of throttle out of the corners, especially onto the straights. The straights are so long here that it's critical to carry a lot of speed into them. I have to give credit to Ford on this one, because the engine was perfect. I mean, this is the best engine I've ever had. We were flying down the straightaways."

Montoya qualified on the outside of the front row and made an aggressive outside move into Turn One to take the lead, but the race was soon red flagged after separate incidents in Turns One and Three eliminated six cars. Hélio Castroneves looped it entering Turn One, taking out Memo Gidley, Max Papis, and Scott Pruett. Meanwhile, Bryan Herta bumped Cristiano da Matta entering Three, spinning the Arciero-Wells car into Mauricio Gugelmin's PacWest entry.

Everyone was allowed to restart after a twenty-five-minute break, and Montoya pulled the same trick around the outside to snatch the lead. He pulled away at the rate of a second a lap from Andretti, Gil de Ferran, and Adrian Fernandez.

On lap twenty-seven, Montoya spun on his own in Turn Five, cutting his lead from eleven to six seconds. "I lost third gear after the first pit stop," he explained. "For a while, it was OK. I figured a way to downshift from fourth to second, skipping over third with just a blip. One time, though, I did it too fast and caught first gear in Turn Five, instead of second and spun—*ziipp*—right around."

JPM was able to nurse the car along in the lead until the transmission finally packed it in on lap fifty of fifty-five. "Finally, all the rest of the gears went too, and we were done," he said. At least he had been spared the disappointment of having his car fail on the very last lap.

Fittipaldi stretched his fuel one lap longer than Andretti in the first two stints and emerged ahead of his teammate after his final stop on lap forty-three. He was clearly making ground on Montoya when the Target car dropped out, and he was convinced there would have been an exciting fight to the finish had the championship leader's transmission not given up the ghost. But the opportunity to race never came, and Christian gratefully accepted the lead and the win.

"Juan had some misfortune today, and we were able to take advantage of it," Fittipaldi said. "It's happened to all of us before. It's unfortunate for Juan, but I'm happy for myself and my team."

Andretti once again heaped praise upon Ford-Cosworth after a one-two-three for the manufacturer; Fernandez' feast-or-famine, top-five-or-break season swung up with a third-place finish, and he was followed by Moore, Papis, and Tony Kanaan. Moore was catching Fernandez rapidly as the laps wound down and he was convinced he would have finished on the podium given a couple more laps of racing. "This is my best finish on this track, so I'm pretty happy," Moore said. "Towards the end of the race, we had one of the fastest cars on the track and we were really coming on strong."

Michel Jourdain Jr. claimed a CART career-best finish at Road America with seventh place. Like the Fittipaldis, Andrettis, and Unsers, the Jourdains were a famous racing family. Michel's father, Michel Sr., competed in the two CART races staged in Mexico City in 1980 and '81 and has been called "the Bill France of Mexico" for his role in founding at least two dozen racing series in his homeland. His Uncle Bernard also raced Indy cars in the late '80s and early '90s and was instrumental in advancing Michel Jr.'s career, establishing a strong sponsorship program with the Grupo Herdez food company. Michel had scraped around the back of the CART field since 1996, the last two years driving for Payton-Coyne Racing, yet he was still the youngest driver on the grid.

"I did some CART and IRL races in '96 and I finished second in the IRL race at Las Vegas," Jourdain recalled. "I started with Dale Coyne in '97 with the Lola chassis, which was really bad. At Milwaukee, I crashed and destroyed the car. We got a Reynard from Bobby Rahal, and we got huge support from Bobby and from Reynard. That was a huge change in my '97 season, and every race I finished better and better. I was the first guy running strong for Dale. Bobby knew it was his old car, and he and Ray Leto were very encouraging. They sold us their worst car, but at Mid-Ohio, I qualified ahead of Bobby, and he came over to talk to me. The respect I gained during that part of the season was important, because '98 and '99 were really bad. But people remembered that when I had a competitive car, I could do it, and those races in '97 saved my career. Bobby and Tim Cindric talked to me about 1999, but I understand why they went with Max Papis. Later, I drove for Bobby in 2002 and '03 and those two years were the best of my career."

Dale Coyne was an SCCA road racing veteran who made his Indy car debut as a thirty-year-old owner/driver at Mid-Ohio in 1984 in an old March converted to accept a stock-block Chevrolet powerplant. He persisted with the bulky Chevy, often failing to qualify for races, and even built his own chassis in 1986.

Coyne gave up driving after the 1988 season and found his niche helping hopeful drivers step up to the CART series. Most of them were no-name journeymen, but Scott Pruett dropped his life savings into driving Coyne's car in the 1988 Long Beach Grand Prix and parlayed it into a full-time ride with Truesports Racing the following year. Similarly, reigning Indy Lights champion Paul Tracy drove Coyne's car at Long Beach in 1991 and the Canadian had a Penske Racing test contract in his pocket by mid-season. But those were the exceptions to the rule, and even after he joined forces with NFL legend Walter Payton in 1994, Coyne's team spent most of the 1990s at the back of the pack. In 1998, his was the only team that used the unloved Lola chassis, but there were a few bright spots along the way, including the well-traveled Roberto Moreno's third-place finish in the 1996 U.S. 500.

"Any guy that comes here has a certain skill level—the guy at the back of the field has to have a certain level of skill to be here," Coyne said. "We've enjoyed trying to get the best out of those guys, whether it's a guy at the beginning of his career trying to climb the ladder and get more experience—because he needs a vehicle to do that, and we can provide that. Or a guy at the end of his career and this has always been his goal. This is a dream for people to do, and yes, money can get you in to do it, but anybody in this field is a world-class driver, because they are tough cars."

TEXACO/HAVOLINE 200

Road America — July 11, 1999 – 55 laps

1. Christian Fittipaldi
2. Michael Andretti
3. Adrian Fernandez
4. Greg Moore
5. Max Papis

CHAMPIONSHIP STANDINGS AFTER 10 OF 20 RACES

1.	Montoya	113
2.	Andretti	95
3.	De Ferran	87
4.	Franchitti	82
	Fittipaldi	82

Paul Tracy was by far the biggest success story to emerge from Dale Coyne's prep school. When he leased Coyne's car for the 1991 Long Beach Grand Prix, he was the twenty-two-year-old, record-setting defending Indy Lights champion, but his accomplishments hadn't gotten him a sniff of an Indy car drive. "We put the money together to race with Dale at Long Beach and had a good qualifying in an old Lola, but then something stupid broke in the race so it was over pretty quickly for me," he remembered. "I finished twenty-second, so there wasn't a whole lot to get excited about."

But Tracy's effort, especially in qualifying, caught the attention of Roger Penske, who offered the young Canadian a testing contract with the opportunity to run a few races alongside regular Penske drivers Rick Mears and Emerson Fittipaldi. His first start came in the 1991 Michigan 500; he qualified eighth for his Penske debut, then crashed and broke his leg on the fourth lap of a 250-lap race. A planned partial schedule in '92 turned full time when Mears crashed at Indianapolis and complications with his injured wrist forced him out of the car a few races later. Tracy claimed his first Indy car pole at Road America, then wrote off the car eighteen hours later in the prerace warm-up. But he also learned how to finish races, notching three podiums, and when Mears decided to call it a career and never returned to the car, PT was in position to take over from the legend.

The rest of Tracy's Penske career was tumultuous. He crashed out of a two-lap lead at Phoenix in 1993 but won a week later in Long Beach—driving bruised and battered from injuries sustained in a karting accident that he neglected to inform the team about. Tracy won five races in '93, finished third in the standings, and gave veterans Fittipaldi and Nigel Mansell all they could handle. The wins kept coming in '94, but at the end of the season, he was farmed out to Newman/Haas Racing as Penske cut back from three to two cars. He was back at Penske for the '96 and '97 seasons, taking three consecutive oval wins in mid-1997. But at the end of the year, he was mysteriously dropped by Penske (see Chapter 2), leading to his move to Team Green.

By 1999, Tracy was a national hero in Canada, especially in his home province of Ontario. And thankfully, his season was unfolding in a much less dramatic fashion than his calamitous '98 campaign. He didn't quite manage to repeat his hometown win from 1993 in the fourteenth annual Molson Indy Toronto, taking second place; but he had the satisfaction of knowing it was his teammate and friend Dario Franchitti who grabbed the headlines with his first win of the year.

Run on a challenging temporary course that combined roads through the grounds of the Canadian National Exhibition Centre with a blast down Lake Shore Boulevard, the Toronto race was added to the CART schedule in 1986, joined four years later by a street race in downtown Vancouver. The two Molson-sponsored Canadian events demonstrated the popularity of the FedEx Championship Series north of the US border and the potential for its success everywhere else. The 1999 edition of the Toronto race drew a record race day crowd of 72,589, with the announced three-day attendance figure of 168,314 also a record.

The Canadian races enjoyed very strong support from Molson, which created its own promotion and production company called Molstar Sports & Entertainment. That drove substantial weekly coverage from the Canadian print and television media. As a result, these races were genuine events that generated the kind of buzz and loyal fan support that promoters of several American rounds of the CART championship could only dream about.

Gil de Ferran took pole, and he was particularly enthusiastic about his Goodyear tires. "There's no magic involved," he said. "The team has

The traditional public driver's meeting for the 1965 Indianapolis 500. Dan Gurney, eventual winner Jim Clark, and pole winner A. J. Foyt stand in the foreground; Rookie of the Year Mario Andretti sits far left in the lowest of three rows of drivers. Directly behind Andretti is Parnelli Jones, adjacent to Bobby Unser, Johnny Rutherford, and Gordon Johncock, with Al Unser at the far end. *Steve Shunck Collection*

Drivers gather for a group photo prior to the 1999 CART season opener at Homestead-Miami Speedway. Championship protagonists Juan Pablo Montoya and Dario Franchitti are near the center; pole- and race-winner Greg Moore waves to the crowd (far right). *Ken Pamatat*

The 1969 front row of (left to right) Bobby Unser, Mario Andretti, and pole-winner A. J. Foyt is one of the most iconic in the long history of the Indianapolis 500. Andretti prevailed over Dan Gurney to score his only Indy win. *Indianapolis Motor Speedway*

Wally Dallenbach raced Indy cars from 1965 to '81, earning five race wins and a best finish of second in the 1973 USAC championship. He's seen here in 1974 after qualifying on the front row for the Indianapolis 500. *Indianapolis Motor Speedway*

A. J. Foyt's record-setting fourth victory in the 1977 Indianapolis 500 is one of the most famous sports achievements of the twentieth century. *Indianapolis Motor Speedway*

BorgWarner celebrated the fiftieth anniversary of Parnelli Jones's 1963 Indianapolis win, and Mario Andretti crashed the party. Jones is seated in front of Bobby Unser, Andretti, and Johnny Rutherford. *Michael Levitt*

Bobby Rahal was one of the top Indy car drivers of the 1980s and '90s, winning three CART-sanctioned titles. Here he shows off the classically simple lines of a 1988 Lola.
Bob Harmeyer / RMA

Al Unser won the CART championship in 1983 and battled his son Al Jr. to another title two years later. By the end of the decade, Unser Jr. was one of Indy car's top stars.
Indianapolis Motor Speedway

Emerson Fittipaldi, a two-time Formula 1 World Champion, became an Indy car star in America and helped popularize the sport in his homeland of Brazil. *Paul Webb*

Rick Mears (left) and Michael Andretti during their duel in the late stages of the 1991 Indianapolis 500. Mears joined the exclusive four-time winners club, while Andretti never did taste victory at Indianapolis despite leading 431 laps in his career.
Indianapolis Motor Speedway

Jimmy Vasser (left) won the 1996 CART championship, but by the end of the season, teammate Alex Zanardi took over at the front of the field. *Paul Webb*

Vasser and Zanardi became close friends and truly enjoyed each other's success on the track. Here they celebrate Vasser's win at Nazareth in 1998. *Paul Webb*

Zanardi's 1998 championship was one of the most dominant in the history of Indy car racing, with fifteen podiums from nineteen starts. *Kazuki Saito*

Alex Zanardi (left) and Jimmy Vasser (right) flank winner Greg Moore after the 1998 U.S. 500 at Michigan Speedway. Moore snookered the Ganassi teammates in the closing laps. *Paul Webb*

Vasser (No. 12) and Zanardi worked together to deny Greg Moore in the 1998 season finale at California Speedway. By finishing second to Vasser, Moore lost out on a $1 million bonus from team owner Gerald Forsythe. *Dan R. Boyd*

Jimmy Vasser thought things would be easier after three years teamed with Alex Zanardi, but Juan Pablo Montoya (right) quickly showed he had championship potential. *Paul Webb*

Paul Tracy and Dario Franchitti spent a harmonious five years as teammates with Team Kool Green. *Michael Levitt*

Tony Kanaan and Hélio Castroneves began competing against each other as teenagers in Brazil. Their careers ran parallel for more than thirty years. *INDYCAR / Chris Owens*

Musician Lenny Kravitz greets Greg Moore on the grid before the 1999 CART race at Homestead-Miami Speedway. *Michael Levitt*

Moore always starred at Homestead, and in 1999, he finally took the checkered flag.
Kazuki Saito

Pole winner Gil de Ferran spun at the start of the Japanese race without hitting anything. *Dan R. Boyd*

Juan Pablo Montoya's Reynard-Honda in superspeedway trim. *Michael Levitt*

Juan Pablo Montoya and Hélio Castroneves engaged in a furious scrap at Nazareth Speedway. Montoya took his first oval win, while Castroneves crashed. *Michael Levitt*

A champagne shower greets Montoya after his triumph at Nazareth. *Paul Webb*

PacWest Racing's Mauricio Gugelmin and Mark Blundell were front-runners in 1997, but their competitiveness suffered with the decline of the Mercedes-Benz engine program.
Dan R. Boyd

NFL legend Walter Payton took a minority ownership in Dale Coyne's team in the late 1990s prior to his shocking death in November 1999. Here he is seen joking with the PacWest team. *Dan R. Boyd*

Four generations of the Andretti family (left to right): Alvese, Mario, Michael, Marco. *Paul Webb*

Paul Tracy (right) credits engineer Tony Cicale for helping him gain the maturity that brought him back to winning form in 1999. PT later earned the 2003 CART championship.
Michael Levitt

Juan Pablo Montoya and Dario Franchitti flank winner Gil de Ferran as they take a Portland victory lap. *Michael Levitt*

The Road America podium (left to right): Paul Newman, Michael Andretti, Carl Haas, race winner Christian Fittipaldi, and third-place finisher Adrian Fernandez. *Michael Levitt*

Paul Tracy and winner Dario Franchitti exult on the podium after Dario claimed his first win of the 1999 season at Toronto. *Michael Levitt*

Tony Kanaan broke through for his first career Indy car victory at Michigan Speedway, but the win came at the expense of his friend Max Papis. Gerald Forsythe stands far left.
Kazuki Saito

From left to right: Paul Tracy, Juan Pablo Montoya, and Dario Franchitti hoist their trophies after Montoya's win at Mid-Ohio. It was one of the best drives of JPM's Indy car career.
Michael Levitt

On race day at Laguna Seca, Greg Moore (left) signs an Uruguayan flag as a memorial to Gonzalo Rodriguez. *Paul Webb*

Paul Tracy after winning Houston: "It's better to have this trophy in my hand instead of up my ass." *Michael Levitt*

Dario Franchitti leads the field into the first corner at Surfers Paradise from pole position. Franchitti won the race to carry a slim lead into the championship finale. *Kazuki Saito*

Dario Franchitti (left) and Juan Pablo Montoya (right) face the media prior to the season finale at California Speedway. *Michael Levitt*

With his injured hand heavily wrapped, Greg Moore worked with Championship Drivers Association executive director Jon Potter to insure he could compete in the season finale. *Steve Swope / RMA*

Greg Moore heads out for the morning warm-up prior to the Marlboro 500 at California Speedway, October 31, 1999. *Michael Levitt*

Moore's car kicks up dust as he runs four wide in the far outside lane to start the tenth lap of the Marlboro 500. Moore would fatally crash in Turn Two. *Michael Levitt*

With flags lowered to half mast, Greg Moore's pit sits empty as the 1999 Marlboro 500 draws to a close. *Paul Webb*

Juan Pablo Montoya accepts congratulations as the champion of the 1999 PPG CART FedEx Championship series. ESPN pit reporter Gary Gerould waits for an interview.
Kazuki Saito

From left to right: Christian Fittipaldi, winner Adrian Fernandez, and Max Papis were emotionally shattered in the post-race press conference at Fontana. *Kazuki Saito*

Wally Dallenbach and his wife Peppy were honored at CART's annual "Runway Madness" charity event to start the Fontana weekend. Dallenbach intended to retire after the 1999 season. *Michael Levitt*

Gil de Ferran (left) won the 2000 and '01 CART championships for Marlboro Team Penske. Hélio Castroneves replaced de Ferran's intended teammate, Greg Moore, and went on to become a four-time Indianapolis 500 winner. *INDYCAR / Chris Owens*

Tim Cindric (second from right, next to Roger Penske) joined Team Penske in October 1999 and expanded the legendary organization into a powerhouse in Indy cars, NASCAR, and IMSA sports cars. *Michael Levitt*

The 2005 St. Petersburg Grand Prix saw Andretti Green Racing score an unprecedented one-two-three-four sweep. Left to right: fourth-place finisher Bryan Herta joined Dario Franchitti, winner Dan Wheldon, and Tony Kanaan on the podium. Wheldon's death in the 2011 IRL season finale featured some similarities to Greg Moore's passing in 1999. *Michael Levitt*

The late Robin Miller interviews Tony Kanaan (left) and Juan Pablo Montoya (right) in 2016. Kanaan won the 2013 Indianapolis 500, while Montoya added a second Indy triumph in 2015, fifteen years after his first. *John Oreovicz*

Dario Franchitti would have achieved more had his career not been cut short by a 2013 accident at Houston. His four championships and three Indianapolis 500 victories put him among the all-time Indy car greats. *Michael Levitt*

In 2021, Hélio Castroneves (right front) gained membership to the exclusive club of four-time Indianapolis 500 winners with Al Unser (left front), A. J. Foyt (left rear), and Rick Mears (right rear). *Indianapolis Motor Speedway*

Twenty-three Indianapolis 500 winners joined Indianapolis Motor Speedway owner Roger Penske (far right) on the IMS "Yard of Bricks" for a group photo in 2024. The "Class of '99" was well represented. *Indianapolis Motor Speedway*

Greg Moore, 1975–1999. *Michael Levitt*

been very good since I came in 1997. The difference is the evolution of Goodyear. They're consistently giving us better tires. It's easier to get the car working, to get into a rhythm, and to get the most out of the car."

Al Unser Jr. was similarly optimistic. "The Goodyears are not an issue as much as they used to be," he said. "Right now, I think they are a faster tire when they're new and I think they are very close on the consistency too. We build our own car in the belief that if we get it right, we'll have an advantage no one else has. That's kind of where we're at with Goodyear. When they get it right, it'll be me and de Ferran with the edge."

Starting from the outside of the front row, Franchitti did a nice job of catching his sliding Reynard/Honda after he was bumped from behind by third-place qualifier Christian Fittipaldi in Turn One. It must have triggered memories of 1997, when as a rookie, Dario took a shock pole for Hogan Racing, only to tangle with Bobby Rahal in the first turn and drop to the back. Mark Blundell drove through the confusion and defeated Alex Zanardi in a straight fight to win that race, one of the few times Zanardi was flat-out beaten during his three-year stint in the CART series.

In '99, Dario successfully made it out of Turn One, passed de Ferran for the lead at the end of the Lake Shore straight, then dictated the pace to lead all ninety-five laps and earn his first race win of the 1999 season. Making things even sweeter, teammate Tracy competed a Team Kool Green one-two, crossing the line 2.624 seconds later.

Even though Canadian hero Tracy didn't come first, the result was popular with the record crowd as Franchitti made up for two years of Toronto disappointment. The Scot duplicated his 1997 pole in '98, and he led most of the '98 race before encountering brake problems and spinning off.

"It's about time I finished a race here!" Franchitti exclaimed. "I had to make it difficult on myself, I guess. But we finally sorted the problems of the last two years out. After I got by Gil, the car was awesome all day. Near the end I was watching the gap to Paul and trying to keep it at two to three seconds. I was just basically driving as fast as I had to. When the car is that good, you kind of wonder what everybody else is doing sometimes."

For years, Franchitti denied that he made a mistake to lose the race at Toronto in 1998. He finally came clean in 2024.

"I really screwed up the '98 race," he admitted. "I think there were only about ten laps to go. Pushing too hard, I hit a bump, I had the pads knock back, I went for the brake pedal, and there were just no brakes. That was just my fault, and I can look back now and say that. At the time, I was like, 'Oh, there were no brakes.' But that was my fault. I should have backed off.

"In '99, Gil qualified on the pole on Goodyears," Dario continued. "I think I got knocked completely sideways going into the first corner, but even with that, the Firestones were so much better at getting up to temperature that I still passed him into Turn Three! Gil had some pretty colorful language after that. I was pretty dominant that day. I loved driving that car on street circuits. We just had such a good setup, and I had such good rhythm with that car almost everywhere. PT was the same."

At the time, the Scotsman was fully aware how important the Toronto win was, given the unexpected emergence of Montoya as the main threat for the championship. But he refused to get carried away in his celebration.

"We surprised a lot of people on the ovals in the first part of the year, but then we were expected to go well on the road courses," he said. "It didn't happen for a bit, and then Cleveland was our least competitive race. To have a good weekend here gives me a little more optimism. But the telling point in the championship will be later in the season. Montoya will be up front at every race, so we have to stay in contention. Confidence-wise this is a big help, but that's it.

"Montoya has been making a lot of headlines this year, which is fine—he deserves some recognition for what he's done," Franchitti added. "It's always surprising when a guy of Juan's relative inexperience comes in and wins races, but he's doing a terrific job. He's with a team that won three championships, so there's no doubt about the car, but at the same time, he's doing the job properly. There have only been a couple times when he's been lucky."

Incredibly, Tracy's second-place finish was his best result on a road or street course since the 1995 season finale at Laguna Seca Raceway. He confirmed that after a pair of controversial incidents between himself

PAUL TRACY

"Dario and I got along great off the track and on the track, but we raced each other super hard. We gave each other just an inch, and sometimes that ended with us touching. In some instances, it was my fault, and a couple were his, though he would never admit to anything being his fault. We just ran each other hard. And Barry let us race each other hard. He never gave us team orders. There were a couple races where we were one-two and we got down to the last ten laps or so—Toronto '99 was one where I was chasing him down and we got through the last pit stops. I chased him down, but they said, 'We're going to finish like this.' Which kind of chafed me a little bit, but the same call came for me later when the situation was reversed. For the team it was, 'OK, we're going to get to the finish and take this one-two.' There were never any team orders at the beginning of the race not to race each other or pass the other guy if you were quicker. Only when we had a one-two in the bag with a giant lead over third place, and that's fair."

and teammate Franchitti at Houston in 1998 and at Gateway in May, team boss Barry Green had established some informal team orders.

"The rule was put in place that if we're running in formation, the guy in front gets to stay there unless he's holding up the guy behind," Tracy explained. "It seemed like every time I was able to put some pressure on Dario today, he was able to respond. He deserved to win today, and I'm not ashamed to say I'm proud to come home second behind him. I've been labeled all my career as inconsistent, so to be knocking down races and finishing them is exactly what I want."

Tracy and Fittipaldi battled throughout much of the afternoon, but the runner-up spot was decided in Tracy's favor after Fittipaldi encountered slow traffic on his way into the pits for his second and final stop. Fittipaldi moved up to third in the point standings after another consistently strong weekend that netted him his second consecutive podium finish.

Since Christian joined the CART series in 1995, Chief Steward Wally Dallenbach insisted he would give the Brazilian his trademark

Stetson hat when he won his first Indy car race. Fittipaldi duly arrived at the Toronto postrace press conference wearing the hat, which was embellished by a Kmart decal to satisfy the longtime Newman/Haas sponsor.

Roberto Moreno matched his best result of the season for PacWest Racing with fourth place, followed by Papis and Fernandez. It was a bad day for many of the other FedEx Championship Series contenders. Montoya was on the edge all weekend, with a couple of spins and a bumping incident with Gualter Salles in practice. His eventful day ended after fifty-nine laps when he tangled with Michel Jourdain. Andretti punted Moore off early, and pole man de Ferran ran second for many laps but lost time to a pit infraction and ultimately spun off on coolant from Moore's blown Mercedes engine.

PacWest owner Bruce McCaw was grateful for how even as a temporary substitute, Moreno brought stability to the team at a turbulent time. Rumors were starting to swirl about Mercedes-Benz's commitment to the CART series as its engines continued to under-perform for a second consecutive season. During the summer, McCaw began working behind the scenes to organize a satellite team to convince himself and Mercedes that PacWest's lack of performance was not team or driver related.

"A lot of our challenge was related to the engine and the engineering challenges related to that," McCaw said. "We had a lot of strength in those years with Mark and Mauricio as our drivers. Mauricio was like a rock. He didn't complain, he didn't fuss. He was such a team player, and I think he really helped keep the wheels on the team. It was a very tough time. He was later also a huge influence for Scott Dixon, especially during Scott's Indy Lights championship year.

"The nice thing about when we brought Roberto in is he wasn't trying to take Mark's seat," he added. "He was a real gentleman about his attitude, and he really tried to adapt himself to fit the team and to work with the engineers. He didn't complain a lot, he just stood on the gas. His whole history is pretty remarkable. He drove for everybody. I still have so much respect for Roberto because he was an absolute gentleman. I just enjoyed being with him."

The battle for the PPG Cup tightened considerably in the wake of Montoya's second consecutive DNF, with his lead over Franchitti cut to seven points and the top eight drivers covered by just thirty-seven as the series headed to Michigan Speedway for what was traditionally a wild-card event—the first superspeedway race of the 1999 season.

MOLSON INDY TORONTO

Exhibition Place —July 18, 1999 – 95 laps

1. Dario Franchitti
2. Paul Tracy
3. Christian Fittipaldi
4. Roberto Moreno
5. Max Papis

CHAMPIONSHIP STANDINGS AFTER 11 OF 20 RACES

1.	Montoya	113
2.	Franchitti	106
3.	Fittipaldi	96
4.	Andretti	95
5.	de Ferran	88

Tony Kanaan hoists the Vanderbilt Cup after winning the 1999 U.S. 500. *Michael Levitt*

CHAPTER 10

CHANGING FORTUNES

Max Papis had a quartet of fifth-place finishes in the first eleven FedEx Championship Series races of 1999, which pretty much summed up his season to that point—decent enough, but not the breakthrough to consistent front-runner status that he hoped for or expected with his move to Team Rahal. His race craft was excellent, displayed in the fact that he finished higher than he qualified in eight of those eleven races. Unfortunately, the three outlier events were the only ones for which he qualified in the top seven. His average starting position for the majority of the first half of the season was fourteenth, so Papis had to work hard for those fifth-place finishes, along with a career-best P4 in Brazil. His results did compare favorably with his Rahal teammate Bryan Herta, who often qualified better (four starts in the top five) but had only a third at Long Beach and a pair of sixths to show for it.

It's fair to say that by mid '99, Papis, team owner Bobby Rahal, and the CART community were mildly disappointed by Mad Max's season to date, and he needed a breakout performance. With the benefit of a couple decades of hindsight, Papis realizes that he did not maximize his opportunity with Team Rahal.

"I wish I would have been less selfish," he said. "I had a respectful relationship with Bryan, but I wanted to demolish him. When I look back, I lost an opportunity to be a better teammate. With today's knowledge, I would have worked harder to help that relationship. We weren't hiding anything, but we were so different as human beings that

I know if I would have made more effort—and maybe he would say that too—we could have helped each other more.

"I also wish I hadn't taken one piece of advice Bobby gave me. When I asked him where he thought I should reside—because I lived in California—he said, 'Go wherever you want, maybe to Florida where everyone is.' He didn't push me to stay in Columbus. And I wish he would have. In my previous contract with PPI, I had to live within one hundred miles of the facility. I really wish he had been firmer on that, because it would have been a better thing for me as a human to live there with the team. I would have learned about the culture and been more an integral part of the team, more of a team player. I still don't understand why I wasn't there."

It would be equally fair to say that Tony Kanaan's career also wasn't on the upswing that had been predicted for the 1998 CART Rookie of the Year. The transformation from Steve Horne's family-oriented Tasman Motorsports team to Forsythe Championship Racing, a single-car satellite with little connection to Gerald Forsythe's primary Player's/Forsythe Racing, had not been without issues. Kanaan beat himself up hard over his crash at Long Beach, where he had secured his first career pole position but was pressured into a mistake by Juan Pablo Montoya. Outside of Long Beach, TK's average grid spot was fifteenth, including six starts of seventeenth or lower; his best result, like for Papis, came on the Rio "roval" where he placed fifth.

Horne, who managed the Forsythe Championship Racing effort, provided some perspective on what he and Kanaan were up against in 1999. "The CART-IRL war was devastating to Tasman," he began. "We were a small team, and two of our sponsors left because we weren't going to the Indy 500. I wasn't in a position or mentally capable of getting my head around the IRL. I kind of felt we were getting near the end, and we were kind of being driven out of the sport—which happened to a lot of teams.

"Jerry Forsythe had been nibbling away at Tony behind the scenes. He wanted Tony, believed he was going to be a star, and he was right. Luckily, I had a three-year contract. Tony came to me and said, 'This guy is offering me this, this, and this.' I said to Tony, 'Let me take care of it and make sure you're treated fairly. But I own you, man. There's no way out.' I sat down with Jerry and said, 'You're undermining me. You have all the money and can do what you want, but this is hurting me.' He really wanted Tony, so he said, 'Tell you what . . . I'll buy the whole team. Period.'

"I didn't know Jerry that well, but I thought it was actually a savior for us as a team," Horne concluded. "Yes, I was going to give up my equity in the team and it was going to be rebranded. But all the people were going to have jobs, and we were going to keep going. That's how the McDonald's team eventuated. We had a pretty good year, but the whole IRL-CART thing was just imploding. Jerry wanted to have another franchise within CART, but they wouldn't give it to him with this team. So, he parked the whole fucking lot for 2000. Just parked it. Paid all of those employees for one year to not go racing. Christine and I just watched the whole thing dribble away. Which was sad, but we were secure. I keep going back to the CART-IRL debacle. There was no single fault there—it was circumstances or egos, whatever you like. But it destroyed us, clearly. If it wasn't for that, I think I'd still be out there."

In short, Papis and Kanaan were two young lions in search of their first Indy car race win, and one of them got it at Michigan Speedway in the U.S. 500. Papis dominated the second half of the race in his Rahal Reynard/Ford, but the Miller Lite car ran out of fuel entering Turn Three on the 250th and final lap. Kanaan slipped past and barely held off a charging Juan Montoya by 0.032 seconds in one of the closest finishes in the ninety-year history of Indy-style racing. It was therefore Kanaan who ended up in the winner's circle, while Papis's only victory was of the moral kind.

In what was becoming the norm for superspeedway events using the Handford Device rear wing, the race was a wild, slipstreaming affair. It started with a rush as PPG Cup points leader Montoya and Michael Andretti jumped pole qualifier Jimmy Vasser on lap two and then unofficially traded the lead thirty-three times between themselves in the first nineteen laps. The pair continued an extended battle until Papis emerged in front on lap eighty-four.

Unlike Andretti or Montoya, Papis was able to pull away once he was in the lead, building margins of up to ten seconds. "I knew what we could do," Papis said. "I just let them play with each other, kept it flat, and pulled away."

Papis, who led a total of 143 laps, was the first of the leaders to make his final stop, on lap 221. He pitted with a six-second lead over Montoya, who was hotly pursued by Dario Franchitti, Andretti, Kanaan, Christian Fittipaldi, and Paul Tracy. The stop looked routine, but the Rahal team did not use the fueling mechanism's vent bottle system on the final stop. In addition, Papis's car-to-pit telemetry again failed after suffering a glitch earlier in the race.

"Our fuel meter quit working after the last pit stop," said Papis's strategist, Rahal team manager Tim Cindric. "We thought we were fine on fuel. I have to say I'm sorry to Max. They did everything right in the pits. Max drove a hell of a race. He was the class of the field without a doubt. To come home with nothing is a bitter disappointment without a doubt. But we showed everybody today who 'Mad Max' is."

Bobby Rahal explained that when the telemetry fails, as it did twice on Papis's car in the U.S. 500, a safety system restores the fuel mixture to full-rich. That's what happened in the final stint at Michigan, causing Papis to use fuel at a faster rate than the team expected.

"The telemetry froze on us earlier in the race and luckily there was a yellow," said Rahal. "We turned it off, and turned it back on, and it worked again. But after the last stop it did the same thing, so we had no idea what kind of fuel mileage we were getting and where we were on the mixture. Max was running quite lean before the last stop, and we thought he could maintain it, and I guess we were as surprised as anybody. Obviously, I am devastated for Max because he dominated. His performance was the most dominating performance I have seen in this place. Like I said to him, he won the race, we lost it for him."

If Papis had the fastest car in the race, Kanaan's Reynard/Honda was nearly a match. Tony lost a lap when the Gurney flap on his Handford Device rear wing became dislodged on lap seventy-eight. But led by Steve Horne, the team was able to strategically guide the McDonald's machine back onto the lead lap, putting Kanaan in position to take advantage of Papis's misfortune.

Kanaan noticed Papis was slowing just in time to realize Montoya was gaining on him as he took the lead entering Turn Four. "At first, I saw [Papis] getting bigger in front of me and my automatic reaction was to lift," Kanaan related. "But I had a lean mixture—since the start of

MAX PAPIS

"I came from road racing in Europe, and I was super brave. On my first ever oval with PPI, I drew number one for qualifying. I was scared to death and didn't know what to do. I sent it so hard into the old Homestead mini-Indy that I had the front end chattering.

"In '99, I went testing at Michigan three months before the race, and I kept observing Michael Andretti, the oval king. I worked with my engineer Tim Reiter and came up with a very unusual setup for the car with all four springs the same, and I learned how to do it like Michael. I started to feel comfortable with oval racing. From not knowing what I was doing to that moment in Michigan, that test was very, very important to me.

"For the race, I had the utmost confidence that I knew exactly what was needed. I felt invincible—until the last stop. I came in, and I felt it was super-fast. I think my lead increased over P2 and I thought, 'Wow! We did an amazing stop.' But it actually felt a little bit too quick. I kept asking the team, 'Should we save fuel?' They made me go to a different fuel setting, but I still kept asking. I never heard anything back, or at least anything that was worrisome to me.

"The other thing I don't think anybody knows is with thirty laps to go, the car started vibrating like hell, on the left rear. After the race, we went back and discovered the left rear shock was cut in half. Every time I lifted, I was almost wrecking. But I learned how to drive it.

"White flag, One and Two, backstretch . . . I put my finger on the radio button to tell the guys 'I'm coming home!' While I was clicking, *bluuaah*. I weaved the car and clutched it, but I was out of gas. I saw Tony go by. After that, I didn't know what I was doing because I put my head down on the steering wheel and I couldn't look up. I know that I stopped at the end of Pit Lane and I couldn't get out of the car. I was devastated. It wasn't losing the race. It was the emotions from executing, pushing through what we later knew was a broken damper, the excitement from a second before. I could see the stand with the guy with the checkered flag, and boom."

the race, I couldn't talk to the team on the radio, and when they told me to richen up the fuel mixture, I misunderstood and leaned it out—and I just lost all the speed. That's why Juan came at me at the end.

"When I saw Max slowing down, I said, 'Luck is turning around to my side today,'" he added. "It was a hard day for me, but a lucky turnaround, so let's keep it going. I feel sorry for Max, but that's the way races are sometimes. I think Max deserved it. He led most of the race and had the strongest car. I was happy to be second, to be honest, but today was not Max's day. It was my day."

Montoya felt he might have challenged for the win, but he was hindered by a couple of longish pit stops. "I lost the rear brakes on the car about the middle of the race, and that cost me positions at each stop after that," he stated. "The first time, I slid past the pit box and that cost a lot of time. But I think it was a pretty good day for us." Juan extended his PPG Cup points lead to thirteen over Franchitti, who led four laps and finished fifth.

Tracy and Andretti fought over the last podium spot, with the position going to the Canadian by 0.053 seconds. The pair demonstrated some admirable racing ethics as they approached the line and encountered the coasting Papis.

"It was super, super close at the finish line," Tracy related. "Michael and I passed each other twice on the last lap, and I have to thank him for giving me room when we came up on Max."

"Everyone drove well today," added Andretti. "Everybody took care of each other. It was a long day for us, but I was very happy to get some points to keep pace with Montoya and Dario in the standings. Max was on it. He was in a class of his own. You have to drive all five hundred miles to win, though. It's too bad for him after running so strong. His day will come, though. Today he proved he could run strong."

Papis sometimes takes some good-natured ribbing for his theatrical "I have the will to win and the heart of a lion" schtick, but on this day, he had every right to be boastful. He showed the class of a true champion in the way he handled the disappointment of losing a sure victory on the last lap, falling to seventh place.

"I had the time of my life all race," Papis said. "I had a fantastic car, and we did a good job. It's sad we didn't win it, but it gives me more confidence that next time we will be on the podium. Today was our day, but just not at the start/finish line. We need to go away from there with a smile on our face knowing that we were the best, because we were, except for the last half lap.

"When the car quit, I said many bad words in Italian that I cannot repeat," he continued with a chuckle. "I can't say much more. Bobby gave me a fantastic car and was with me all the way. We are a very tight team. Today we showed what I told you guys at the beginning of the season. Just wait, because when we get our chemistry right, we will dominate. But I am very glad for Tony because he is a nice guy and deserves to win."

Though well down on the record sixty-three lead changes in 1998, it was still an exciting race, despite hot, humid conditions and a high level of attrition that saw just eleven of twenty-six cars reach the finish. That allowed perennial backmarker Dennis Vitolo to score two PPG Cup points for an eleventh place finish, despite being eighteen laps behind the leaders at the flag. Richie Hearn was forty-three laps down and not running at the finish, but he claimed the twelfth and final points-paying spot.

There were thirty official lead changes and only four caution periods (all for similar one-car incidents in Turn Two involving Gil de Ferran, Scott Pruett, and P. J. Jones), making for a near-record race average of 186.097 miles per hour.

U.S. 500 PRESENTED BY TOYOTA

Michigan Speedway — July 25, 1999 – 250 laps

1. Tony Kanaan
2. Juan Pablo Montoya
3. Paul Tracy
4. Michael Andretti
5. Dario Franchitti

CHAMPIONSHIP STANDINGS AFTER 12 OF 20 RACES

1.	Montoya	129
2.	Franchitti	116
3.	Andretti	107
4.	Fittipaldi	101
5.	Fernandez	96

TONY KANAAN

"We lost a gurney on the rear wing, so I had to get it replaced and went a lap down. It was chaos. Plus, I lost the radio in the middle of the race. In those days we still had the pit board, but you're going past at 230–240 mph. But I knew where I was running because I could see the pylon. I knew I was running second and I was trying to look at the pit board every couple laps. Then I saw the white flag and thought, 'Not a bad day, P2 after being a lap down in a five-hundred-mile race.'

"I knew Max was the leader because I was looking at the pylon. Then all of a sudden in Turn Four, I see Max slowing down. So, I get distracted, and I lift. I get back on the throttle, and here comes Montoya, the guy that took my job, in the car I was supposed to be driving, and he has a run. We crossed the finish line in thrilling fashion, so close.

"Obviously it was the worst day of Max's life. We're good friends, and that was a hard phone call to make because it was the happiest day of my career at that point and the worst day of his career. Max was pretty depressed, and with reason. Back in the day we were pretty tight, and we would have drivers' parties. There were no cameras and social media and stuff. Every race weekend we would stay and celebrate. We decided not to that day.

"I remember I went home that night, and I flew through Atlanta. Cristiano da Matta was with me—we both lived in Miami—and he said, 'C'mon, man, we have to celebrate!' People that know me know that I don't drink a single drop of alcohol. I never did, I just don't like it, never found a drink that I enjoy. But Cristiano was like, 'You have to have a beer!' The only way I can drink is to do it fast, since I don't like the taste. So, I chugged a full beer at the Atlanta airport, dehydrated after a five-hundred-mile race. By the time I got to Miami, I don't think I remembered a lot. That was my celebration—a beer in the busiest airport in the United States with my good Brazilian friend Cristiano."

MAX PAPIS

"Obviously, I was devastated. Tony won. I remember going back on the plane. Some of the people that worked with Tony, like his manager and agent, they had the trophy, and they were not very nice. I joked something like, 'Are you going to share that trophy with me?' And they said 'Well, you had a shot to win it, so we don't care.' And then I never heard from Tony as well. Maybe I made a little of this up in my mind, you know? But it took us a long time to mend the situation. That really massively dampened the relationship with Tony, and it took maybe a couple of years to rebuild. I knew him since he was fifteen, and I was expecting an acknowledgment or something. I had to do a lot of inner searching to mend that moment because I love Tony. But that was very difficult for me. I didn't talk to him for a long time—not because he won, but I felt if this was happening to him, I would have really showed my sympathy in my heart. We discussed it later, and now there is a stronger bond than we ever had."

August started poorly for Christian Fittipaldi, who on Monday the second became the latest to crash while testing at Gateway International Raceway. Briefly knocked unconscious, Fittipaldi suffered a subdural hematoma and was expected to miss several weeks. For the second time in three years, Newman/Haas Racing turned to "Supersub" Roberto Moreno, who was once again available since doctors finally cleared Mark Blundell to return to action in the No. 18 PacWest car at the next race, the Tenneco Automotive Detroit Grand Prix. Moreno had impressed during his races with PacWest, leaving Blundell in an unenviable position for his comeback to the team he had driven for since 1996.

Perhaps the most disappointed man leaving Michigan was Greg Moore. Already coming off a disappointing DNF in Toronto that dropped him to seventh in the standings, Moore was optimistic that his traditional superspeedway form could help lift him back into championship contention. "One bad outing by Juan and one good one by us and it's a new ballgame again," he said prior to the weekend. "We've always been competitive on this big oval, and we expect that to continue." But Moore qualified twenty-first, almost 6 mph off Vasser's pole speed, and his race lasted just sixty-three laps before he was eliminated by a broken transmission. He was now forty-eight points behind championship leader Montoya.

While his shot at the 1999 championship seemed to be slipping away, Moore had his future to focus on. He'd been a free agent since July 1 and had drawn plenty of interest from within and outside the CART series. His experience competing in the International Race of Champions (IROC, a four-race mini-championship featuring stock cars very similar to NASCAR Cup cars) cast away some of his concerns about venturing out of his Indy car comfort zone. Moore also enjoyed the two FIA World Endurance Championship races he ran in late 1997 at Sebring and Laguna Seca in a factory AMG-Mercedes CLK GTR, co-driving with F1 star Alexander Wurz.

"CART is where my heart is because it's what I've wanted to do since I was a little boy," Moore said. "It would be difficult to leave here, but being in a race car, be it in NASCAR, Formula 1, or CART, they're all enjoyable for me. At the beginning of the season, I might have looked at NASCAR and said, 'I don't think there would be any opportunities there or any chance I would enjoy doing it.' But after doing the IROC series, that has opened my eyes and made me say, 'Hey, I could go down there and still have plenty of fun.'"

In truth, Moore and his pal Dario Franchitti were engaging in a bit of mischief. "That IROC race was Greg's one race at Indy. There were lots of rods in the fire and Greg and Dario got a rumor started that he was going to go to NASCAR, just for fun," revealed Moore's friend Al Robbie. "It was picked up in the press, and they were both involved in that. They were out there working and being professional but still took a lot of time to make everyone laugh and enjoy themselves."

While declining oval attendance was a worrying trend across the schedule, CART's poor drawing power at Michigan was also likely affected in 1999 by the fact that the next race on the FedEx Championship Series schedule, two weeks later, was just seventy miles away in Detroit. Indy car attendance at Michigan was traditionally soft compared to NASCAR's, though CART set a Michigan attendance record of 104,000 for the inaugural running of the U.S. 500 in May 1996. The crowd at the rural track near the small city of Jackson had steadily diminished since then, with the '99 attendance estimated at forty-five thousand. The lack of spectators was accentuated by additional empty grandstands that were continually being added to increase capacity for NASCAR, which at its early twenty-first century peak attracted around 150,000 spectators to MIS twice a year for Winston Cup Series races.

The Michigan slump also raised questions about the fundamental ability of longtime track owner Penske Motorsports to fill the stands for any of its CART events. The crowd for the May CART race at Nazareth Speedway, another Penske-promoted track, was similarly disappointing, though Penske had generated a crowd of over ninety thousand for the Marlboro 500 at California Speedway in November 1998.

By the time the 1999 Michigan 500 rolled around, there was a new conspiracy theory: In May, Roger Penske sold Penske Motorsports, which owned and operated Michigan, Nazareth, Rockingham Speedway, and California Speedway—along with an interest in Homestead-Miami Speedway—to International Speedway Corporation (ISC). That essentially put those tracks under the same France family ownership umbrella as NASCAR, which by the late '90s was already starting to reap the benefits of the Indy car split. Common wisdom said ISC needed its tracks to host additional events beyond NASCAR, but it did not want those Indy car events to appear more popular than its bread-and-butter stock-car races.

But slim crowds at his now-former tracks were the least of Roger Penske's racing-related problems as the calendar turned to August 1999. Given the level of funding and the quality of personnel, Marlboro Team Penske was dramatically underperforming, magnified by the handicaps of running Mercedes-Benz engines and Goodyear tires. Al Unser Jr. missed two races after breaking his leg in the season opener; never a great qualifier, he managed to start fourteenth or better only twice since then and brought home only three top-ten finishes. Rookie Tarso Marques produced similar results in his six starts, three in a second car alongside Unser.

After fielding a pair of Penske PC27s at Michigan for Unser and Alex Barron, Team Penske was set to revert to a Lola for Unser at the Tenneco Automotive Detroit Grand Prix. A second Lola would be run for rookie Gonzalo Rodriguez, the first driver from Uruguay to achieve international success; he had won two races on the way to third place in the 1998 FIA Formula 3000 championship behind Juan Montoya and Nick Heidfeld. Rodriguez won the F3000 race at Monaco in May, and when he traveled to America to race in Detroit, he ranked second in the '99 standings, fresh off a second-place finish at Spa-Francorchamps.

Following the Brazilian race in May, Penske had summoned Unser to his corporate office in Bloomfield Hills. As Junior detailed in his book, *A Checkered Past*, the meeting was not about a contract extension as he had hoped. Instead, he was confronted about his suspected drug use, and when forced to admit he had marijuana in his system, he was given thirty days to produce a clean test. As many suspected, that's why he showed up nearly bald at Cleveland. He was subjected to an on-the-spot screening at Road America in early July, and by the first of August, the results were in: Unser had tested positive for pot. On the eve of the Detroit race weekend, he was ordered to meet with a late-arriving Penske at his hangar at Wayne Metropolitan Airport.

Unser learned he again tested positive for marijuana—he claimed to have taken a single toke, twelve days earlier—and was ordered to produce a clean test on the spot or he would be out of the car with immediate effect. To the relief of all, he passed. But Penske had additional news for the struggling former champion. "Tomorrow morning, I am announcing my drivers for the next three years, and they are Greg Moore and Gil de Ferran," he said.

Unser was stunned, as was the rest of the CART community when Penske revealed the bombshell signings the afternoon of Friday, August 6. "This states clearly that I'm not backing off and shows that I have committed to the future, and not just the next six months," Penske stated. "When you look at these two drivers, they've got experience, they've won races, and they're at the top of their game. We're counting on both Gil and Greg to work with us to meet the challenge of the close competition of CART racing."

Moore's teammate Patrick Carpentier had an inkling that something was up. "I think Greg knew he was leaving in Toronto," Carpentier recalled. "We rode together in a pickup truck; we must have qualified close to one another at that race. He invited me to dinner, said, 'Let's go to dinner sometime.' I think he had already signed his deal with Penske. He wasn't happy about a few things and wanted to leave.

AL ROBBIE

"I went to Woodstock '99, the concert. CART was racing at Michigan Speedway that weekend. On the Saturday afternoon, I had to go out to my car in the parking lot to charge my phone. When it powered it up, I had like six messages from Greg. I got hold of him, and he says, 'What's going on over there? It's all over the news that people are rioting.' I said, 'No, it's great!' So, the race happened on Sunday, the last day of Woodstock happened on Sunday, and we all got kicked out of Woodstock because people really did start rioting. The state troopers came in and sent everybody packing at three o'clock in the morning.

"I drove an hour up the highway and pulled over because I hadn't slept. I woke up to another six messages from Greg, because he had seen the news that everyone was trying to burn down Woodstock. So finally, I wake up at the side of the road Monday morning and phone him. 'Where the hell are you?' He says he's worried about me. I ask, 'Where are you?' He says he was at Alan Miller's house in Detroit, his attorney's. I said, 'I thought you'd be heading back to Vancouver by now.' He says, 'No. But I've got news though. I just signed for Penske!' There was a delay, and he said, 'Yep. I'm driving for Penske next year.' I said, 'You could have been a bit less nonchalant,' and he said, 'I was just slow playing you there!' Of course, he said not to tell anybody."

"I was not the type of guy to go to dinner all the time, and I think Greg was a bit the same as far as teammates were concerned," he continued. "But he had a great relationship with his group of friends. Those guys remained friends, and I think that was part of the popularity that Dario and Tony and Greg had for such a long time. That was very unusual, and they had a super fun ride. I struggled with that, because you're racing against each other really hard. Like Lando Norris and Max Verstappen in F1 right now—their friendship didn't last very long. But Greg changed completely when he knew we were not going to be teammates. He started playing tricks and jokes and things."

Driving for Penske Racing was obviously the opportunity of a lifetime for Moore and de Ferran. "I don't look at this move as a gamble,"

DARIO FRANCHITTI

"If you remember, he left Detroit Friday afternoon to do the IROC race at Indianapolis, and I think he crashed, had a big shunt. [On the second lap, Dale Earnhardt took the air off Moore's rear spoiler in the south short chute, he spun 180 degrees and whacked the Turn Two wall with the left side of the car. 'You know what they call that Benny?' said ABC analyst Darrell Waltrip to broadcast partner Benny Parsons. 'That's the hospital wobble.'] Then the announcement happened.

"I get out my Motorola flip phone, and I'm like, 'Hey asshole! Thanks for the heads-up!' And he was very much like, 'Ah, business is business.' But I saw that a year earlier. We were driving Greg's bus from Mid-Ohio to Elkhart Lake—and I mean Max, Greg, and myself took turns driving Greg's bus—bloody hell, it was terrifying! Max, at that time, was trying to do a deal with Bobby Rahal, I think I was possibly trying to do an F1 deal, and Greg was trying to get out of his Forsythe contract. We're driving along, and whoever's phone would ring would go into the back of the bus and have this secret call. That showed how we separated business from fun."

Moore commented. "I look at it as a challenge. They haven't had results for the last couple of years, but in the long run, it comes down to the guy with the horsepower, and that's Roger. One reason I went with Roger is he's one of the world's best businessmen, but he's also a racer. I know he's not happy with where he is on the grid. You can see how serious he is about changing that by looking at the two drivers he has selected. I believe Gil and I represent one of the strongest driver pairings in the series."

"I think the timing is good," added de Ferran. "It puts an end to the speculation about what we're going to do and allows me, Greg, and Roger to concentrate on what we have to do this year. It's a great team; they have all the capabilities, and they have all the resources. Roger is as committed as he's ever been, and you can see it in the two drivers he has selected. The last three years haven't been as successful for the team, but Roger is doing all he can to get back to that level. I'm just one of the pieces of the puzzle."

Penske declined comment on his chassis/engine/tire combination for 2000 and said sponsorship details would be revealed later. "I assume we'll remain loyal to our current suppliers," Penske remarked. "Penske Cars will be part of our operations, but I'm at the 90 percent mark assuming we won't run a Penske chassis. We'll run a Reynard or a Lola. We can take a chassis and enhance it with our ability and our people over in England."

He noted that accusations he had poached drivers from other teams were wide of the mark and wished Unser success in the future. "We certainly didn't invade their teams," Penske stressed. "Their contracts were open. I was one of many who was pursuing these drivers. Al and I talked in May, and we again talked recently, and the both of us decided that it would be best to go our own way. He and I were very open, and we're going to support him for the rest of the season.

"Sometimes a change of scenery can be good," he added. "Look at Paul Tracy—he's doing a great job with Barry Green's team."

Understandably distraught, Unser refused to discuss his future with reporters. "I have a strong feeling about what I'll do," he said. "My wife's lawyers are asking me the same question, and until our divorce is final, I won't be talking about it. I'll be driving race cars, now and next year. If the best deal is to drive a Winston Cup car, you bet I'd do that. If the best deal is to be teammates with John Force, I'll do that."

He continued to discount speculation that his private life and lifestyle adversely impacted his driving. "My life off the track is nobody's business, to begin with," he told *Autoweek*. "But believe me, it has not affected what I do on the track, or anything I do around the racetrack. I'll have a drink after the race, but so will a lot of people. The worst thing is that I haven't been able to quit smoking, so maybe I'm probably breathing a little harder than some of those boys out there. But it doesn't make the car go any slower, and if I quit, the car wouldn't go any faster.

"People think it's partying or something. It ain't. It's trying to figure out how I can help my little girl get back on her feet, and dealing with lawyers, instead of thinking about my race car. The only time I've been truly happy this year is when I'm in that seat, by myself, doing what I do. The race car has saved me from a lot of frustration."

It was fellow Penske Racing castoff Tracy, in fact, who set the provisional qualifying pace in Detroit ahead of Montoya and Andretti on the same day "The Captain" sent out the press release announcing his Moore/de Ferran news. Neither of Penske's 2000 drivers were present; Moore was fourth fastest, and immediately after the session, he and Unser flew to Indianapolis for the final round of the 1999 IROC (International Race of Champions) series. Adrian Fernandez was slated to join them, but he failed to make the trip after crashing heavily in practice. Fernandez flew separately to Indianapolis, where Dr. Joe Baele inserted a plate and screws to close the fracture. The Mexican was expected to miss up to four weeks.

Fernandez crashed in Turn Two, a fast, off-camber fourth-gear lefthander that was one of the most challenging street course corners on the entire schedule. "I caught it, and it got away again," he stated. "The right front hit the wall, but before it did, I thought I was going to catch the car, so I left my hands on the steering wheel. At first, I thought it was just a bruise, and I was saying to myself that it couldn't be that bad, but inside I knew it wasn't good. It's too bad for our championship hopes, and I feel bad for the team, but it's important that I have it taken care of properly and come back 100 percent."

With one driver out of action, Patrick Racing was left with a single entry for Jan Magnussen, in his first race in the No. 20 car normally driven by P. J. Jones. Jones arrived in Detroit Friday evening, but Patrick decided to withdraw the No. 40 for the rest of the weekend. Fernandez laments 1999 as the year that got away, when there was so much potential but comparatively little reward.

"We were competitive in '99, but if we had just stuck with the Reynard and had a steady driver situation, we could have fought for the championship," he reflected. "Unfortunately, I also broke my wrist in Detroit. I missed four races and still finished sixth in the championship. Just imagine if I had raced those four races, so that was a shame.

"IROC was an amazing experience, and a sad experience in a way because I have great memories with Greg Moore," he added. "We did all the training and testing together with Dale Earnhardt, who is also no longer with us. He was the one that helped us get used to the tracks. The radios were set up so he could talk to us as we were running around the track. We had to follow him in another one of the IROC cars so he could teach us the line and how to get very close to the outside wall, and those are moments I miss a lot. It was such a nice experience."

Shortly after action resumed at Detroit, Hélio Castroneves appeared to pile into the Turn Two wall even harder than Fernandez, but he emerged uninjured. Then in the Saturday morning practice, Magnussen planted the Patrick Swift into a tire barrier lining Turn Three. A closely following Moore was unable to take evasive action, his car slamming into the No. 20. Both crews faced a serious thrash to get their cars ready for qualifying. Meanwhile, Franchitti was playing catch-up after crashing Friday afternoon and failing to set a time.

In the Saturday afternoon session, Montoya put together a ragged pole position lap captured in full by onboard camera that remains a YouTube favorite among Indy car fans all these years later. JPM staged a car control clinic and overcame a couple of brushes with the walls of the notoriously tight Belle Isle temporary course to claim the fifth pole of his rookie campaign. Having already smashed Alex Zanardi's 1996 rookie mark of 610 laps led, the brash youngster set his sights on the seven pole positions Nigel Mansell achieved in 1993.

"I just pushed a little too hard," Montoya said with a broad smile. "It just touched the wall. That didn't help me, but it didn't slow me."

Tracy, who held the overnight pole, managed second. "I made a few mistakes," he admitted. "I actually did my time on the seventh lap on the tires, which is impressive." De Ferran claimed third in one of his last runs for Walker Racing, followed by a rebounding Franchitti. "The lack of track time Friday really hurt us, and I've been playing catch-up really," Dario said. "There's a lot more traffic in the first qualifying group and the track isn't usually as fast. I'm thrilled to be starting fourth."

Rodriguez (sixteenth) outqualified Unser (twentieth) in his first run for Marlboro Team Penske. "I've never experienced so much power before," enthused the Uruguayan rookie. "The car is much heavier than the Formula 3000 car I am used to, so the reactions are a bit slower. But I am enjoying the experience. I hope I get to drive this car on a natural road course." He was scheduled to get his wish at Laguna Seca later in the season.

The Racetrack at Belle Isle, as it was officially called, almost always produced memorable races since the Detroit GP was moved there from a forgettable downtown street circuit in 1992. The 1999 version was arguably the strangest one yet. From pole position, Montoya and his Target/Ganassi Reynard/Honda were once again the class of the field. But a rare miscommunication resulted in Montoya staying out while the rest of the field pitted under yellow on lap forty-four.

With a much lighter fuel load, Juan steamed away to a 15.6-second lead before he came in for his final stop on lap fifty-eight. That dropped him to eighth place, 10.1 seconds behind new leader Franchitti. Would there be another fighting comeback from the sensational rookie?

Maybe at any other track. Instead, Montoya soon tangled with Moreno while disputing sixth place. That brought out a yellow, during which the Ford Mustang pace car developed a fuel leak. A second pace car was dispatched to the start/finish line to wait for the field, but when the stricken Mustang peeled into the pits, several drivers thought it was for the restart—including Castroneves, who cannoned his Hogan Racing Lola/Mercedes into the back of Montoya's car.

"I saw the pace car pull off the track, and I assumed the race was going to go green," Castroneves explained. "People started to speed up and the team told me it was going to go green. I never knew they were bringing another pace car onto the track. By the time I knew that the track was still yellow, I had already hit Juan."

Franchitti had passed Tracy on the twelfth lap, and when Montoya encountered his misfortune, they were able to cruise home in that order under yellow to another Team Kool Green one-two, trailed by Moore, Andretti, and Vasser. Remarkably, it was Moore's first podium finish at a road racing venue since Mid-Ohio in 1997, twenty-four months earlier. "Our two pit stops were great," he said. "I'm super happy to score points and get back into contention in the drivers' championship."

Detroit 1999 won't be remembered as Franchitti's prettiest win, but it still counted for twenty points. "It was a very interesting day, although I don't think it was a particularly nice race to watch," he said. "I told the guys on the radio it was an ugly way to win a race, but we'll take them any way we can. I was a little worried that Juan might catch us at the end because we were saving fuel, but we were ready to go for it if we had to. Then I looked up at the jumbo screen and saw Juan walking away from his car."

Despite having only two wins to Montoya's four, Franchitti departed Detroit with a five-point lead in the PPG Cup standings. Given the turn of events that unfolded at Belle Isle, the feeling existed it could have been the turning point in his championship campaign.

"It's great to be leading the championship now," Dario said. "But the time to do it is after the last race at Fontana. I hope we can keep it till then."

TENNECO AUTOMOTIVE GRAND PRIX OF DETROIT

The Racetrack at Belle Isle — August 8, 1999 – 71 laps

1. Dario Franchitti
2. Paul Tracy
3. Greg Moore
4. Michael Andretti
5. Jimmy Vasser

CHAMPIONSHIP STANDINGS AFTER 13 OF 20 RACES

1. Franchitti 136
2. Montoya 131
3. Andretti 119
4. Tracy 106
5. Fittipaldi 101

Juan Pablo Montoya drove one of his best races to defeat the Team Green duo at Mid-Ohio.

Michael Levitt

CHAPTER 11

SUMMER OF JUAN

The 1999 CART season was two-thirds completed, and to some, it looked like Juan Pablo Montoya had finally encountered a slump. The rookie had managed to score just nineteen points in the three races since the Cleveland Grand Prix at the end of June, and sixteen of those points were the product of his second-place finish in the U.S. 500 at Michigan Speedway.

But in truth, Montoya was in position to win at both Michigan and Detroit, only for a variety of factors out of his control to knock him out of contention. The only place he looked truly uncomfortable and out of his normal place as an absolute Indy car front-runner was the tricky street course in Toronto, the type of stop-and-go track that Dario Franchitti tended to thrive on. Coming off a victory at Detroit, in the lead of the championship for the first time all year, and with three of the final seven races to be staged on temporary urban circuits, Franchitti entered the final third of the campaign with confidence and momentum.

That was vividly on display as Dario dominated the first day of action at Mid-Ohio Sports Car Course, a rustic road racing facility nestled in rolling terrain halfway between Columbus and Cleveland. Mid-Ohio was built in 1961 and updated in 1983 to '70s standards by Jim Trueman, the Red Roof Inns magnate who formed Truesports Racing and launched Bobby Rahal's Indy car career. Not much has changed another quarter century down the line, but despite its lack of amenities and penny-pinching current owners (Kevin Savoree and Kim Green, brother of Barry Green), Mid-Ohio remains a charming favorite among fans and racers. It's what drivers like to call a "technical" track, with a variety of off-camber corners that feature blind entrances and little or no runoff.

Franchitti blitzed the competition on the opening day of the Mid-Ohio weekend by half a second with a track record lap of one minute, 5.347 seconds, a benchmark that wasn't bettered until 2016. "At the end of the season the single point for the pole today may make all the difference in the championship," he said. "We spent four days testing here over the past couple of months, and the track seemed a lot slicker today than it did in testing. To do a 1:05.3 in that session was really a bit of a shock. I looked down at the dash and saw the time and said to myself, 'Where the hell did that come from?'"

Saturday qualifying was rained out, meaning Friday results determined the grid. Bryan Herta made it a Franchitti-Herta front row at Mid-Ohio for the second year in a row, followed originally by Mark Blundell in an encouraging result for PacWest Racing. But Blundell's time was disallowed when his car failed to meet the two-inch ground clearance rule. "We can't buy a break, but you've got to take the rough with the smooth," said the disconsolate Brit.

Paul Tracy inherited third, followed by an encouraging performance from Tony Kanaan, whose Forsythe Championship Racing entry was still being run out of the old Tasman Motorsports facility in suburban Columbus. Tasman owner Steve Horne served for many years as team manager for Truesports, and Team Rahal now occupied the former Truesports facility just up the street in Hilliard. Those two teams enjoyed enthusiastic support from the loyal local fan base at the Cleveland and Mid-Ohio events.

The Saturday rain also prevented Montoya from improving on his provisional qualifying position of eighth, and he was not happy with the Target Reynard/Honda. "We came to Mid-Ohio with high hopes after we had a very good test here, but I just couldn't drive the car," he said. "At one point, I actually told my crew 'This car is dangerous to drive!' We made some changes for qualifying but were still way off."

When Montoya was still unhappy with his car in the Sunday morning warm-up, engineer Morris Nunn conjured up a completely different setup for the race. But starting from the fourth row at a track where it is considered very difficult to pass, few gave him a chance of winning. Instead, the focus was on Franchitti and Herta, who in 1998 came together on the opening lap to trigger a multicar crash at the apex of the Turn Four-Five-Six sequence called The Esses that took out Jimmy Vasser and sparked some lingering hard feelings. Franchitti had been involved in at least two first lap incidents in the last two years after starting from pole position, and several of his rivals thought he tended to be too conservative at the start.

"I remember what happened last year when Bryan came up beside me," Franchitti said. "This year, I'm going to get through the first corner and get on with the rest of the race. I'm not going to concede anything to Bryan at the start. I aim to be leading after the first corner."

Mission accomplished, because Franchitti emerged cleanly at the head of the field. For good measure, Tracy passed Herta for second place on the third lap and settled in behind his teammate until they made their first routine pit stop on lap thirty. Meanwhile, Montoya failed to make any ground from his grid position. But he had been saving fuel, and when the majority of the field stopped on the thirtieth tour, he ran one lap longer and emerged from the pits in third place. "It was a pretty good in lap, and then the guys did a fantastic job in the pits," he related. "My first pit stop was brilliant."

Still, Montoya faced a twelve-second deficit to Tracy, not to mention Franchitti was another four or five seconds up the road. But he went to work and soon started cutting into the cushion the Team Green drivers enjoyed. "Chip told me over the radio, 'You're catching them quickly,'" said Montoya. "So, I pushed harder."

On lap forty-five, Franchitti started reporting over his radio that his car was starting to bottom out in an unusual manner. It transpired he had a slowly deflating right-rear tire, and Montoya suddenly started eating into Franchitti's lead at the rate of a second a lap. Dario finally had to pit on lap fifty-five, about five laps earlier than he had intended. Now his strategy for the final stint was compromised, because he would have to conserve fuel to make the finish.

Montoya swept past Tracy into the lead on the fifty-sixth lap, and after they both completed their final stops, the Colombian retained the lead over Tracy and Franchitti. Following the only caution of the race, Montoya simply drove into the distance, pulling out a 10.927-second margin over Tracy before the checkered flag flew. Franchitti trailed home in third and saw his championship lead over Montoya slashed to a single point.

"On the first stint, the car was great," said Franchitti. "We had everything under control. The tire cost us the race, really; it was pretty costly, to be honest. That and the backmarkers. What can you say about the backmarkers—it was a bit of a joke, really. Obviously, it's nice to get on the podium, but from the way the day started to the way it ended, I'm kind of disappointed."

Conversely, Tracy was pleased with the podium finish and jumped up to fourth place in the standings. "I drove my heart out in the second half of the race," he related. "I was quite surprised at the pace Juan ran. When he passed me, he got a nice run on me going into the corner. I tried to protect the line, and I made him go wide, but Juan went in a little deeper than me and he braked late. It was a good pass. They ought to put Superman on his car.

"He's an incredible driver," Tracy continued. "He doesn't worry about anything. He drives the car sideways to its full potential. He's young, and there's nothing that bothers him. I guess that's the way I used to drive, but as you get older, you think about other things and you're maybe not as fearless as when you're younger. That the way Juan is."

Herta looked set for "best of the rest" honors until his Ford/Cosworth engine blew with eleven laps to go. The lost podium was salt on the wound for Herta, who learned earlier in the week that he would not be back with Team Rahal in 2000. "It's a tough deal, but this can be a tough business," said Bobby Rahal. "I think I've been fair and patient. Bryan is a fast driver, but our results haven't been there." Herta's misfortune allowed Montoya's Target/Ganassi teammate Jimmy Vasser to claim fourth place, ahead of Max Papis and Gil de Ferran. Championship contenders Michael Andretti and Greg Moore finished eighth and eleventh respectively.

Herta couldn't really argue with Rahal's decision, as he reflected on that era years later. "You always wish for more," Herta said. "I enjoyed my time with Rahal and felt we were always on the cusp of something great. I don't think from one year to the next I ever had the same combination of tires and chassis. But I hate to use that as an excuse. As a driver, you're supposed to get the best out of whatever combination the team owner throws at you. I think you have to say, no, we didn't get everything out of it because we had good sponsors and good people in the team, and I don't think we won enough at that time. That's not the team's fault or my fault, because everyone was trying the best they could. We just weren't quite getting it done."

Both Team Green drivers were left wondering what they had to do to defeat Montoya. Winning from eighth on the grid matched a Mid-Ohio record, and his fastest race lap was 0.6 seconds better than anyone else in the field could manage. It topped Franchitti's best by 0.8 seconds. Overall, it was arguably the most impressive performance of Montoya's brief Indy car career to date, and it matched the rookie record of five race wins established by Nigel Mansell six years earlier. Generally nonplussed, JPM seemed to take great pride and joy from his latest accomplishment.

"This was a good day after what happened Friday," he said. "Morris did a great job—I never expected to win. The first pit stop was the difference. After the first pit stop, I wanted to prove that I was quicker than them. I was catching them and catching them quick, so I just kept pushing and pushing and pushing until the end. We came here looking to get some good points out of this and we did, so we're happy."

Decades later, Montoya looked back with a hearty laugh on what he considers one of his best races in CART. "Qualifying was always difficult," he said. "The team always felt like they could find a lot of time and I didn't. But when the race came, I knew there was not even a question whether I had enough pace to win. You know, at Mid-Ohio, we were miles off the pace in practice. This is funny, we went upstairs in those old garages they have at Mid-Ohio and looked at the Team Green cars to see what they were running. You could see they had massive springs, and we didn't. So, Morris, on the basis of that, put on big springs and we beat them!"

MILLER LITE 200

Mid-Ohio Sports Car Course – August 15, 1999 – 83 laps

1. Juan Pablo Montoya
2. Paul Tracy
3. Dario Franchitti
4. Jimmy Vasser
5. Max Papis

CHAMPIONSHIP STANDINGS AFTER 14 OF 20 RACES

1.	Franchitti	152
2.	Montoya	151
3.	Andretti	124
4.	Tracy	122
5.	Fittipaldi	101

Juan Montoya would never admit it in public, but he pretty much dreaded the prospect of the week that lay ahead. Not because Chicago Motor Speedway was a 1.029-mile oval that was new to everyone, built on the grounds of the old Sportsman's Park dog (and later horse) track near Midway Airport. No, because this was effectively a Target Chip Ganassi Racing home event. The track itself was nicknamed "The Chipyard," in honor of Chip Ganassi's co-ownership role with Charles Bidwell III, a character of some notoriety in Chicago business circles. Target was fully on board, and despite the oval racecourse, the race was billed as the Target Grand Prix. Ganassi and Bidwell, president of the National Jockey's Association and owner of Sportsman's Park, split the construction costs.

"The last thing the world needs is another car race," Ganassi said. "If we can make this an event, we'll succeed. I don't think there's any secret to it. We had the location, the money, and the political capital. We tried to take all the positives of a permanent facility and all the positives of a temporary urban facility. We have five expressway interchanges within a mile and a half. You're seven miles from the Chicago Loop, and thirty-five thousand hotel rooms and good restaurants. We don't have to put it up and tear it down every year and put everything else in the area on hold in the meantime. You take all the good stuff about Toronto or Long Beach, and add good, close, fan-friendly racing."

Given Ganassi's first-time involvement as a race promoter and Target's massive investment and promotion, it was an important event for CART, but Montoya was never one to relish spending the week facing banks of television cameras and microphones. To his credit, he got on with the job, and he did it well. But he saved his best for the racetrack. Chip Ganassi may have built the playing field, but it took Montoya to complete the dream. The spectacular first-year driver did it by driving Ganassi's Target Reynard/Honda from tenth on the grid to victory in the inaugural Target GP, leading 132 of 225 laps to beat Dario Franchitti in a straight fight and retake the FedEx Championship Series points lead with five races to go. Compounding race promoter Ganassi's joy, Jimmy Vasser secured the remaining podium position in the second Target/Ganassi car.

While pole-winner Max Papis jumped into the lead, Montoya moved quickly from tenth to fifth. He got by Hélio Castroneves on lap forty-seven for fourth, then caught and passed Vasser on lap fifty-one. Seven laps later, he eased under Franchitti in Turn Three before taking the lead from Papis on lap sixty-four. At the same time, Michael Andretti had moved from eighteenth to third when the yellow flag flew for Greg Moore's stalled car.

After all the leaders pitted under yellow, Montoya led from Andretti, Franchitti, Paul Tracy (up from seventeenth on the grid after a great pit stop), Vasser, Papis, and Castroneves. Franchitti took second from Andretti on the lap seventy-six restart, but the yellow again flew on lap eighty-six for a crash involving Jan Magnussen and Roberto Moreno. Tracy got the jump on Andretti for third place entering Turn One, but Michael remained inside as the two cars ran neck and neck down the backstraight. Andretti was still alongside when Tracy turned in sharply entering Turn Three, and both cars spun into the wall.

"Unbelievable—normal Paul Tracy driving," fumed Andretti, who came out of the car limping from a bruised right Achilles tendon. "What was he thinking? Does he have a death wish? He was swerving down the straight at me and then he turned into me. He pinched me down and I had nowhere to go. He took us, both of us, out and I hope he's happy with himself."

Not surprisingly, Tracy didn't see it the same way. "It looked to me that we were going for the same piece of real estate," he said. "This track is such a one-line place that you've got to turn in sometime." Vasser, who watched the whole situation unfold, called it "The Paul and Michael Ego Show."

Almost unnoticed, Franchitti was making an inch-perfect pass for the lead on Montoya through Turn Four as Andretti and Tracy crashed. When the race went green for the final time on lap 114, Dario held the point for thirteen more laps before Montoya slipped by on the inside of Turn One. Juan held the lead through the final round of pit stops and built a three-second gap.

Montoya's only scare came with forty laps to go when he caught P. J. Jones, who was running in seventh place subbing for Adrian Fernandez in Patrick Racing's Tecate/Quaker State No. 40 car. Juan would be stuck there for the rest of the race as Jones resolutely ignored waving blue flags. Jones had been the chief subject of Franchitti's displeasure with the backmarkers one week earlier at Mid-Ohio and was known to be the most difficult driver in the field to put a lap down.

"In the driver briefing, we had a bit of a discussion about this," said Montoya. "If I [the leader] get alongside, you let me by. He did it to me two or three times. It was a joke—people like that shouldn't be allowed to race."

Jones's tactics allowed Franchitti to catch up, but he never had a real shot of passing Montoya for the lead. In fact, ninth-placed Moreno (who had resumed from his earlier spin and was running two laps down) passed Franchitti with seven laps to go and prevented him from making a final charge on Montoya.

"I was just waiting for Juan to make one small mistake in traffic," Dario commented. "Then when we were stuck behind PJ, Moreno came steaming by me on the inside to unlap himself and that was basically the end of my race."

Vasser had similarly been held up for an entire stint and was unable to capitalize. He finished fifteen seconds behind the leaders. "I didn't realize they got bottled up that bad," he said. "I guess I could have gotten up in the mix."

Tying a CART career-best fourth was Papis, who said, "The car just got too loose at the start. We probably had a better car than fourth, but we'll take it for now." Castroneves was next, claiming his third consecutive top-ten finish, while Patrick Carpentier and Jones rounded out the lead-lap runners.

"I'm so pleased," said Montoya. "All weekend the car was so bad. We couldn't get the car working. Last night I stayed really late with the guys and with Morris, and he made all the right changes to the car. I was fastest in the warmup, and I thought, 'This could be good.' The car was just flying all day long."

The incredible difficulty in getting past slower lapped cars was yet again the result of the inappropriate aero package with small speedway wings that CART utilized for short ovals in 1999. It was as frustrating for fans and team owners as it was for the drivers. The paper clip–like Chicago layout was supposed to race like Milwaukee, but CART never tried running there with a higher-downforce setup, and by 2003, the $65 million track was defunct.

"If you have a follow-the-leader procession on short ovals, that's not doing justice to our audience," fumed Gerald Forsythe. "I wrote a letter to every team owner and told them point-blank that we have taken the best racing CART has and turned it into a parade. They took a vote and decided to stay with smaller wings. Does that make sense? To me, absolutely not."

There was a significant new winner in the Indy Lights support race at Chicago. Scott Dixon, an Australian-born New Zealander who just turned nineteen, led flag to flag from pole position to finish 0.326 seconds ahead of Guy Smith to score his first major international victory. Dixon finished in the top four in his first three Lights starts but then endured a four-race mid-season slump. The Chicago victory made him the second youngest winner in Indy Lights history behind Greg Moore.

Dixon's family had supported his career on a shoestring budget, and his performances coming up the ladder in New Zealand and Australia convinced former Formula 1 and Indy car driver Stefan Johansson to take on a management role. Surprisingly, Dixon scored the majority of his points during the 1999 season on oval tracks despite his total lack of prior experience.

"I don't know what it is," he said. "I've always enjoyed the road courses more than the ovals, but we've had better luck on the ovals. This win is very big, especially after the bad luck we've had, some of it my fault. It's a real boost for us, and hopefully it will help us get more money when we get home!"

TARGET GRAND PRIX

Chicago Motor Speedway — August 22, 1999 – 225 laps

1. Juan Pablo Montoya
2. Dario Franchitti
3. Jimmy Vasser
4. Max Papis
5. Hélio Castroneves

CHAMPIONSHIP STANDINGS AFTER 15 OF 20 RACES

1.	Montoya	172
2.	Franchitti	168
3.	Andretti	124
4.	Tracy	122
5.	Fittipaldi	101

Scott Dixon had plenty of time to return home for a break, because the Indy Lights support series did not accompany the FedEx Championship Series to its next venue, the downtown street course in Vancouver, British Columbia—Greg Moore country. Moore was probably wishing he had headed directly home from Chicago, but instead, Player's/Forsythe Racing detoured to greater Los Angeles to test at California Speedway, site of the October 31 season finale.

Moore had enjoyed great success on oval tracks throughout his Indy car career, and he adapted quickly to the style of superspeedway racing required by the introduction of the drag-inducing Handford Device rear wing in 1998. But the August 28 test at Fontana went poorly. Nearly two years into the evolution and development of the Ilmor/Mercedes-Benz IC108E engine, it was still temperamental and unreliable. Lapping Indy car racing's fastest circuit at 230 miles per hour in the days before the invention of the SAFER Barrier, Moore suffered an engine failure and crashed heavily. He was still feeling the effects three days later when he made a promotional appearance at a Vancouver area sporting goods store.

SCOTT DIXON

"I actually made a trip at the end of 1997 with Steve Horne's team to the Vancouver CART race, on the weekend that Princess Diana died, and then also to Laguna Seca. Steve Dickson was with the Tasman team at that time, and I had a weird moment in Vancouver. I checked in to the hotel and they gave me the key to Steve Dickson's room. I go in, and there is he laying on the bed naked! I'm like, 'Sorry man, I think I'm in the wrong room!' That was kind of my welcome to IndyCar.

"That was my first awakening to it, and honestly, I was just blown away by the competition. At Vancouver, Zanardi had some kind of issue and drove through the whole field. It was so cool to watch, because in most other formulas even if you have a good race car and drive a good race, it's difficult to make it through. I loved the fan atmosphere and how close you could get to everything. Even in V8 Supercars, you couldn't get the access you did to Indy cars. It was mind-blowing. It was much more expansive back then, the scale of the manufacturers and the way the cars were being updated, and the speed and the sound of the cars was just so cool. The whole scene was much bigger back then, for sure.

"In 1999 I was driving Indy Lights for Stefan Johansson's team and living in an apartment on the west side of Indy. It was fun, because there were Blair and Anton Julian and Kane Williams and bunch of Kiwis at that team. It was a pretty wild year in the sense of never knowing whether you were going to catch on and stay. Obviously, that happened the next year with getting the PacWest deal. I remember the win at Chicago and the Cicero track and there were some other good races, but man, I was having a lot of fun that year. There was just no real expectation.

"I did get to test an Indy car at the end of '99, some kind of Mercedes test for PacWest. The late '90s were an exceptional era, for sure. I was kind of bummed I missed it. I think '99 and 2000 was kind of like the last real push for CART. By 2001, it was slipping a little bit. The split was still at full strength at that point."

"The engine broke just as I was entering Turn One and I hit the wall at about 210 mph backwards," Moore told reporters, adding that he sustained bruises to his upper and lower back and knee. "I think your body shuts off for a few seconds. It's such a big hit that your body just says, 'I don't want to remember that.' And you just sort of black out for a few seconds. It's not a lot of fun; probably the biggest one I've had in my career. But other than that, I'm fine."

Moore's teammate Patrick Carpentier recalls how he and the other Mercedes runners often had to resort to black humor in reaction to the poor engine performance and reliability.

"Neil Micklewright was the head of the team back then," Carpentier chuckled. "He had a meeting with Mercedes; I think it was at Laguna Seca. The engines kept blowing up and they were not fast. At Player's we had pistons on the middle of each table at the hospitality area to be used as ashtrays, because people smoked a lot back then. The guy from Mercedes was sitting there and he said to Neil, 'Wow, those pistons, that's really cool. We should have some of these.' And Neil Micklewright said, 'Well, just walk around the circuit—you'll find a few more.' That kind of summed up what the relationship was with Mercedes."

As always, Moore was cordial with the local beat reporters, many of whom he had known for nearly a decade, as he talked about the difficult season he had endured and the optimism he felt about his upcoming move to Team Penske. "We had a lot of bad luck this year, things going wrong, the car running perfectly all day in practice and qualifying, then all of a sudden, in the race something happens," he said. "You know, it's just kind of been the wrong place at the wrong time. But just because I'm moving on to a different team doesn't make me any less hungry or anything like that. If anything, it may make me try to win a little bit harder because it's my last three or four races with these guys. They've given blood, sweat, and tears over my race car the last four years. It would be nice to be able to repay them with a victory sometime this year."

Alas, the Vancouver street course—especially in the tighter, revised form it took starting in 1998 as urban development encroached on the original circuit—was not the ideal venue for Moore or any of the other Mercedes drivers to shine. Mark Blundell managed to qualify fifth in one of PacWest's Reynards; Moore lined up P9.

Tracy and Franchitti slotted their Team Green Reynard/Hondas onto row two, the Scotsman disappointed after topping the timing charts in provisional qualifying. "We went from having a great car this morning and yesterday to having an undriveable one for qualifying," said Franchitti.

Meanwhile, Montoya claimed his sixth pole of the season, joined surprisingly on the front row by his recent nemesis P. J. Jones, who produced by far the best qualifying performance of his Indy car career. "I think I'm in a pretty conservative position where I can get some good points and finish ahead of Dario," Montoya observed. "We had a problem [Friday] where we blew a motor, so we qualified the backup car. Then this morning I blew up the engine again. So, we stayed with the backup, but Morris Nunn made some good changes for qualifying, and the car felt pretty good."

Montoya was not happy with his car in the wet race day warm-up, but Nunn again worked his setup magic, and the Colombian was much happier once the event got underway after eleven laps in the rain behind the pace car. Montoya immediately pulled out to a five-second lead over Tracy, Blundell, a rapidly fading Jones, Moreno, and Franchitti, whose car did not handle well in full wet conditions.

But by this time, the rain had stopped. Several drivers who had not taken care of their rear tires found them going off and started dropping down the order. The problem even affected leader Montoya, who saw his lead dwindle to nothing over Tracy by lap thirty-five. Meanwhile, Moreno had moved up to third and was reducing a twenty-eight-second deficit to the leaders.

On lap thirty-six, Tracy dived inside Montoya for the lead in Turn One, then promptly spun in Turn Three. He rejoined, now just in front of Moreno and some twelve seconds behind Montoya. But the yellow soon bunched the field when Herta punted Team Rahal teammate Papis off. At half of the scheduled ninety-lap distance, Montoya led from Tracy, who was being hounded by Franchitti. Six laps later, Jones's eventful day continued when he spun at the chicane right in front of the Team Green battle. In the confusion, Franchitti slipped by Tracy and set off after championship rival Montoya.

After yet another yellow, Franchitti resumed the chase on lap fifty-nine. One tour later, he made his move on Montoya at Turn Four. But the attempt was unsuccessful, and Franchitti spun. He subsequently had to pit for a new rear wing and dropped back to fourteenth before he gained a few places in the final laps to finish tenth.

"We worked really hard to get back to second place and then I made a mistake," Dario admitted. "I got halfway alongside Juan when he started to turn in. Then I hit the brakes pretty hard and lost the back. It wasn't a clever move, I'll put it that way. It's pretty frustrating to get back from a bad start and then throw it all away like that. Who knows if we would have had something for Montoya if we had gotten through there clean. He's doing everything right, and I'd just like to forget about today and move on to next weekend."

"It was a clean move," Montoya confirmed. "I knew he couldn't get me there, but he went for it. If I would turn in, I would spin as well, so I just gave him more room and he touched me and he spun. When he hit the tires, I thought, 'These cars are strong,' but I could see he damaged his rear wing."

Almost simultaneously as Franchitti spun, Blundell thumped the wall, and then Tracy did the same thing. "We could have finished one-two if we had just kept it off the fences," Tracy lamented.

Moore was one of ten drivers who were eliminated by contact or crashes, his coming on lap sixty. The local hero had never finished the Vancouver race in four attempts. "I just locked it up and put it into the tire wall," he said. "I made a mistake there, and then we made the

DARIO FRANCHITTI

"Vancouver was completely my screw up. I think it rained. Vancouver had a double-apex right, a bumpy left, and then a hairpin right onto the backstraight. And I made a stupid move on Monty. I tried to avoid hitting him, locked up, and spun. That was an interesting part of Monty and I's relationship. Especially that year, we were at times hammer and tongs. But there was a respect there, and there was never contact, there was never bullshit, there were never mind games, and I loved it. It was such a pure fight. I could have jumped off the brakes and smashed into him or whatever, but I spun trying to avoid him. And that was my fault for trying to make a stupid move."

switch to slicks a little too early, and the gamble didn't quite pay off today. Unfortunately, when you hit the cement walls, they suck you in."

Now Montoya led from Carpentier, Vasser, and Mauricio Gugelmin, and that's the way the race finished when the checkered flag flew after seventy-four of the scheduled ninety laps, due to CART's two-hour rule. Montoya won by a margin of 7.585 seconds.

While Montoya was the race winner, Carpentier received the biggest cheers on the podium. "I'm very happy," he said. "There is no better place for this than Canada. It's the best day I've had in a long time. It's also very gratifying because it's contract time!"

Never one to hog the spotlight, Montoya was happy to allow Carpentier to bask in the damp crowd's cheers. "The only time I was worried was when Tracy passed me," said JPM. "My car was sliding around a lot, but he just spun off in front of me three corners later. I thought, 'Well, he wasn't as quick as I thought he was.' Dario got a couple of points, but having all twenty-two points [a clean sweep of pole, most laps led, and the win] in my pocket feels good. A really good day for us."

Indeed, Montoya now led Franchitti by twenty-three points—more than achievable in a single race weekend, and the largest cushion he had enjoyed since building a twenty-five-point bulge over Gil de Ferran following his win at Cleveland in late June. Juan Pablo then endured his weakest point-scoring stretch of the campaign, allowing Franchitti to creep back into contention. And make no mistake, the 1999 CART championship had become strictly a two-man show. Third-ranked Andretti was now a massive seventy points out of the lead; de Ferran had fallen to seventh in the standings, having scored just nine points in the seven races since Cleveland. With four races remaining, who would prevail between Franchitti and Montoya?

MOLSON INDY VANCOUVER

Concord Pacific Place – September 5, 1999 – 74 laps

1. Juan Pablo Montoya
2. Patrick Carpentier
3. Jimmy Vasser
4. Mauricio Gugelmin
5. Cristiano da Matta

CHAMPIONSHIP STANDINGS AFTER 16 OF 20 RACES

1.	Montoya	194
2.	Franchitti	171
3.	Andretti	124
4.	Tracy	122
5.	Fittipaldi	101

Gonzalo Rodriguez negotiates the Corkscrew during Friday practice at Laguna Seca.
Michael Levitt

CHAPTER 12

GONZALO

From 1995 to 2000, CART scheduled its races in Vancouver, British Columbia, and Monterey, California, on successive weekends. It was not logistically feasible for teams to return to their shops between a pair of West Coast races—most were based in Indianapolis, but Newman/Haas Racing and Payton-Coyne Racing operated out of greater Chicago, and Team Penske's home at the time was Reading, Pennsylvania—and it made little sense for most personnel to fly home and back. Almost everyone in the CART community was therefore able to enjoy a pleasant Pacific Coast interlude for a couple days before getting back to business at one of America's most historic road courses.

Like Road America, Lime Rock Park, and Watkins Glen, to name a few others, Laguna Seca Raceway was built in the late 1950s in the postwar sports car boom, on land midway between Monterey and Salinas that was part of the Fort Ord military post. The track winds around a dry lakebed before taking the racers up a hillside, through the fast and challenging left-hand Turn Six, onto an uphill ridge, and over a blind rise. Then it's immediately hard on the brakes for Laguna Seca's signature corner(s)—one of the most difficult and unique sequences in the world. Listed in the program as Turns Seven, Seven-A, and Eight, the Corkscrew is a sharply descending left-right-left sequence that draws comparisons to a rollercoaster. The track is located on public recreation grounds and is a favorite among fans; you can sit on the hillside and see three-quarters of the circuit while getting a full day's worth of exercise just walking to your vantage point. Or hike all the way up to the Corkscrew and watch the cars grab some air as the drivers wrestle with the wheel.

Michael Andretti endured a different kind of tension than typical racing-related stress over the Laguna Seca weekend. His wife Leslie was scheduled to deliver the couple's first (Michael's third) child on September 19, but the date was moved up a week to the twelfth—race day. "She promised me she would wait until I got home late Sunday night—I hope she keeps her promise," Michael said. "If I was in another sport like golf or one where you are an individual rather than a team, I might be able to leave if she goes into labor. But I have obligations to Kmart, Texaco, and the team. They're relying on me. Leslie and the baby are my number one priority, but she understands I can't miss a race. I'll just hope and pray it doesn't happen until at least Sunday night." To Michael's relief, Lucca Andretti waited until September 16 to arrive.

One driver had a particular mastery of Laguna Seca like no other: Bryan Herta. The Michigan-born, California-raised Herta qualified on the front row for all four of his previous Laguna starts, and he dominated the 1996 race until Alex Zanardi's spectacular (and these days, illegal due to track limit rules) pass for the win at the Corkscrew on the last lap. Herta finished sixth at Laguna Seca after starting on pole position in 1997, before finally converting pole in 1998 into his first Indy car race win. His team owner Bobby Rahal had also tasted plenty of success at the famous venue, winning four consecutive CART races from 1984 to '87; the uphill run from Turn Six to the Corkscrew was later named the Rahal Straight.

"As a kid I remember reading about Laguna Seca in car magazines and dreaming about racing here, and I remember how excited I was when I came here for the first time in 1976," Rahal said at the 2003 dedication. "I've had a lot of success here, but to have my name on this circuit, along with Mario Andretti [Turn Two, Andretti Hairpin] and Wayne Rainey [Turn Nine, Rainey Curve], is a tremendous honor."

No one was surprised when Herta set the pace in provisional qualifying on Friday, a stout 0.404 seconds up on Tony Kanaan in the Forsythe Championship Racing entry. "I don't have an explanation or a reason why things have gone well for me here," Herta remarked. "But if I knew why I was fast here, I certainly wouldn't tell anybody! I don't feel any different when it comes to driving here. I don't say that I am going to try hard this week because I am supposed to be fast here. This track just suits my style. But there is, really, more pressure in a place like this because everyone expects you to do well here."

Max Papis made it a one-three for Team Rahal. "I think things are coming together pretty good," he said. "We are not where we want to be, but I don't think we are too far off. My job is to just go faster than Bryan." Greg Moore, Michael Andretti, and Mauricio Gugelmin claimed the next three positions, while Adrian Fernandez returned impressively to run seventh in the No. 40 Patrick Racing car after missing four races.

Dario Franchitti crashed hard at the fast Turn Six after turning the twelfth-best lap. "The car bottomed out and I lost the steering," he reported. "Then I caught the curb on the exit. I hit the wall on the right, then came across the track and hit the wall on the left. I'm a little upset; I think a fourth-gear corner should have a bit more runoff area than that one probably does."

PPG Cup leader Juan Pablo Montoya also spun in Turn Six, but the damage was limited to a broken right-front wing. He ended the day sixteenth fastest, three spots behind Target/Ganassi teammate Jimmy Vasser. "Not a very good day today," was Montoya's succinct comment. "But we've had a few bad Fridays recently and then gotten things OK on Saturday."

This time, circumstances prevented him from having the chance. As was often the case at Laguna Seca, lingering coastal fog delayed the start of the Saturday morning practice by more than an hour. Less than ten minutes into the session, the red flag flew, and silence fell over the circuit. Gonzalo Rodriguez, the Formula 3000 frontrunner from Uruguay who was preparing for his second race in Penske Racing's second car, locked the brakes of the No. 3 Lola/Mercedes entering the left hander that leads into the Corkscrew. The car bounced at virtually unabated speed over a gravel trap into a head-on 140-miles-per-hour impact with a concrete wall protected by a thin band of tires. Almost in slow motion, the car catapulted directly over the wall and landed upside down on its roll bar in loose dirt about thirty feet down a steep embankment.

Rodriguez was transported to Community Hospital of the Monterey Peninsula where he was pronounced dead from massive head and neck injuries at 10:10 a.m. PST by Dr. Robert Kearney. He was twenty-seven years old.

"It was the impression of those on the scene that he was killed instantly on impact with the wall," said Dr. Stephen Olvey, CART director of medical affairs. Olvey later confirmed that was the case, noting it was the first basilar skull fracture in the twenty-one-year history of CART.

Olvey and Roger Penske contacted Rodriguez's family in Uruguay with the tragic news. Olvey recalled the immediate aftermath of the accident in his book *Rapid Response*. "We were stunned; shock and disbelief," the doctor wrote. "Some of our safety guys were new and had never seen anything like it. They wandered around in a daze. In the emergency room, Rodriguez's body looked as if he had simply gone to sleep. There were no visible signs of injury, not a mark anywhere—the sight was macabre. No one from his family was at the race. He had come to America alone to race for Roger Penske."

One of the few people that Rodriguez knew in the CART paddock was Montoya. They had competed against each other in Formula 3000 in 1998, shared the podium at Spa and the Nurburgring after races won by Rodriguez, and become friends in the process. "When he was on form, he was blindingly fast," Montoya said. "He was always one of the guys I had to worry about."

Reflecting on the brief time he spent with Rodriguez at Detroit and Laguna Seca, Montoya added: "When he got to IndyCar, I asked him how he was doing, how are things. I wanted to help him. I said, 'You want to do this here, do that there.' And when he tried it, he couldn't believe it actually worked. That was a big thing. But for me, I was so comfortable. I could tell anybody what I was doing because I knew I could get the job done. In my mind, even if you knew what I was doing, I always felt I could beat you. It wasn't relevant."

Observers initially believed Rodriguez's throttle may have stuck on the approach to the Corkscrew, a point where the drivers reach around 160 mph before braking hard. However, Ilmor Engineering managing director Paul Morgan immediately ruled out any issues with the throttle mechanism in the crash. "We downloaded all the data from the data logger. The throttle was acting in a perfectly normal way at the time

DR. STEPHEN OLVEY

"Terry and I got to being scientific about it, looking for cause and effect with the injuries. We started working with the car designers and team managers trying to get changes made to the cars to prevent injuries. What we were doing coincided with what Dr. Sid Watkins did in Formula 1. Jackie Stewart got Sid into it, playing the role of Wally Dallenbach in F1. Through the International Council of Motorsport Sciences, which is an organization I started with Terry and Hugh Scully, we started doing things in concert with Formula 1 and that collaboration continues to this day. I'm on the FIA Medical Commission, and we do all the rules and regulations for medical care in motorsports around the world. That's still going on today. We all work in the same direction now. All these years later, we're as involved in that now as we were back then. Terry and I talk to each other two or three times a week. We still have a real close relationship, actually.

"In CART, we were the first ones to make the HANS Device mandatory. Formula 1 did a year later, and NASCAR didn't until after Dale Earnhardt was killed. The SAFER Barrier was a combined thing between NASCAR and Indy, and that's been fantastic. There's no way to know how many lives it's saved. Those are the two biggest safety advances we have seen, in my experience.

"I'm often asked how we separate personal friendships with the drivers when we have to tend to them professionally. Terry and I answer it the same way. When you do what we do at the hospital, day in and day out, you learn to turn everything off except what you are doing. You don't think about the guy's wife you just met, or the kids in the waiting room. You have a job to do, and you do it. You don't have those feelings until it's all over. Then you get them on the way home, when you're off call and you've had a particularly bad case. That's happened to both of us on the racetrack. We just did what we had to do. We couldn't get upset until later, when our part was done. That's when it hits you."

of the accident," said Morgan. "The throttle was doing as it was commanded by the driver. Immediately when he got to the top of the hill, he took his foot off the throttle, and it did close."

Several competing drivers and three-time PPG Cup champion Rick Mears theorized that a bump in the braking zone for the Corkscrew may have caused Rodriguez's right foot to be jarred off the brake and onto the accelerator, or that his foot got wedged between the pedals. Jan Magnussen, like Rodriguez, a right-foot braker, said his relatively minor Friday accident at the Corkscrew was caused by that problem. Michael Andretti added that while he normally is a right-foot braker, he brakes with his left foot at Laguna Seca because of the bump in the Corkscrew braking area.

Al Unser Jr. had his own theory. "That model of Lola would jam into neutral if you tried to downshift too fast," Unser said. "I believe the gearbox jammed into neutral."

CART President and CEO Andrew Craig stated that the car was impounded for a full investigation. A National Highway Safety and Transportation Association (NHTSA) investigation of the car's telemetry later revealed that Rodriguez stayed on the throttle momentarily longer and braked one hundred yards later for the corner than he had previously attempted.

"Obviously it was a huge blow to the sport," reflected Paul Tracy. "A horrible accident—he just sailed off the track. At that point in time, that whole top section of Laguna, although it was better than it was in the '60s, '70s or '80s, it was still pretty unsafe. You think about the speeds we were doing up that straightaway and the line to that braking zone, there was not much runoff or gravel trap or anything if you have a big problem. Laguna has made a lot of safety improvements, but there's not much you can do there because there's a huge slope downward into the valley. It's just dangerous—that's how motorsports is."

Rodriguez was making his second appearance for Marlboro Team Penske; he drove to a twelfth-place finish in his debut at the Detroit Grand Prix, consistently outpacing lead Penske driver Unser. While no additional opportunities awaited him at Penske given the announced 2000 driver lineup of Moore and Gil de Ferran, Rodriguez was scheduled to test for Patrick Racing with an eye toward running the penultimate race of the season at Surfers Paradise, Australia. Some sources reported that he had already signed a contract to join that long-running team.

"Gonchi was a very nice guy, and I think he had a letter of intent and was very close to signing with Patrick," said Adrian Fernandez. "He was probably going to be my teammate in 2000. When Scott Pruett departed, they hired P. J. Jones and they were not very happy with him, to the point where they had to pick another driver. Jan Magnussen is a great driver, and I don't know why he struggled in Indy cars. They were looking for a strong candidate for the following year and Penske was not possible for Gonchi because they had signed Greg Moore and Gil de Ferran. Patrick was really inclined to sign him, and I remember early that Saturday morning we had a meeting with Gonchi and he was very excited. I was looking forward to working with him, and unfortunately, he had that horrible accident."

Rodriguez loved his brief time racing in America. "He was optimistic and full of passion for the USA," wrote Simon Arron, a Formula 3000 journalist who was close with Rodriguez. "I asked Gonzalo about his race at Detroit and was detained for half an hour. He loved the cars, racing, and atmosphere, and was tittering because old F3000 adversary Juan Pablo Montoya was kicking him under the desk during the driver's briefing. [IndyCar] racing represented the step forward he wanted, a big chance to put Uruguay on the map. He would have had a marvelous career in America. The paddock will be a duller place without him, but it was at least a privilege to have known him."

It was the first driver death during a race meeting in the forty-two-year history of Laguna Seca Raceway, and it had been more than three years since the last driver fatality in the CART series. That occurred in July 1996 when Jeff Krosnoff's Reynard/Toyota locked wheels with another Reynard driven by Stefan Johansson on the backstraight of the Toronto street circuit. Krosnoff's car shot airborne and pinwheeled along the catch fence before the cockpit struck a tree and a lamppost with unsurvivable force. Track marshal Gary Avrin also died in the incident. The only other driver death at a CART-sanctioned race was way back in 1982, when Jim Hickman died at Milwaukee in an accident caused by a stuck throttle. In the aftermath, CART required all cars to include a steering wheel–mounted kill switch. CART's more recent safety record was marred by the deaths of three spectators in the 1998 U.S. 500 at Michigan Speedway when a detached wheel from Adrian Fernandez's crashed car flew into the grandstands. That led to CART mandating a wheel tether system beginning in 1999.

At noon, news of Rodriguez's passing was formally announced at the circuit. By then, the decision had been made to cancel on-track activity for the rest of the day. "At the drivers' request, there will be no qualifying this afternoon," stated CART CEO Andrew Craig. "The clock will run, but the cars will not leave the Pit Lane. The race will take place tomorrow [Sunday], and yesterday's [Friday's] times will stand."

Indy car racing was considerably safer in the 1990s than at any time to that point in history. CART was cautious about embracing the groundbreaking carbon-fiber composite chassis construction pioneered by John Barnard and the McLaren Formula 1 team in the early '80s, but the introduction of that technology and other changes recommended by Doctors Olvey and Trammell had significantly reduced the severe leg injuries that occurred so frequently in the first fifteen years of the CART era. CART's safety record was significantly better than that of the IRL, which hospitalized dozens of drivers in the late '90s. But it was obviously still a dangerous arena, as evidenced by the fact that Al Unser Jr., Naoki Hattori, Mark Blundell, Christian Fittipaldi, and Adrian Fernandez all missed multiple races due to injury during the 1999 season.

All forms of racing have historically learned from and reacted to tragedies, and the Rodriguez accident was no exception. "Obviously, it was a big deal," said Tony Kanaan. "Thanks to Gonzalo, the HANS Device was created. You never want to lose a human for anything, but that is sometimes how we improve safety in society. Something needs to happen for us to react."

The relative safety of the modern sport arguably made it even more difficult for drivers to get back into the car in the aftermath of a death or serious accident. It was thankfully a scenario that was not nearly as common for them as it once was, especially across the decades that Indy car racing's original Greatest Generation competed. Pat O'Connor died while competing in the 1958 Indianapolis 500, which was A. J. Foyt's rookie start; by the time Foyt retired in 1993, twenty-seven other Indy car drivers had perished.

Mario Andretti recalls chatting with Billy Foster, his best friend among drivers, in 1967 prior to practice for a NASCAR stock car race at Riverside Raceway. A few minutes later, Foster was deceased. Andretti's Formula 1 teammate Ronnie Peterson succumbed to complications from injuries he suffered in the Italian Grand Prix at Monza on the day Mario clinched the 1978 World Championship. But by the late '90s, dying in a race car was pretty much a foreign concept to drivers born in the 1970s.

They went back to work, because that's what racers do. And once the green flag flew for the 1999 Honda Grand Prix of Monterey, it looked a lot like the last few Laguna Seca Indy car races. Herta once again demonstrated his amazing command of the tricky circuit to win for the second year in a row, this time a 1.825-second triumph over Roberto Moreno. Asked if he had a secret formula, Herta said, "There isn't one, but they told me if I win a couple more, they're going to rename it LaHerta Seca."

Herta led all eighty-three laps in a sleepy but incident-filled race that saw FedEx Championship Series points leader Montoya finish eighth after a conservative run. That still enabled the Colombian rookie to widen his lead in the PPG Cup to a season-high twenty-eight points with three races to go because his closest rival Franchitti retired after he clashed with Gugelmin and Moore in separate incidents. Meanwhile, Paul Tracy quietly moved up to third in the standings after a steady run to fourth place.

From pole, Herta was able to pull out as much as 2.7 seconds over Kanaan by lap twenty-one, but the Brazilian driver in the McDonald's car was able to cut the gap to less than a second a few laps later. The top nine remained the same after the first round of pit stops under a yellow for a tow-in for Hélio Castroneves on lap twenty-five.

On the lap twenty-eight restart, Fernandez, on the way to fifth place in his first race since breaking his right wrist at Detroit five weeks earlier, barged inside Moore into Turn One and banged wheels. That contact momentarily slowed the cars behind, so Franchitti tried to dive inside Gugelmin in Turn Three. They bumped and the PacWest car spun, but Franchitti caught his slide and continued. Then on lap thirty-two, Dario tried to outbrake his friend Moore into Turn One, but Moore

MARIO ANDRETTI

"Billy Foster and I were really like brothers, almost. Because it was not just he and I, it was the families—the girls and the kids. Even though we were far away from one another as far as the bases in this country—one east, one west, he lived in California—that didn't matter. So that was one of the toughest losses. Jud Larson was another one. He and I were good buddies. To save money going to some sprint races or even midget races, we used to room together and stuff like that. And he was killed. We went through too many of those. Dick Atkins, I really didn't know him that well, but he was my teammate at Ascot when he and Don Branson were killed. I loved Don Branson because as a young lad myself, he was the only one that I felt that I could go to and get a straight answer for a question that I had. On the dirt especially, because he was a master of that. If I would ask him something about the cushion or whatever, the approach, he would be the one to tell me honestly what to do and I always had a special appreciation for that. You bond with people like that.

"Ronnie Peterson was another one. We were buddies. He'd come over to the States and we'd go off to the lake and just run each other into the ground doing all the stuff. Everywhere we went, we used to play tennis together with Niki Lauda. To lose somebody like that at a time that probably should have been one of the most important moments in my life in the sport . . . I clinched the World Championship and then my good buddy is gone. You cannot celebrate.

"I lived through this era, and there were some terrible moments. You couldn't help but thinking, you know, 'When is it going to be my turn?' Not that you want to dwell on that, but the reality was there. I always think back as to not myself as much as the wives. Most of us had young families, and my wife was a rock. I knew what she was going through whenever we would lose one of our close ones who maybe had young kids, and she would be thinking, 'OK, when is it going to be me like that?' But she never, ever, ever expressed that to me to make me feel guilty, that I was trying to satisfy myself by risking so much. These are all the things that when you start reflecting, come back to you. How important certain individuals were to keeping your mind clear. There couldn't have been another person at that point better than Dee Ann. That's where you count your blessings."

turned in and the resulting contact trashed the Kool car's right-front suspension.

"Greg was definitely holding me up a lot," said Franchitti. "We really needed to get by him to make inroads on the guys in front—you can make up only so many places on pit stops. He was braking deep, and I got alongside him a few times, but I had to get out of the pass each time. I went in there hard, and he didn't give me any room. It's just one of those things."

Years later, Franchitti saw things a bit differently. "When I crashed into Greg at Laguna trying to pass him, that took a bit of repair because that was my fault," he said. "I had to put my hands up and just say, 'Fuck, I'm sorry, dude.'"

Herta lost a seven-second second lead when the yellow flew on lap fifty-eight for Naoki Hattori's spin, and after pit stops, Andretti ran second. Drama ensued as Herta nearly lost it in the last turn as he prepared for the lap sixty-one restart, balking Andretti and allowing a cluster of cars running behind to get a run. "I almost threw it all away," Herta admitted. But Andretti made a similar mistake, allowing Herta to ultimately hold Moreno off to the finish to score his second career Indy car victory.

"If that was easy, I don't know what hard is," said Herta. "Although I was leading all the time, there was always someone lurking behind me. After what happened on the last restart, I said to myself, 'No mistakes,' and I just stayed focused and kept on."

Second place in his fill-in role for Fittipaldi at Newman/Haas Racing marked Moreno's career-best finish in the CART series, a great effort from eleventh on the grid. But the happy-go-lucky veteran had to be reminded by Herta and Papis to control his typical over-the-top enthusiasm in the postrace press conference given the tragic events of the day before.

"We are race drivers, and we have to have a blocking system in our minds to do our job," said Moreno. "We just go out and drive every corner until the checkered flag. But you don't forget what happened. This was my best result, but when I think about it, it's always going to be in my mind a sad day.

"I can only say 'Supersub' came through today," he added. "I couldn't believe it when I gained three positions on my last pit stop. Thanks, guys."

Papis was delighted to finally earn his first podium visit as an Indy car driver, though no champagne was sprayed out of respect to the Rodriguez family. "I'm so glad," he said. "This is a tremendously sad weekend, but the Miller car ran fantastic and it's a great result. I want to remember that Gonzalo is here in my heart. I think he had a great passion for racing, like all of us. He would have wanted us to race hard the next day. And we did. This race was my tribute to him."

Sixth place matched Gil de Ferran's best finish since he reeled off three consecutive podiums including a win at Portland from June into July. His downfall since then was marked by five DNFs in seven races. A reporter asked de Ferran if the slump had any connection to his upcoming move to Team Penske and a rumored $3.5 million annual retainer.

"I think it's exactly the opposite from what you see," he responded. "Although I know my future lies somewhere else, I want to make absolutely sure that I do my utmost to bring Derrick Walker, team owner, the best result I can. Obviously, since the announcement the results have not been good, but I think that is more of a coincidence than focus or effort on my part. It's a tough thing, because I feel very responsible for all the guys on the team. I have struck a lot of friendships within the team, with different personnel, and I simply can't brush that aside and just forget about it. Derrick employs over forty people, meaning forty families are involved in this—and I can't just forget about that fact."

Montoya almost couldn't believe his luck after extending his championship lead despite being less of a factor at Laguna Seca than any other 1999 race weekend outside of Toronto. On that occasion, he lost twenty-one points to Franchitti; this time, an inconspicuous drive to eighth place netted him a gain of five. "We were really struggling with the car," Juan admitted. "In the race, I didn't want to push too hard and make any mistakes. But we leave here with some points for the championship, and now we'll get ready for Houston."

Out of respect to Gonzalo Rodriguez' passing, Marlboro Team Penske withdrew Al Unser Jr.'s entry from the Laguna Seca race. A few days later, Roger Penske made one of the most important decisions in the history of Penske Racing. He called Tim Cindric, the thirty-one-year-old team manager for Team Rahal.

"I took a look at myself and said, 'What do I need to be doing as far as the race team is concerned as we head into the year 2000?'" Penske later recalled. "People said, 'Are you really committed to racing or not?' I think I made the statement that I was committed, but I had to make the decision to put somebody in charge of our organization that could pull the team together and take it to the front.

"I was fortunate enough to know Tim Cindric. His dad was a key to our success in running the Offy engines and working with Herb Porter. So, I contacted Tim and asked him if he would be interested in coming in to be president of Penske Racing, and also to be a shareholder—not just coming in as a team manager. He could bring the team together from the top—Tom Wurtz and Clive Howell really had to wait in the past until I called before they could make the important decisions."

For Cindric, the call from Penske was totally unexpected and overwhelming. "He contacted me out of the blue. He called my house; I remember it was a Wednesday night after Gonzalo passed away. He called my unlisted number at like nine or ten o'clock at night. My wife thought it was Ray Leto, so she hands me the phone while we're watching TV, and he says, 'This is Roger Penske.' I had to sit up in my seat! I had never talked to him on the phone; I'd said hello to him at the track or whatever and helped him during that whole mess when they didn't qualify at Indy in '95. That's kind of how we got to know each other.

"He was going on about how he hadn't won a race two and a half years, how he needed somebody to run the team, and how he needed a partner in the team, not just a team manager," Cindric continued. "He's going on and on, and I'm like, 'Who can I tell you about?' I honestly thought he was calling me for a reference. I was thirty or thirty-one years old. Austin was like six months old; my other son was a couple years old. He says, 'Can you meet me in New York this week to talk about this?' I said I'd be there, because I at least wanted to hear what he had to say."

Cindric was under no illusions about how big a job it would be to rebuild Team Penske, which was in the longest Indy car slump in the organization's thirty-year history.

"Roger's team hadn't won a race since Gateway 1997 with Paul Tracy and was stuck on ninety-nine wins for two and a half years," TC observed. "At that point in time, it was a revolving door at Penske, if you remember the number of drivers they had in '99. They tried to run a Reynard, they ran a Lola, they tried all kinds of stuff. That thing was in a bit of disarray. Penske wasn't even considered a frontrunner for a couple of years there.

"Then I spent a few weeks trying to understand, meeting him in hotel rooms and stuff during race weekends to talk, because he doesn't have any time during the week. I wanted to talk to him about 'Why me?' It didn't have anything to do with money or anything else. I knew all these other guys, at Penske Cars and everybody else, and he was going to drop me in to be in charge of Penske Cars and the Marlboro Racing School, and the race teams—everything but NASCAR. And I was like, 'I don't understand. This isn't going to go over well.' He says, 'You won't understand until you're here.' Well, I wasn't going to sit in my rocking chair and wonder what it was like. Worst case is it doesn't work out, and that's pretty much an 'I told you so.'"

Cindric made the life-changing decision to pursue the opportunity.

HONDA GRAND PRIX OF MONTEREY

Laguna Seca Raceway — September 12, 1999 – 83 laps

1. Bryan Herta
2. Roberto Moreno
3. Max Papis
4. Paul Tracy
5. Adrian Fernandez

CHAMPIONSHIP STANDINGS AFTER 17 OF 20 RACES

1. Montoya 199
2. Franchitti 171
3. Tracy 134
4. Andretti 127
5. Fernandez 105
   Papis

(Left to right) Max Papis, Greg Moore, and Dario Franchitti enjoy a bit of downtime on Australia's Gold Coast. *Michael Levitt*

CHAPTER 13

FRANCHITTI FIGHTS BACK

Barry Green's memories of CART's first visit to Houston for a race on streets surrounding the George R. Brown Convention Center weren't all warm and fuzzy. Sure, Dario Franchitti had prevailed to win the inaugural Texaco Grand Prix in October 1998. But along the way, he was nearly spun out by his Team Green running mate Paul Tracy. PT crashed, and upon returning to the pits, television cameras captured him being engaged by Green in a heated conversation that turned into a shoving match with the irate team owner. "It was the low point of the year, and it was unfortunate," Green said. "Luckily, one of my guys stepped in and prevented any punches from being thrown."

The Houston crash wasn't the straw that broke the camel's back for Tracy, but it was the most public in a series of incidents throughout 1998 that prompted CART Chief Steward Wally Dallenbach to suspend the Canadian for the '99 season opener. Despite starting the championship on the back foot, Tracy had kept it clean and driven without significant incident through the entire season, and now he was the last man outside of Juan Pablo Montoya and Dario Franchitti who still had a mathematical chance of winning the PPG Cup championship.

"[Nineteen ninety-eight] was probably the worst year of my career," Tracy admitted. "I knew that the Reynard/Honda/Firestone combination was everything that you wanted as a driver. But I went into that year pissed off at Penske. I just wanted to beat Penske and that wasn't the right approach. I was driving angry, and sometimes I drive better when I'm angry and sometimes I don't."

Green found the key to unlocking Tracy's potential when he hired longtime race engineer Tony Cicale, not so much to engineer PT's car but to get his head in the right place. "Paul was in a funk and didn't know what to do," Cicale related. "He thought what he was doing wasn't wrong, but he was too angry to find the right direction. Yet he was quite talented. He believed if he had the car beneath him and confidence in the team, it wouldn't bother him to start last. He had very good car control and he was very brave, but he didn't quite understand that it was important to have friends on the track. One of my main goals in the first year was to get him to understand the importance of working not only with his own team but making sure that other drivers weren't continually going to be trying to get back at him for things he had done to them on the track."

Cicale's calming influence was clearly working, because in 1999, Tracy put together the most consistent season of his Indy car career to date. Since dropping out of the Long Beach Grand Prix with suspension damage, he had finished nine of fourteen races in the top five, including a win at Milwaukee and four consecutive summer podiums. Houston '98 had marked a breakthrough for Tracy in terms of speed in a season when he had qualified in the top ten only four times in sixteen races to that point. A year later, on the same, bland, concrete canyon street course, he qualified third, just ahead of his teammate Franchitti and beaten only by CART championship leader Juan Pablo Montoya and Laguna Seca winner Bryan Herta.

"I had a really fucking horrible year in '98," Tracy now admits. "Luckily, I was able to stay on, because like I said, it was a shit year. For whatever reason, I couldn't come to grips with the car and the engineer I had, John Dick. I had him as my engineer a couple times in my career. In '98, I couldn't get the car working the way I wanted, and nothing was clicking at all. After that, I got Tony Cicale in '99 and that's when things began to take off for me. I had a good year in '99—I sat out the first race and was still third in the championship. In fact, I won the 'Most Improved Driver' award, and I had to laugh at that.

"It wasn't that I didn't like John Dick—he's a nice guy. But it didn't work. Late in my career when I was driving for Jimmy Vasser at Indy, he was already on their staff and they had him engineer me. I told Jimmy,

'I worked with him before, and it fucking did not go well.' I like the guy, but for whatever reason, it just didn't work. That was the year I didn't qualify at Indy."

The Houston pole was Montoya's record-tying seventh of his rookie season, matching Nigel Mansell's benchmark for a first-year driver in the CART series. But Juan was visibly annoyed when he was asked about the achievement. "Maybe in ten or twenty years it will mean more, and I'll think, 'Oh, that's good,'" he said. "Right now, I'm just trying to win the championship. The car wasn't perfect, but we tried to improve it every time we came into the pits, and it was good."

A surprising seventh fastest in qualifying, just one place behind his Walker Racing teammate Gil de Ferran, was Japanese rookie Naoki Hattori. Despite breaking his leg in the season opener at Homestead and finishing no better than fourteenth in his four subsequent starts, Naoki was still held in higher esteem than his countryman (and nonrelated namesake) Shigeaki Hattori. "The Shigenator" intended to run thirteen races, but after making the show just seven times (and spinning or crashing eighteen times in the process), the elder Hattori had his competition license revoked for good by CART Chief Steward Wally Dallenbach.

Montoya blasted away in the lead at the start, with Tracy slotting into second ahead of Herta. Meanwhile, Franchitti was overtaken by Max Papis shortly after the start and was soon freight trained by a line of cars, dropping to eleventh place by the tenth lap. But Dario was about to get the biggest break of his season, because Montoya finally made the rookie mistake so many had been predicting for so long. Hélio Castroneves had been struggling with difficult drivability like all the Mercedes-Benz runners, and on the twelfth lap, he failed to negotiate Turn Eleven, the final corner of the lap, nosing his Hogan Racing Lola into the tire barrier.

Seven cars passed the scene, but Montoya failed to slow. Blind corner entries were a hallmark of the Houston course, and the unsighted Montoya's right-front wheel clipped Castroneves's stationary car hard enough to snap the Target car's suspension and end the championship leader's day. Unrepentant, he put the blame squarely on his team. "It was just a miscommunication," he said with frustration. "It's happened before, and it will happen again. I saw a yellow flag, but I thought it was for something else. Then I heard, 'Full course yellow, stay out,' and I backed off. I hit the brakes and tried to get the front around, but it didn't make it.

"I didn't know Dario was running at the back," Montoya added. "I was surprised no one told me that, because that means you can take a different approach."

The resultant full-course caution was exactly what Franchitti needed, because he was struggling with a visibly oversteering car. "I have to say thanks to the guy upstairs, because that yellow was timely," he said. "I had a car that I couldn't drive. Every time I tried to turn left, it would go right. When I saw Juan in the wall, I thought, 'Okay, things are bad, but they could be a hell of a lot worse.'"

With new tires, the handling of Franchitti's car was transformed, and he had climbed from eighteenth to fifth when he caught a well-timed caution just past the halfway point when Jimmy Vasser spun. Franchitti passed Jan Magnussen for fourth place on the restart, then claimed another position from Tony Kanaan on another restart brought on by Hattori's second spin of the day. That put him third behind Christian Fittipaldi, back in his No. 11 Newman/Haas Racing car, and keen to end his season on a high note after missing five races to injury.

JIMMY VASSER

"By the time you got to the end of the season, you could tell that Montoya was hardened. He was a phenomenal driver. He established himself early on in his rookie year. A lot of things came at him, the biggest thing probably being the death of his friend Gonzalo Rodriguez at Laguna. They were friends. Nobody really knew Gonzalo Rodriguez on our side, and his passing didn't shake the paddock like others have done. I know it was big for him, and maybe it got to him a bit during that championship run."

JUAN PABLO MONTOYA

(RESPONDING TO VASSER'S THEORY)

"No. I just wanted to fucking win the races."

Fittipaldi kept Franchitti at bay for more than twenty laps until Dario tried a forceful overtaking lunge at Turn Three, a corner not generally considered a passing point. Franchitti said he knew Fittipaldi still had to make another pit stop, but he thought he still stood a chance of catching Tracy if he could somehow get past the Brazilian. The cars made hard side-to-side contact, but Franchitti emerged ahead.

"He was very lucky," Fittipaldi said. "He bumped into me big time, and it worked out for him today. If it wouldn't have worked out, he would have thrown away the championship." Countered Franchitti: "I was lucky, and he was lucky. Christian was blocking. Every time I made a move he made a move. So, I made a move that he countered a little too late, and when he turned in, there was a green car there."

While Fittipaldi went on to finish seventh, Franchitti now looked like a lock for a podium—and even a win, if team owner Barry Green were to institute team orders. But the call never came. Green couldn't bring himself to do it to Tracy, who had performed faultlessly all season long and was the clear class of the field at Houston. His winning margin over Franchitti was 13.733 seconds, with Michael Andretti another twelve seconds back in third, followed by the Team Rahal duo of Max Papis and Herta.

"I just hope we don't miss the championship by four points," Green said. As it stood, Franchitti's second-place finish reduced Montoya's points cushion from twenty-nine (he got a bonus point for the Houston pole) to thirteen.

"Barry said to me, 'I hope you're not upset.' But I don't think today was the day for team orders," said Franchitti. "If I had been under Paul's gearbox, maybe, but he was ten seconds ahead. It wasn't an issue because he was dominant."

Decades down the line, neither driver had any qualms about Green's decision to allow Tracy to remain in front at Houston, despite the championship implications for Franchitti. "Paul was so far ahead, and I think he was still in championship contention," Dario said. "I never felt that Paul should have pulled over. And I screwed up Vancouver and Laguna Seca."

"I had the big drama at Houston the year before with Dario," Tracy added. "We were running one-two and I was catching him on the drying track. I tried to pass him, and he squeezed me and knocked my front wing off, then I got into an argument with Barry on the radio. So, to come back the next year . . . I remember I just dominated. Just left everybody, smoked everybody."

Tracy carried the Houston winner's trophy—a gold-plated cowboy boot—into the postrace press conference and showed that despite having matured on the track, he still had plenty of youthful swagger. "I hate to say that any place owed me one, but I definitely stuck that boot right in my rear last year," he said. "It's better to have the gold boot in my hand than in my ass. I got it right this year." When told that Montoya said he wasn't warned about the caution that led to his crash, Tracy said, "Maybe Chip [Ganassi] was looking at his reflection in the monitor."

Pressed about the possibility of team orders that would have given Franchitti additional help in his quest for the championship, Tracy feigned radio static before replying: "I was never asked, so I'm not going to just pull over to the side of the road. I'd like to think that I helped Dario's situation by pressuring Juan and forcing him into a mistake. I think Dario realized he had a fortunate day, getting sixteen points, and it was my day today."

After the Houston race, Tim Cindric made up his mind to leave Team Rahal. He faced the tough task of informing Bobby Rahal and Scott Roembke, his close friend, boss, and mentor.

"I wanted to tell Bobby because that way there would be no question about intellectual property or any of this other stuff that could come up if he'd heard that I had already committed to this thing," Cindric related. "So, I called Bobby and went to lunch with him and Scotty Roembke on the Saturday before we left for Australia—which I had never done before. I told them I was leaving, but I couldn't tell them where I was going; Roger didn't want a press release out there or anything before he could tell the team. They asked me if it was a competitor; I said yes it was.

"Bobby was really disappointed, because he thought I was going to manage Morris Nunn's new team," Cindric continued. "He was pretty bummed out after the opportunity that they gave me, and I think they assumed it was just financially motivated or some ego thing, that I'd have a bigger title or something. I said, 'I can't explain it to you. Just it's the opportunity of a lifetime, that's all I can tell you. It may or may not work out, but I've just got to try it.'

"I said I would really like to finish out the season with you guys, and Bobby was like, 'Hey I respect all that,' but just couldn't go forward. Bobby said I should stay home from Australia the next week and get everything organized for an easy handoff to whoever gets the job. I said, 'Fine, thank you. I respect that you have the confidence to leave me there to do that.'

"I had been out to dinner a night or two before with Kenny Bräck, who was coming to drive for us the next year. All that was signed; he was going to come replace Herta. I walked into the shop Monday morning, and Kenny was there getting his seat fitted to get ready for testing. He says, 'Why aren't you in Australia?' 'Well, I've got something to tell you . . .'"

TEXACO GRAND PRIX OF HOUSTON

George R. Brown Convention Center — September 26, 1999 – 100 laps

1. Paul Tracy
2. Dario Franchitti
3. Michael Andretti
4. Max Papis
5. Bryan Herta

CHAMPIONSHIP STANDINGS AFTER 18 OF 20 RACES

1.	Montoya	200
2.	Franchitti	187
3.	Tracy	155
4.	Andretti	141
5.	Papis	117

Montoya had plenty of time to dwell on his misfortune, because the three-week gap between Houston and the next race on Australia's Gold Coast was the longest of the season. The 2.795-mile circuit paralleling the Pacific Ocean through the resort town of Surfers Paradise was arguably the finest street course in the world, with long straights broken up by a series of unique chicanes. Travel from America was difficult, but the Honda Indy 300 was the one event on the CART schedule for which drivers were happy to show up early for promotional work. The event's

PR director Brett "Crusher" Murray was incredibly effective at his job, and he knew the prospect of beaches, bikinis, and cold Australian beer would appeal to the CART "Brat Pack."

Montoya was copacetic about the additional media load in Australia, but he wasn't entirely happy with his grid position by the end of qualifying. The No. 4 car was set to start the sixty-five-lap race from the outside of the third row, and making matters worse, Franchitti had uncorked an amazing lap to claim pole position by the enormous margin of 0.892 seconds over Bryan Herta. "We had a decent car, and I got a pretty clear lap," Herta said. "Dario's lap was just fast." Montoya was a full 1.3 seconds off Franchitti's blistering benchmark.

Franchitti later called his 1999 Surfers Paradise pole one of the most satisfying of his career. "That '99 street course car, that's the happiest I think I ever was behind the wheel of an Indy car. There's a reason that's the only Indy car I've got in my garage. To pull those guys by three-quarters of a second or whatever it was, that was the day of days. I remember that very clearly. But here's something that has always pissed me off—there's that Monty qualifying lap at Detroit on YouTube, but there's no video of my lap in Australia."

But if Montoya had shown anything over the course of his first eighteen races in the FedEx Championship Series, it was that he could never be counted out. While Franchitti led from the start, it took Juan just twenty-seven laps to move from sixth to second. It looked like the championship protagonists were about to engage in an epic head-to-head duel.

It came as a surprise when Team Green elected to pit Franchitti when Mark Blundell's spin brought out the caution on lap thirty-five. But almost everyone except Papis, who had started eleventh, followed suit. Max led laps thirty-six through forty-six before making his own stop, handing the lead back to Franchitti, who now had Fernandez between himself and Montoya.

But Montoya never got to challenge Franchitti for the lead. On lap forty-nine of sixty-five, having just been told to turn up his fuel and go for it, Montoya misjudged his braking for the left-hander at the end of the backstraight from Main Beach Pride to Breaker Street. He thumped into the tire barrier, his race over. "Juan Montoya has had two chances

BRETT "CRUSHER" MURRAY

"A couple weeks before the circus arrived in town, I decided to remarket the entire event as a 'Title Fight' between my good friend Dario Franchitti and new boy Juan Pablo Montoya. We took on a whole boxing theme, and somewhere in the hype, I thought it would be a good idea to attend the annual Gold Coast drivers' breakfast at Conrad Jupiters Casino acting as wild boxing promoter Don King.

"At the breakfast, I helped introduce the first half of the field to the audience of four hundred or so guests, media, and fans. Then I snuck away to a room at the back to put on a suit, vest, gold chains, a well-puffed wig . . . One punter actually asked for my autograph, so it must have been reasonably convincing.

"The theme song from *Rocky* came on, and I entered the room to flashing strobe lights, applause, and stunned looks from the crowd and the drivers. I was then interviewed as 'Don King' with Dario and Juan to talk about the 'Title Fight' that was about to unfold in front of us. A photo of the three of us is one of the most memorable from my career, and if I had a dollar for every time someone has mentioned that stunt to me, I would be a very rich man.

"Montoya had a reputation of being difficult to work with, especially on the media side. I made it a point to get to him early and to break the ice with activities like jet skiing and Miss Indy lunches, and he reciprocated with some of his own time for some media and promotional appearances. Hell, he even turned up to the famous Wednesday night 'Indy' party at my house, where he and the majority of the field signed the felt of my pool table. Greg Moore signed on pole position, right in the 'D.' Greg had become part of a quartet including Franchitti, Tony Kanaan, and Max Papis who had become known as the 'Rat Pack,' and much of the group's notoriety was created under my watch on their annual trip to the Gold Coast."

to wrap up a championship, and both times, he's blown it!" exclaimed Paul Page on the ESPN2 broadcast.

"I'm mostly disappointed because we had a winning car and a shot at a spot on the podium. I locked the brakes, turned around, and tagged the wall," Montoya stated. "We lost a place in the pits, and I was driving hard trying to make up for it. Obviously, this isn't the way I wanted to end the day," he added for understatement.

Franchitti led the final twelve laps and won by 2.61 seconds over Papis, a result orchestrated by Team Rahal chief operating officer Scott Roembke's sharp pit strategy. Fernandez took third ahead of Herta and Andretti.

Montoya is still seething about the events of Houston and Surfers Paradise 1999 many years later. "In Houston, there was no yellow flag," he said. "But I remember, for me, Dario was so arrogant about Australia, I just wanted to kick his ass. I was coming and I caught him, and I wasn't thinking about finishing second. I was thinking about beating him, and I made a mistake."

Franchitti's memories of the race in Australia are, not surprisingly, far more positive.

"The race is going on, and next thing you know, Monty is second," he recalled. "I'm like, 'Fuck!' Let's be clear here, I had maximum respect for him, the Ganassi team, and Morris Nunn. They were good. So, I start pushing harder and harder to see if I could get him to make a mistake, and he crashed. Before that, I was almost driving on pace because I was so comfortable. I was in trouble championship-wise. I needed something special. I felt like I needed to get pole, fastest lap, and win the race just to stay in contention. I did, and Monty crashed, which I didn't see coming.

"I loved being in Australia; I loved everything about it. I felt comfortable there. Actually, the year after that, I took Monty out at the first corner at Surfers in 2000. And he and I went straight back to my hotel room and sat and watched the race while eating cheeseburgers from the balcony of the Marriott hotel!"

Team Green crew member Dave Popielarz was especially happy to see Franchitti turn in strong performances at Houston and Surfers Paradise after chiding the driver in the aftermath of his collision with Greg Moore at Laguna Seca.

"Dario came to life midyear, but we had a tough time at Laguna Seca and I rather stupidly lipped off to him about not winning the championship," said Popielarz. "Then he goes out and wins Australia. He could just lift himself up like that."

"You think, 'Oh, Zanardi's leaving!'" Poppy added. "But then Montoya comes along and he's another throat-stomper. It showed how Chip had a pipeline, and he really picked a couple winners there with Zanardi and Montoya. But Dario was a force to be reckoned with and could go head-to-head with Montoya. There was definitely a rivalry, but Juan was always friendly to us."

It had been a remarkable turnabout for Franchitti. From a twenty-nine-point disadvantage after Montoya took pole position twenty-two days earlier at Houston, Dario now led the CART standings by nine points heading into the championship's twentieth and final round. It had been a very successful trip to Australia for the Scotsman.

"We came here with a thirteen-point deficit and came away with a nine-point lead," he mused. "We came to Australia hoping for a twenty-two-point weekend and it happened. You can't ask for any more than that. When I heard Montoya was out, I thought this was a perfect weekend. You never give up, and I think the only pressure we take into California is what we place on ourselves. I'm especially happy to get Barry Green's first win in Australia."

It had been a long time coming for Green, whose journey came full circle with the victory. Born in Western Australia in 1952, Green emigrated to England when he was nineteen to claim his stake as a driver in Formula 3 while building his resume as a mechanic for Surtees and later Chevron. A hard testing crash at Mallory Park in 1978 left Green with a broken leg in a cast and forced him to reconsider his future as a driver. He accepted an offer to spearhead Chevron's attempt to enter the SCCA Can-Am sports car series in America with a team co-owned by Paul Newman. Over the last twenty years, Green had advanced to the status of team owner in the CART series, and Franchitti's victory at Surfers Paradise rivaled Jacques Villeneuve's win in the 1995 Indianapolis 500 as the greatest achievement of his career. "I think this feels even better," Green exclaimed.

Most of the drivers attended Crusher's annual Sunday night afterparty, but the race winner was notably absent; Franchitti flew immediately to Japan for a previously scheduled Honda appearance. Among those who did enjoy a big night out was Moore, who had suffered a dip in fortunes following the announcement of his move to Team Penske in 2000. In Australia, he qualified twelfth and dropped out with an electrical issue two-thirds of the way into the race. Moore, in fact, hadn't cracked the top ten since he finished third at Detroit six races earlier. And while he felt duty bound to finish out the season strongly with his longtime friends and teammates at Player's/Forsythe Racing, he also craved the fresh new start and bright future that awaited him in just a few weeks.

Perhaps surprisingly, Montoya was among the postrace revelers. Tracy was certainly shocked to see the former championship leader out and about instead of licking his wounds. Tracy was upset in his own right, having been assessed a drive-through penalty for passing a slow-starting Herta before the green flag. He rallied to finish seventh.

"If I was Juan, I would be kicking myself for making a mistake like that," Tracy said. "But it didn't seem to bother him. He was having a good time, chatting up all the girls. Seemed like he was enjoying himself as much as anyone."

"It's like he just puts it behind him and goes on," added Blundell. "Maybe it's a strength."

Two weeks later in Southern California, Montoya, Franchitti, and the rest of the FedEx Championship Series field were going to need all the strength they could muster. Before that, Tim Cindric faced a daunting event of his own—his introduction as the new President of Penske Racing.

TIM CINDRIC

"Between Gil and Greg and Roger and I, we had already figured out who was driving what car, who would be strategist. Greg was going to run No. 3, Roger was going to be his race strategist, and I was going to be Gil's race strategist. The day after the Australia race, Roger picked me up at the Ohio State University airport in his plane to go to Reading to tell the team that I'm coming to work for them. He hadn't told anyone yet. I had worked with Tom Wurtz and Clive Howell and these guys at the racetrack, and I thought, 'Man, this is going to be really awkward.' I get in his plane, and there's Rick Mears, Dan Luginbuhl, Greg Moore, Gil de Ferran, and Roger. I didn't know to wear a tie or not wear a tie, so I wore a sport coat, and I had a tie in my pocket. Everybody in the plane had ties on, so I was glad I brought mine.

"We walked into the race shop, where I had never been. First day. Everybody was cool with everything except for this part of it. They didn't have any idea this part of it was coming. I knew that I wasn't a popular decision. I mean, I had only been around two victory lanes in my time at Rahal's, right? This wasn't somebody coming in that had all the answers. But what I did know was that anybody who was working for that team who was just trying to ride that Penske rollercoaster, they had already left when the grass was greener on the other side. The ones that were left were the core of the team. They had all stuck together, and I thought, 'Man, with a little bit of success here . . . hell if we qualify in the top ten, they're going to have a big party.' They were really struggling in 1999, and then you throw Gonzalo on top . . . there couldn't have been lower morale. When they announced Gil and Greg, that brought the morale back up to a point. Then they lost Gonzalo, and that hurt. I obviously wasn't there at the time, but I still felt the pain when I came there a couple months later, because he was a popular guy and a great guy from everything I understood.

"After they introduced me at Reading, we actually went to the UK the week after Australia. One of Roger's motivations for hiring me was the fact that I had worked with all these people in the industry. His team had always done their own engines and their own cars; I had a relationship with Honda, obviously, through Bobby, and we had run Reynards and Firestones. I already knew the landscape there. He never came out and said it, but I'm sure that was part of it. That's kind of how it all started."

HONDA INDY 300

Surfers Paradise, Queensland — October 17, 1999 – 65 laps

1. Dario Franchitti
2. Max Papis
3. Adrian Fernandez
4. Bryan Herta
5. Michael Andretti

CHAMPIONSHIP STANDINGS AFTER 19 OF 20 RACES

1.	Franchitti	209
2.	Montoya	200
3.	Tracy	161
4.	Andretti	151
5.	Papis	133

With his injured hand heavily wrapped, Greg Moore worked with Championship Drivers Association executive director Jon Potter to insure he could compete in the season finale.
Steve Swope / RMA

CHAPTER 14

CHAMPIONSHIP WEEK

If Juan Pablo Montoya was affected by the consecutive crashes that dropped him out of the lead of the PPG Cup point standings, he certainly didn't show it. It was Tuesday, October 26, and for the first time since his race at Surfers Paradise ended in a tire wall, he was back on the job, participating in a CART media teleconference with his championship rival, Dario Franchitti.

What had Montoya been doing for the last week and a half in preparation for the championship-deciding season battle at California Speedway? "Just relaxing, you know," he chirped. "I went to Bahamas for the weekend, and that's it."

If Montoya felt any pressure or trepidation about the five-hundred-mile superspeedway finale, he didn't show it.

"I'm pretty relaxed about it," he told reporters as best he could while the call moderator battled through technical difficulties. "We won seven races. Nobody else has done that this year. We just had bad luck in other races. We gave away I don't know how many points by silly mistakes. That's the way it goes. We just had a bit of bad luck in the middle of the season, and it just came back when it shouldn't have come back. We had a problem in Houston, miscommunication. The car was there, but we had an accident. And I think the last race I just made a simple mistake.

"We'll see what happens," he concluded. "I'm just going to try to take it as cool as I can, get there, and see what happens. It's another race. Another day in the office. You know, it will be an interesting race for me, so we'll see."

Franchitti started the season as a championship favorite, but he went through what was perceived as a slow start to his year while rookie Montoya caught fire. Capped by a thirty-seven-point swing in the last two races, the strong second half to his campaign seemingly gave the more experienced Scotsman the momentum heading into Fontana.

"Obviously, my position is slightly different from Juan's in the fact that I don't need to go out and win the race," Franchitti said. "I just sort of need to be within a place or two, I guess. But I would like to get out there and try to win this thing. I'm going to be out there pushing. The number one priority is the championship, but you've got to treat every race the same as we have for the whole year. I'm going to get out there and do the best job I possibly can. I want to be right up in front. I know we're capable of getting the job done. We had a good test at Fontana, and we ran well at Michigan, so I think we'll be alright. We're not going to worry about what Juan is doing or anything else that we have no control over. A total team effort has got us into a position to win the championship, and it will take a total team effort to clinch it at Fontana.

"The championship is the big prize," he added. "Obviously, I'll be disappointed if I don't win it. But as Juan says, through the year we have both done very good jobs, so I don't think you can be too disappointed—although I'm sure one of us will be."

The championship protagonists were asked what they would each do to celebrate a victorious title outcome. "Well, I think the first plan after the race is Juan and myself are going to go out and have a small party, because we agreed some time ago whatever the results, win or lose, we are going to have a small party after the race," said Franchitti.

"Little one, by the way," Montoya chimed in.

Even without cars on a track, the two weeks leading up to the race could hardly have been more dramatic. On October 19, CART announced the cancellation of the Hawaiian Super Prix, a non-championship race with a $10 million purse that was to be staged November 13 on runways of the Barber's Point Naval Air Station and broadcast via Showtime pay-per-view. Then the same day that Montoya and Franchitti chatted with the press, Goodyear announced its total withdrawal from Indy car racing—both CART and IRL. Goodyear had already pulled out of Formula 1 earlier in the year but pledged to continue as the sole tire supplier for NASCAR and NHRA drag racing.

"Our decision is based, in part, on open-wheel racing's present state of affairs in North America and the ongoing split between CART and IRL," stated Stu Grant, Goodyear's general manager for global race tires. "Our long-standing commitment to racing made this an agonizing decision. However, it is becoming increasingly difficult to justify the significant capital and resources the company devotes to CART and IRL. Like many suppliers, we are certainly disappointed that no reconciliation between the two groups is in sight and therefore believe it is in the best interests of our shareholders, customers, and the racing division to take a sabbatical from the CART and IRL series."

Unmentioned in the Goodyear release was the fact that it had managed to win just two of the last forty-nine races in the CART series. Firestone agreed to remain the sole tire supplier for the FedEx Championship Series until a competitor to replace Goodyear could be found. Twenty-five years later, that still hasn't happened.

"In one way, it's a time for celebration," said Firestone program director Al Speyer. "On the other hand, it's extremely disappointing not to have competition. When we're the only supplier, it takes away the possibility that the tires could be the difference between winning and losing. So mixed emotions, because our success on the racetrack is certainly part of Goodyear's decision to withdraw."

On Thursday evening, Carl Hogan announced he would shut down his team with immediate effect after the Fontana event. The bombshell decision left Hogan's crew and driver Hélio Castroneves suddenly scrambling to secure their futures. "I'm very upset—it came as a complete surprise," said a shocked Castroneves. "Let's just concentrate on finishing the race strong and worry about next year later."

Behind the scenes, Hélio began frantically working the paddock, looking for any possible way to keep his Indy car career from ending. He felt like a pawn in a complicated contractual game.

"I had a proposal from Bobby Rahal at Detroit that year," Castroneves recalled. "I thought, 'Holy shit, this is amazing!' Back then, Emerson Fittipaldi was my manager. He wasn't at Detroit, but I gave it to Emerson's attorney. Nobody had exercised my option yet, and we didn't have to bring sponsorship or do anything. It was a five-year contract. It would have been fantastic. Then suddenly the next week, the attorney told Carl, and Carl said, 'No, I'm signing your option for 2000.' I thought, 'What the heck?' The attorney ended up telling Carl that to negotiate a better situation, I guess. But they had ties to Mercedes, when we didn't even know if Mercedes was going to be around.

"Coming towards Fontana, Carl called me on Wednesday, and he broke the news," Hélio continued. "I'm like, 'Carl, I can't believe it. I had a contract in my hand—how can you do that to me?' This couldn't have happened now—it had to have happened right about that time in Detroit. I was upset about that. I didn't want to go back to Brazil, thinking my career is over. So I went to Roger Penske, I went to Bob Rahal, I went to Ganassi, I went to Valvoline, which was Derrick Walker back then. I went to everyone and said, 'I need a job!' But they were all fully booked. They all said sorry, and the only one that was available was Derrick Walker because Gil was going to Penske. We started talking and talking."

Hogan took aim at a wide array of targets when he met with a small group of reporters in his motorhome in the Fontana infield. "I don't look at this as bittersweet—it's just bitter, forget the sweet," he fumed. "It took me four years to spend my own money on this team and it took me forty-five years to make it. I'm very discouraged. You hate to be bitter, but there are a lot of guys in this business where $6 million is nothing. To me, it's my livelihood. I didn't inherit any money. I've worked all my life to earn this money. I bought my trucks from my father. Now, look at what I get from these guys."

Hogan was unhappy with Ilmor Engineering and Mercedes-Benz. "Why does an engine get worse as the season goes on?" he asked. He was unhappy with the business climate in the CART series. "I've had companies not come forward on their promises—Brazilian companies, naturally."

But he directed most of his ire at CART itself. "They kissed Tony George's tail trying to get back together with the Indianapolis Motor Speedway and he drug them down the Primrose Path until he was ready to make a statement," Hogan said. "Then the stock went from thirty-three dollars a share down to nineteen dollars a share. What has my investment of 400,000 shares gone down? It just went down $6 million.

"I'm so upset," he concluded. "It's just been going on and on and on. The problem with CART is all these owners have a conflict of interest. What we have on the board is all the guys who own racetracks or sell race cars. It's mind-boggling. The problem is not many people want to come to work for CART because everyone has heard about the board and how difficult it is to work with."

At this point, Mercedes and Ilmor held the rights to Castroneves's contract, and Hélio and Hogan were seemingly unaware of efforts taking place behind the scenes to create a place on the 2000 grid for the young Brazilian involving PacWest Racing owner Bruce McCaw. With the Mercedes engine program in disarray—on October 11, Roger Penske had announced that Team Penske would field Reynard/Hondas in 2000 as he effectively turned his back on the engine program he founded—it was left to McCaw to try to salvage the marque's participation in the CART series. He was trying to create a new team, targeting Ganassi's Mo Nunn as the possible front man.

"By Vancouver, we pretty much knew Penske was leaving, then it became apparent that Forsythe was going to leave, and Hogan was getting sideways at the time," McCaw said. "Vancouver was a fiasco for Mercedes. Virtually every Mercedes engine blew up, it was terrible. The 'E' engine was just a bad concept. But Roger had obviously pushed it, looking for his unfair advantage, and forced Ilmor, being a shareholder, into making decisions that were not prudent for Mercedes-Benz. Roger told me personally that he still had confidence in Ilmor, but that his sponsors had demanded that he go to Honda. It always left me wondering a bit because Roger usually doesn't succumb to anybody—he usually sets the demands himself. But obviously, Mercedes's focus really became Formula 1 and the CART program clearly was becoming more and more second fiddle. I had enough fears about what Mercedes and Ilmor were likely to do that I became very concerned that the program was losing critical mass. And further, frankly, I wanted another credible team so that if the engine failed, we didn't get blamed for it. Not that I was looking for failure to occur, I just could see enough of the handwriting on the wall that if it didn't work, we needed to be able to protect ourselves or it was going to wipe us out. I think our conduct through the entire process is well documented."

The idea to try to convince Nunn to forego his planned retirement for a role as a Mercedes-powered team owner was hatched by AMG president Domingos Piedad. The original goal was to field a German driver with sponsorship from Warsteiner beer.

"They were hoping to get Mo Nunn to come in and engineer this and they had approached me about how we could help set them up and put them in the business," McCaw related. "At that point I had a shop on Gasoline Alley in Indianapolis that was pretty much vacant. I had agreed to help them run the business and get their feet on the ground. We had the mainstay of those discussions in the summertime and probably into September. Then Paul Morgan finally said he thought they could put something together with Mo Nunn. We had a meeting on that and pretty much agreed terms, including to hire Hélio Castroneves. Mercedes actually held his contract at Hogan's. Those pieces were in place, and we would step up and help make the team successful, giving them support with facilities and stuff like that. I think Mercedes was going to fund most of that, and Hollywood was part of it. Hollywood liked Hélio. They wanted a younger driver in IndyCar. Mauricio Gugelmin was too old and too clean cut for them, which is one of the things I admired about him. Of course, Castroneves was perfect, so I went to Hollywood and said, 'We're going to start a team, I'm going to be a shareholder, and we want to put Castroneves in there. It's a perfect fit.'"

Hogan's belief that the rich just keep getting richer in the CART team owner hierarchy was solidified Friday, when Chip Ganassi dropped a stunner of his own by announcing his team would move to Toyota engines in 2000. He said reports of his intention to change to Lola chassis were "just rumors." Ganassi, remember, was a partner and founder in Reynard North America.

Ganassi refused to address the belief that Toyota had offered him considerable financial inducement to make the change. But Honda Performance Development president Robert Clarke eventually went on the record.

"We knew Chip was being courted by Toyota," Clarke said. "Up until that time, all our teams had paid for the engine program. There was never any kind of subsidized program. Chip paid full boat price, and he had no problem doing that until Toyota came along and offered him a lot of money. He never told us what he was being offered, only that basically we had a long way to go. And we did go—for us—a long way. We felt that we offered him a lot. We made our final offer at Laguna Seca, but he basically indicated it was going to be difficult for him to accept it considering what he was being offered elsewhere."

Clarke added: "When we first found out about Ganassi and the actual numbers that Toyota was throwing, I met with Andrew Craig and said, 'A bad thing is starting to happen here, and you really need to get a handle on it. Every team in the paddock is going to want that kind of deal.' The problem is that the teams will become dependent on the manufacturers to a level like never before. The manufacturers were going to have even more control, not only of the teams, but ultimately of the series."

Despite Honda's dominance of the last four years in CART, Ganassi insisted his decision was based only on Toyota's performance and potential. "I just think it's time to change 'The Package,'" Ganassi said. "Switching engines today is not about a bad job that anybody else has done—I agree Honda is still today the number one engine. This is not about any offer Honda had to match or any level of performance Honda doesn't have. It's about a new program, staying at the leading edge, and remaining a winning team.

"As you can imagine, leaving Honda was one of the most difficult decisions I've ever had to make," he added. "It's an intangible, a hunger I see in Toyota's attitude. I see it in their eyes, in the level of commitment they personally make, and the level of commitment the company is making. They've brought key people into the program over the last year. I've been to their facility in Japan, and the commitment is there. They just need a winning team, and I expect Toyota cars, not just Chip Ganassi Racing cars, will be running in the top five and winning races next season."

As if on cue, Scott Pruett and Arciero-Wells Racing delivered Toyota's first Indy car pole position Saturday at Fontana, on a gusty and unseasonably hot autumn day in the Inland Empire. Max Papis had paced practice with a 238.231 miles per hour lap—which despite the high-drag Handford Device wing, was just 4 mph down on the unofficial record set by Mauricio Gugelmin just two years earlier. The afternoon heat and wind were at their peak when Papis was last to qualify, and his 234.544-mph effort fell short of the 235.398-mph benchmark Pruett laid down earlier in the session.

"Actually, I'm surprised they made us run between three and four o'clock," said Papis. "Whenever we test here, the wind always comes up at about two thirty and makes it difficult to run. I think these are the worst conditions I've seen at this track in two and a half years."

"We knew we had to get the car as loose as we could, and it was right on the limit," said Pruett, who had recently announced that he would leave the CART series in 2000 to drive a Tide-sponsored car for Arciero-Wells Racing co-owner Cal Wells in the NASCAR Cup Series. Pruett's Indy car career was blunted when he broke his back and multiple bones in his feet and ankles in a testing accident while driving for Truesports in early 1990. His path back to a full-time ride came via the lead testing role for Firestone in 1995 to prepare for the tire maker's successful return to Indy car racing. He won a pair of races for Patrick Racing and played a key role in stabilizing the troubled Toyota engine program through its gestation.

"It feels great," Pruett said. "Everyone on the team and at Toyota has worked so hard. Being my last race in CART, it couldn't be any sweeter. Look at my trace . . . I was sideways for a period of time. We've all got to cope with it, but three hours in this wind would be problematic, for sure."

Both championship protagonists played down the importance of qualifying after Montoya set the third fastest speed of 234.251 mph. Franchitti lined up eighth at 232.713 mph.

"It doesn't say much," Montoya said. "When you get to the race, you have to finish it first. This is a tough race, and anything can happen. If we're good enough to win, we'll win. If not, we won't."

Until late Saturday afternoon, the mere participation of one of the favorites to win the race was in question. Greg Moore did not make a qualifying run because earlier that day, he collided with a delivery van that was backing out of a parking space when he was riding his scooter though the garage and paddock area. Moore was thrown from the Honda Cub, and he sustained a broken pinky finger and a scaphoid fracture in a bone in his right wrist, along with several lacerations that required fifteen stitches. The treatment was handled at the track in CART's state-of-the-art mobile medical center. Dr. Stephen Olvey recalls that Greg's father, Ric, did all the talking as he implored doctors and series officials to allow his son to race the next day.

Dr. Terry Trammell determined that the wrist could be temporarily splinted prior to a permanent fix. Player's/Forsythe Racing hastily stitched a unique four-fingered glove to accommodate Moore's injured digit, and he was granted dispensation to run a few practice laps at the end of the day to assess his pain level and ability to drive.

"As Director of Medical Affairs, I was ultimately responsible for a driver's return to competition," Olvey recalled. "Greg quickly got up to speed. He ran a series of laps that would have qualified him on the front row. Telemetry from the car's data recorder showed he had used the steering wheel perfectly during the test. After a brief discussion, we cleared him to race. His father was especially happy . . . Ric Moore thanked Terry and me again and again."

Moore's hastily scheduled late afternoon test run wasn't the end of Saturday's activities. By the late 1990s, the CART paddock was truly impressive in its scope. Almost every team provided high-end hospitality to sponsors and guests. The journalists were even luckier; those well-connected could enjoy healthy gourmet meals from Penske, Green, Forsythe, PacWest, Newman/Haas, and others while on the job, a far cry from typical media center or concession-stand fare. Only Chip Ganassi's hospitality was truly a closed shop to outsiders.

The party scene was particularly vigorous for the season finale at Fontana. Friday night was highlighted by "Runway Madness II," a gala assembled by Championship Auto Racing Auxiliary (CARA) Charities in the Lockheed hangar at nearby Ontario International Airport. Items up for bid included laps in a PPG Pace Car driven by Paul Newman or Rick Mears, a day on the set of the television drama *ER* with actor Anthony Edwards, and the retiring Wally Dallenbach's iconic cowboy hat.

PacWest Racing created a large and complex modular hospitality area called "The Summit" in 1999, and Saturday night at Fontana, the team and Mercedes-Benz hosted "World Party '99," inviting the entire paddock to watch the Formula 1 championship showdown at Suzuka,

AL ROBBIE

"I went down to Fontana with two other buddies. We went to Runway Madness on the Friday night. The next morning, Greg had the accident in the paddock. We had just left his bus, and I think he was going to the trailer to get changed into his driving suit to go onto the track. When he didn't go on the track, we wondered 'What the hell is going on here?' We heard what had happened and caught up to him about an hour later after he had gotten his stitches in the bus. He said, 'Well, I'm still racing.' We were all like, 'Really?' He said he had to go onto the track in the afternoon and do four or five laps. They said if he was at pace, he could start last.

"I wasn't present at any of the conversations in the transporter where he and Ric and the team were talking, but everybody agreed that he was alright to race. Roberto Moreno was kind of milling around just in case. He always came to the track with his helmet. But I don't think that led to Greg being more driven. Whether we were playing pool or racing home from Vancouver to meet for dinner or whatever, Greg always had to be first. So, it was no surprise. It was his last race with Player's. He had won a race at Michigan and been competitive almost every year they had raced at Fontana. He went out and did the laps and came back and said, 'It was fine. No issues.' There were no indicators anything was awry with his hand."

Japan, between Mika Hakkinen of McLaren/Mercedes and Ferrari's Michael Schumacher. To the delight of most in attendance, Hakkinen and Mercedes prevailed in Japan, a stark contrast to the three-pointed star's dismal performance in CART over the past two seasons. That futility was forgotten in the moment as almost every driver in the FedEx Championship Series field stopped by to join the revelry celebrating the impending conclusion to the 1999 season.

As a Mercedes-Benz driver for one more race, Greg Moore was obligated to make an appearance at the World Party, but it was exceedingly brief. But not because he was worried about his injured hand and wrist. He was determined to represent Mercedes to the best of his ability and leave Player's/Forsythe Racing on a high note, with the kind of thrilling performance he had become known for at a type of track where he frequently excelled. But in truth, Moore's focus was already on his long-term future with Marlboro Team Penske.

"He just had signed with Penske and was going to be Gil's teammate the next year," said Tony Kanaan. "I remember Saturday night . . . we all stayed in buses at the time. We went to his bus, and he's like, 'Hey, come here!' I walked in, he takes me to his bedroom, and on top of his bed is his Marlboro suit. That, in the day, was *the* suit. He's like, 'Look at this, we're doing a photo shoot on Monday!' Now finally he was making the big bucks, and he had ordered a brand-new bus that was white, red, and black, the Marlboro colors. He was showing me the renderings. Just buddies, talking about stuff—young kids who have a lot of money from being very successful."

TIM CINDRIC

"For Fontana, Roger was going to be the strategist on one car. I was going to be on another car, but I told them that I didn't want to do a car. I just wanted to take time to stand back and watch how the team works and understand what exists, rather than getting stuck in one pit and calling the race.

"That was a crazy weekend. Hélio had just been told that he was out of a ride, that Hogan's team was folding. Hélio was walking around trying to find a ride. He came by and talked to Roger Friday or Saturday that weekend. At that point, we were like, 'Thanks for coming by.' I'd never met the guy before, and just pretty much told him, 'Thanks but no thanks. We don't have anything.' He was hoping we could start a third car or could run a car at Indy for him.

"We were going to do a tire test with Firestone at Portland after Fontana. That was going to be Greg's first opportunity to drive the car. That Saturday night, Greg and I were finishing the design of his Marlboro helmet in his bus. You know how he was, all about his helmet and stuff. We worked on this gold helmet with checkered flags and Marlboro red and got that all sorted out."

Greg Moore makes it four-wide into Turn One on lap ten of the Marlboro 500. A few seconds later, Moore crashed fatally in Turn Two. *Phillip Abbott*

CHAPTER 15

SEE YOU AT THE FRONT

It couldn't be better . . . the championship coming down to the very last race of the season. For Dario Franchitti, it's really pretty simple. He just has to keep Juan Montoya in sight. A little ahead of him, a little behind him, Franchitti will be the champion. But for Montoya, it's a whole different story."

That's how Paul Page led off ESPN's live broadcast of the final race of the 1999 CART FedEx Championship Series, the Marlboro 500 Presented by Toyota at California Speedway. Franchitti could clinch the championship with a third-place finish, no matter what happened to Montoya. The Colombian, on the other hand, would need a bit of help to overcome the nine-point deficit to his Scottish rival. Even if Franchitti failed to score a point by finishing in the top twelve, Montoya would still need to finish fifth (or sixth with a bonus point) to walk away with the title.

It was Halloween, and it couldn't have been a more pleasant day, with sunny skies and a comfortable temperature of eighty degrees for the 12:10 p.m. green flag. Despite starting from the back of the twenty-seven-car field due to the paddock scooter accident that injured his wrist and caused him to miss qualifying, nobody was more upbeat and eager to race than Greg Moore. "See you at the front," he told his friends as they interacted during prerace driver introductions.

"He sat right next to me in the drivers meeting, and I was asking him, 'Why are you racing?'" said Adrian Fernandez. "Greg had this confidence, maybe overconfidence in himself that you could not convince him from doing anything. Greg could feel like he could walk on water, he was so confident, and I loved that part of him. I always admired his youth and his talent. Obviously, that was part of his attraction. I remember he said, 'No problem, I'll be at the front in however many laps.' I said, 'Well take it easy, it's a long race.'"

Max Papis also has memories of his interaction with Moore in the lead-up to the Fontana race. "In '99, after I pushed Greg to the wall on the front stretch in St. Louis—I didn't crash him, but it was close—we didn't talk," Papis reflected. "It was tough to have those conversations. It was tough to be real. I remember we were not talking so much—we were talking, but we were not super, super close—but when we were in Fontana, after he got hurt with the scooter, I went to see him on Sunday morning. I told him, 'You crazy son of a bitch! I know I'm going to see you in my rearview mirror in like twenty laps.' And he told me, 'Actually, about fifteen.' And I left with a smile, because it had been a couple months since we had a conversation like that. Then I never saw him again. I'm happy that was my last conversation with him."

Papis immediately jumped into the lead from his outside front row starting spot, while pole-winner Scott Pruett found his Toyota race motor was nowhere near as potent as his special qualifying engine and immediately dropped to fifth place. He would last only forty-eight laps. Michael Andretti drafted past Papis into Turn One on the second lap to take the lead. Meanwhile, Moore moved up quickly through the field, gaining twelve places in the first three laps.

On the fourth lap, Richie Hearn spun the Della Penna Motorsports Reynard/Toyota 180 degrees at the exit of Turn Two. Upon reaching the infield grass, Hearn managed to whip the car back around facing forward, but it made hard left-side contact with a concrete wall lining the infield along the backstretch. Uninjured, Hearn quickly tossed his steering wheel from the cockpit and awaited the quick arrival of the CART Safety Team.

"Very strange to see a car come off the corner that late and still turn around," observed analyst Parker Johnstone on the ESPN broadcast. It appeared that Hearn's car was affected by turbulence from the pack running ahead, and Johnstone noted that the CART cars were restricted to half the downforce they were able to utilize just two years earlier.

There was nearly a disaster under the ensuing caution. Papis inexplicably dove inside Andretti into Turn One, only to nearly collide with the slow-moving pace car. During the six laps run under the yellow flag, ESPN aired a feature on the CART Safety Team.

The green flew to start lap ten. Montoya passed Papis into Turn One for second place, and ESPN's cameras followed the leaders into Turn Three. Suddenly, the director cut to the image of a light-blue racing car hurtling backwards through the grass before being flipped ninety degrees as if by a spatula, slamming the top of the cockpit into the same concrete infield wall that Richie Hearn hit at nearly the identical spot just a few minutes earlier.

Greg Moore wasn't as lucky as Hearn. After exiting Turn Two, Moore's Reynard/Mercedes snapped into a spin and followed the same trajectory that Hearn's car had. But it was carrying more speed, and instead of whipping back around 180 degrees on the grass before it hit the wall flush with its side, Moore's car skimmed across the infield and was still skidding sideways in full yaw when the right side of the chassis and rear wheel dug into where the turf met an asphalt access road for safety vehicles. That's what flipped the car onto its side and into a top-first impact with the unprotected concrete wall. There was a brief fireball as the Mercedes engine and rear end separated from the Reynard chassis, which barrel-rolled four times before coming to a stop upside down in the grass. Moore's arms could be seen flailing from the cockpit during its crazy gyrations.

"Oh, an enormous crash," Page shrieked. "Oh my God."

Safety workers were on the scene within twenty seconds, and after a brief delay to determine which of the two drivers in similar-looking Player's cars was involved, Page revealed it to be Moore's No. 99. The accident did not look survivable.

Dr. Terry Trammell confirmed as much on the CART Safety Team's private radio channel. "I don't think he's gonna make it! I'm coming in with him," Trammell shouted. Medics unsuccessfully tried to intubate Moore in the ambulance, and Dr. Stephen Olvey observed that the stricken driver was in near cardiac arrest when he arrived at the track heliport. Once Olvey and paramedics were quickly able to place a breathing tube in Moore's trachea, cardiopulmonary resuscitation efforts (CPR) were instigated.

HÉLIO CASTRONEVES

"I remember I almost spun at the same point Greg did. In fact, as soon as I passed that bump, I said, 'Ooh, if somebody is not careful, they're gonna spin out here.' [On footage from Adrian Fernandez's onboard camera, you can see Hélio's car twitching at the exit of Turn Two.] Right after I said that Richie Hearn spun out there. In my mind, I said, 'I knew that was going to happen. And it could happen on the restart.' Then I remember me backing off, because that was a great place to pass, but I remember because of the bump thinking, 'I don't want to take a risk, this is too long a race.' And I saw Greg Moore passing by me and I was getting pissed because we both had the same engine. Then he hit the bump and then he accelerated. He crossed over in front of me and I thought, 'Oh my God, I just hope he's okay,' because I saw the car jumping in the grass, and then I didn't see anything anymore. But then obviously on the next lap, when the yellow came and we passed through, I was like, 'Oh shit, that's a lot of debris.' Oh my God, the car was so destroyed, and I was like, 'Oh shit.'"

Olvey described Moore's condition in his book *Rapid Response*. "His heartbeat was undetectable, with a chaotic heart rhythm visible on the cardiac monitor. His head had assumed a grotesque appearance, being purple in color and very swollen. The pupils of his eyes were fixed and dilated with the empty stare that accompanies a severe head injury. Moore was near death."

In the track Medical Center, Richie Hearn was checked and cleared. He had learned of Moore's early progress through the field as he watched on TV, and then he saw the accident. ESPN reporter Jon Beekhuis asked Hearn whether there was something on the track that might have caused two such similar-looking incidents.

"I don't think so," Hearn said. "For me, it was just purely a turbulence issue. I had a really good run off of Turn Two, I pulled down low, and there's about three or four guys running three-wide in front of me. It just gets really unpredictable, and I just lost the rear end slightly. That's all she wrote. You're on a knife-edge out there. I'm okay—I slowed the car down quite a bit and hit pretty square.

ADRIAN FERNANDEZ

"At the beginning of the race, I remember it was so close and getting so crazy—everybody was running like it was a sprint race. I told John Ward, 'I think I'm going to lay back a little bit and pay attention because everybody is driving a little bit too aggressive too soon.'

"I remember the restart after Richie Hearn's crash perfectly. We were coming into Turn One three abreast, and then here comes Greg on the outside of me. I was starting to drop back on purpose, and I still vividly have the image in my mind of when he passed me. I said to myself, 'Greg, take it easy, slow down. It's too early, just relax.' I was right behind Greg on the outside of Turn Two and that's where he lost it. He lost it right in front of me—right in front of me."

"I didn't know what happened to Greg," he added. "It could have been the same thing—it's pretty busy at the back."

With trackside rescue efforts ongoing, the remaining cars in the race continued to circulate behind the pace car. On the twenty-second lap, Patrick Carpentier coasted into the pits with a dead Mercedes engine. Twenty-five years later, the events of Fontana are still vividly clear for him.

"Coming into that weekend, the atmosphere within the team was really weird," Patrick remembered. "It started before the race weekend. Greg had been with Steve Challis for a long time. Steve was not only his engineer, but kind of half of him. Steve was his mentor. He would guide him, he would calm him, he would coach him. Steve and Tony Cicale were great engineers like that. They kept Steve home before Fontana because they knew Greg had signed with Penske. I don't know if it was to get back at Greg, or what it was. But Steve Challis was not there, and to me, that was a big error, a big mistake."

"The weekend kind of started this way, and then Greg was all over the place," he continued. For some reason, he was not 100 percent, with the conflict they had at that race with the team and his dad and everybody pulling away. He hit that truck in the parking lot, and he should have stopped. I think if Steve would have been there, he would have said, 'No, you're not racing tomorrow, Greg, it's nonsense.' But they gave him some anti-inflammatories and other things and he wanted to race."

Carpentier is convinced that Moore's injury was not significant enough to affect his driving. But he believes Moore's head space did have an impact.

"It would have been okay for Greg to race with his injured hand," Carpentier said. "But he was starting at the back of the field, and I think Greg went into that race with revenge in mind. He wanted to prove absolutely that the back of the field was not where he belonged—it was up front. I guess he wanted to show whether Steve Challis was there or not, he had the winning car.

"When he crashed, it was after only a few laps, and he was already coming up behind me. I saw him; I was looking in the mirror. I saw in the mirror as—*whoooop*—his car started to spin. When I drove by the next lap, I couldn't really find the car, because the only thing left was parts, and the way the tub was laying down was hard to see. I could see his number drop on the scoring tower, so I knew it was him.

"The funny thing—not funny, but the weird thing that happened is everyone thinks the team told me to come in the pits and that was it, but that's not what happened. My engine shut down, just before the pit entrance. It was an electrical problem, and I was able to coast to my pit. But it's almost like it was a sign that he was gone. It was a weird, weird thing."

Franchitti's crew member Dave Popielarz is among those convinced that Forsythe pulled the plug on Carpentier's race in the wake of Moore's accident.

"Somehow, right from the start, we saw Greg's accident on the video board in the pits," Poppy related. "Then somebody said something on the radio about 'Code 5' and 'Go to landlines,' and we knew from Gonzalo what Code 5 was. We knew that it was bad and probably curtains. Then I remember Forsythe pulling in the other car, and they said they had an electrical problem. I've talked to guys on the team, and they still say they had an electrical problem. But I think they pulled the car. I saw that, and to me, that meant they pulled the car because Greg was gone. Well, fuck.

"Keith Badger was fueling, and I was doing the right rear, so we stood around together. I didn't want to say anything to Keith because I didn't want to fuck him up on the pit stops. He and Greg were a lot closer than I was. So, I just let it lie."

Looking back, it seems inconceivable that the race was not red flagged. Yet after just fourteen laps under caution, competition resumed, with Andretti running out front. But this was a race that refused to truly get going, because after just a handful of laps, Alex Barron pancaked the Turn Four wall with the right side of Team Penske's part-time No. 3 entry at the end of lap twenty-eight. Almost simultaneously, the med-evac helicopter carrying Greg Moore departed the track.

Barron was one of the following drivers who witnessed Moore's accident as it happened. He called it "the most horrifying crash I've ever seen in front of me. The car exploded in a thousand pieces. I've never seen anything so violent."

Most of the leaders stopped on lap thirty-two under a full-course yellow, which put Michel Jourdain Jr. in position to lead the first laps of his Indy car career. Paul Tracy gained four positions on the pit stop exchange to run directly behind Montoya on the track.

On the forty-fourth lap, Andretti led Tracy by 2.8 seconds when Dr. Olvey gave an update on Moore's condition to ESPN pit reporter Gary Gerould. Olvey's voice quivered, and he admitted his hands were shaking. "Greg has severe head and internal injuries," said the head of the CART Safety Team. "He's being sent to Loma Linda [University Medical Center] hospital for further resuscitative efforts. Dr. Jeff Grange, who is the chief emergency doctor here in this area, is with him in the helicopter and is going to report back to me soon."

When Gerould asked if this is a life-threatening situation, Olvey replied, "Yes, it is."

The race finally settled into a rhythm, with Andretti extending his comfortable lead over Tracy, Papis, Montoya, and Franchitti to more

PATRICK CARPENTIER

"We knew right away. As he got in the helicopter, we kind of knew. Everybody was silent. I remember we were sitting in one of the motorcoaches and everybody was in shock. 'Oh my God, what just happened?' I still get chills when I talk about it. Everybody was crying and hugging each other. We just couldn't believe it. For me, that was one of the toughest moments."

AL ROBBIE

"We were all up in the grandstand. Greg had gotten us some seats between the start line and Turn One. We saw he had gone from twenty-seventh up near the top ten in the first few laps. They didn't have very good jumbotrons, just one screen that was behind the pit row suites. I actually didn't see the impact—I saw him spin coming out of Turn Two. The last I saw, the car had looped around backwards and was going down the track. The announcer said there was an accident on the track, and we saw that Greg didn't come by. I was there with Ryan and Scott, my two friends, and Greg's kind of girlfriend Tammy was with us too. She saw it on the screen, I guess. She was obviously very upset, so I said, 'Don't worry, the cars are very safe' and things like that. We went down and actually convinced a guy on a golf cart to drive us around to the infield. We got to the pits, and there was nobody in the pits. We asked a couple questions and were told they were over at the medical center.

"There were a bunch of other people outside the medical center, and when they started up the helicopter, you kind of knew things were not good at all. Ric and Donna came out, and they just said, 'We're going to Loma Linda, come to the hospital.' But our rental car was about five miles away, and I didn't know where the hospital was. I went back to the IndyCar office, and Mike Zizzo [CART PR] was in there. We had spent a lot of time with Mike the year before in Australia, so I knew him quite well. Mike gave us a ride to the hospital.

"I was with Greg in 1994 when Ayrton Senna had his accident. I think we got home really late from somewhere, and he flipped on the race. We didn't actually see it happen, but we saw the announcement as it happened. Senna being Senna, the legend that he was, obviously it was a huge impact for everyone in the racing community. For me, that was a 'Holy fuck' moment. Greg was obviously a little bit rattled by it, but it's one of those ones where clearly something happened or went wrong. Like they say, you know the risks, but it still hits you when it happens."

than ten seconds. But Tracy and the rest fought back, and Andretti's margin was less than four seconds when he pitted from the lead on lap seventy. The stop was a disaster. Michael overshot his pit box by a good five feet, and he had been sitting there for a solid twenty seconds when his overheated rear brakes sparked a small oil fire in the engine compartment of the Newman/Haas Swift. Exit the day's dominant driver.

Franchitti stopped at the same time, and his pit visit was almost equally as damaging. Accelerating back up to speed, Dario correctly surmised something didn't feel right with his Reynard/Honda and he drove a slow lap, swerving back and forth to try to determine the cause of the imbalance. He immediately pitted again, with the right-rear wheel locked up as he entered the box. Crew member Dave Popielarz tried to hammer the incorrectly seated right-rear wheel into place before ultimately removing it and replacing it with the one that had just come off the car. One of the spring-loaded pins that locks the wheel into place on the hub had snapped out of place, and the smallest of misfortunes dropped Franchitti to eighteenth place, two laps down from the leaders after he stopped again for further investigation and a replacement right-rear wheel. Meanwhile Montoya ran in third behind Papis and Tracy after an untroubled pit stop.

"What happened to Greg must have been under my skin or something because I sure didn't do a good job the next stop," said Popielarz. "The championship fell apart in my hands. There were other factors, but you know how it goes—it's always the last chip to fall. I probably started standing up too soon, and if you stand up too soon, it cocks the gun. When you cock the gun, it starts hammering; when it starts hammering, you turn off the gun and get away from it, which means it's tight. It wasn't tight. Dario got to the middle of One and Two, and he says, 'I've got a loose wheel.' Fuck! He comes around, and the problem is, driving around, the wheel locks did a good job of holding it on, but it killed the threads inside the nut and then the wheel lock. Every time you took the wheel on or off, you had to force it over the mangled wheel lock. Each time, it took thirty seconds to pound the nut off again. I should have changed nuts—I've thought about that since. After, it was just drive around."

The race lost an interesting contender on the 110th lap. Hélio Castroneves had scythed from twentieth place to third, only to be let down once again by a Mercedes "E" engine. The Hogan team had blown through five motors in the Vancouver weekend alone. The yellow flag flew, and on the television broadcast, Page lamented the loss of most of ESPN's in-car camera cars through retirement or technical issues, leaving Fernandez as the only driver transmitting on-track visuals. It was the first time the broadcast made significant mention of Fernandez, who had started thirteenth and quietly moved up to fourth place.

As the bunched-up field came into the pits, leader Papis locked his rear brakes and slewed sideways into the grass, losing several positions. "Don't worry, guys, everything is fine," Max assured team owner/strategist Bobby Rahal over his radio. But he exited the pits in seventh place, the race now led by Tracy over the Target/Ganassi duo of defending Marlboro 500 winner Jimmy Vasser and Montoya. Franchitti took advantage of the caution to regain one of his lost laps and ran in thirteenth.

During this caution, as the cars were running their 118th lap, it was announced in the media center that Greg Moore died from the injuries he sustained in the accident on lap ten. There would be no postrace ceremonies. It was 1:44 p.m., about ninety minutes since the race started. Moore had been pronounced dead at Loma Linda University Medical Center more than twenty minutes earlier.

"The doctors there had tried unsuccessfully to resuscitate him for more than twenty-five minutes," wrote Dr. Olvey. "They had even opened his chest hoping to find a treatable injury. There was none. Moore's body and head had been virtually destroyed in the crash."

The race continued. On the 134th lap, the out-of-sequence Franchitti made what was supposed to be a routine pit visit, but Popielarz again struggled with the car's damaged right-rear hub. The nineteen-second stop left Dario three laps down on leader Christian Fittipaldi. A bad day for Team Green was compounded a few minutes later when a blown Honda engine eliminated Tracy. It had been a redemptive season for the Canadian, who was guaranteed to finish third in the final standings.

"I think everything motivated me, and I really wanted to show what I could do this year," Tracy told Beekhuis on the ESPN broadcast. "I want to thank Wally [Dallenbach] for what he did, because I think that changed my focus and my direction for what I had to do in the future. We'll move on from here and try to win the championship."

CART's indecision and lack of communication in handling Moore's passing was evident when Tracy added, "I hope Greg's feeling okay, because he's a close friend of mine and I heard he got hurt pretty bad. All our hearts go out to the Moore family. We hope he feels good." Tracy's voice was trembling.

On the 153rd lap, the caution flag was shown for debris, and ESPN went to a commercial. Upon return, Gary Gerould's voice identified the two men on the screen, Doctors Jeff Grange and Stephen Olvey.

"Gary, I regret to announce that driver Greg Moore has been pronounced dead at Loma Linda hospital," Olvey stated. "He died of massive head and internal injuries. He was pronounced dead at twenty-one minutes after one o'clock." Paul Page offered some spoken condolences to Moore's family and friends over a fifteen-second highlight reel of Moore's career, followed by a few seconds of silence and another commercial break. It was 2:07 p.m.

At this point, the three flags in the grassy area between the pits and the start-finish line of the track near the scoring pylon were lowered to half-mast. In the TV booth, Page was furious.

"CART management wanted to make a spectacle of his death," he revealed in his autobiography, *Hello, I'm Paul Page.* "They wanted to wave the caution flag to slow the cars, lower the flag to half-staff, and make a dramatic announcement. A tragedy shouldn't be showcased. I looked to Chief Steward Wally Dallenbach through the glass separator between us and Race Control, and I saw the same pain in his eyes that I'm sure he saw in mine. The higher-ups insisted. But in the end, it all got bungled. By then, the families had been notified, so we sent a camera to Dr. Olvey to simply confirm the injuries were fatal. We were done with it. We just wanted that miserable day to end."

The professionalism that Page maintained on the air was highly commendable. The race simply went on, even as pit reporter Beekhuis admitted he and many pit crew members were struggling to concentrate after the confirmation of Moore's death. The drivers remained unaware.

Papis took over from Fittipaldi out front as the contest headed into its final ninety laps. The leaders had just made stops for fuel when Mark Blundell's troublesome PacWest Reynard/Mercedes finally stalled for good and brought out the yellow at lap 201. Franchitti, Fernandez, and

TONY KANAAN

"Greg crashes, and nobody would tell us anything. You're racing, and I remember going on the front stretch at Fontana there's a pylon and a big American flag in the middle of the track. And halfway through the race, which I thought was so inappropriate at the time, and disrespectful to us drivers, because we didn't know and were still racing . . . fuck . . . halfway through, the flag goes to half-mast. I mean, right there, I knew. But no way, man. Being a Brazilian, that's a world thing. That's bad—that means somebody died. And obviously I knew the accident had happened.

"We never went red flag. It went yellow, they took him out, helicopter takes off, and life goes on. We've improved procedures since then. The previous era, those guys were used to that. They used to see two or three people die every year. Mario Andretti used to say, 'When we started the year, we didn't know if we were going to finish it or not.' And by finish, I mean alive. So, in a way, I see why it didn't go red. But nowadays? No way."

Al Unser Jr. topped off their fuel near the end of the six-lap caution to open the possibility of making the finish without stopping again. Attrition had elevated Franchitti up to tenth place and into the points, but he was still two laps adrift of the leaders—and more importantly, four points behind Montoya.

Up front, Papis led Montoya and Fittipaldi and the race began in earnest. Fittipaldi moved past Montoya into second on lap 213. Montoya had raced hard to that stage, but he was finally convinced to back off a bit given his comfortable position in the championship compared to Franchitti. Papis and Rahal, meanwhile, with the memory of running out of fuel while leading at Michigan three months earlier fresh in mind, committed to running as hard as possible and making a late splash-and-go stop.

Papis pitted from the lead as he completed his 237th lap, locking his right-front wheel as he braked for the start of the speed zone. Fresh tires were laid out but went unused as Team Rahal held the car for a surprisingly long time, determined to not repeat what happened at Michigan,

MICHAEL ANDRETTI

"I actually left before the end of the race. I wasn't there to the end, and I didn't know they had done all that. It's an unfortunate part of the sport. It's like at Indy when my brother crashed in '92, I didn't know if he was alive or dead. I literally didn't know. The hardest thing I ever had to do was just try to drive, because nobody was telling me. They told me Dad broke his feet and was going to be okay, but I was asking 'What's up with Jeff?' at every caution. And there was no report. Then you start thinking. I saw the car when it was up on a wrecker, and it was gone all the way up to the dash. And I'm like, 'Oh, God.' That was tough, so I can see how hard it was for those guys to go through that."

---

where Papis lost the race when he ran out of fuel on the final lap. Fittipaldi stopped next time by, also eschewing tires, with Newman/Haas Racing opting for about two seconds less engagement of the fuel hose. Montoya also took five seconds of fuel when he stopped with ten laps remaining.

Now Fernandez led from Mauricio Gugelmin, who was also trying to stretch his fuel to the finish. Papis ran third ahead of Fittipaldi and Montoya. After all his travails, Franchitti was ninth, putting him ahead of Montoya 213-210 in the championship battle with just twenty miles of competition remaining. Alas, it was short-lived, because Franchitti also had to stop for a splash of fuel, dropping him back to tenth. Chip Ganassi was going berserk on the radio, extolling Montoya to pass Gugelmin. With four laps to go, Montoya slipped by the fuel-saving Brazilian for fourth place. The points were now tied on 212, with the championship still in favor of Montoya, and the drama shifted to whether Fernandez could make it to the finish line.

Fernandez won the race earlier in 1999 at Twin Ring Motegi by stretching his fuel, and he duplicated that feat at Fontana. He was 7.634 seconds to the good over Papis and Fittipaldi when he crossed the line to claim his fifth career race win in the CART series and the $1 million check that came with it. More significantly, Montoya took the flag in fourth place to clinch the championship. He and Franchitti finished the year each with 212 points, but Montoya's seven race wins to Dario's three made him the 1999 CART FedEx Championship Series champion.

There was nothing for anyone to celebrate. Most of the participants in the race were still unaware of the death of Greg Moore. The news left the drivers in a state of shock and rendered meaningless the thrilling battle between Montoya and Franchitti for the CART championship.

ADRIAN FERNANDEZ

"I didn't run in the top ten for the first two or three stints, but as the field started getting more wide open, we started going to the front. We had a very fast car. Some of the drivers like Bryan Herta said they saw the flags go down, but I never noticed that. To be honest, at that point I thought Greg was fine and I was not worried about him. I didn't have any communications from the team, and I was really focusing on the race.

"When the checkered flag came, and obviously we won what was a very important race for us, coming back to the pits I remember the team telling me not to go to the winner's circle but to go straight to the pits. The first thing I remember is how stupid I looked shaking my fist after winning the race, because maybe I did something wrong. I didn't know if they had disqualified us for some issue or what. Never to my mind came the situation of Greg—ever."

MAX PAPIS

"I don't think I have ever shared this with anyone. We dominated, right? We led many laps. They never told me anything. I knew there was an accident, but I never noticed anything. I had no idea. When I crossed the finish line, nobody ever told me, or maybe I didn't hear that Adrian Fernandez had won. I never considered that, all day long. I was 110 percent sure I won the race. I crossed the finish line, and I was cheering, was super excited about it, and I could not understand why they were not telling me anything on the radio. I went through One and Two, and Bob Rahal came on the radio and said, 'Your friend Greg didn't make it.'

"From there it was like a blur. I started driving to the podium and they steered me away from P1 and I was like, 'I won the fucking race!' And they're like, 'No, Adrian won.' I was so mad, I exploded. I couldn't understand what happened. I was 100 percent convinced I won the race. I think Fernandez did one less pit stop and was super slow at the finish. I was convinced I won the race. And in the press conference, I said, 'Thank you God for not winning this race, to be my first win.' I was very grateful I didn't win."

MARLBORO 500

California Speedway — October 31, 1999 – 250 laps

1. Adrian Fernandez
2. Max Papis
3. Christian Fittipaldi
4. Juan Pablo Montoya
5. Jimmy Vasser

FINAL CHAMPIONSHIP STANDINGS

1.	Juan Pablo Montoya	212*
2.	Dario Franchitti	212
3.	Paul Tracy	161
4.	Michael Andretti	151
5.	Max Papis	150
6.	Adrian Fernandez	140
7.	Christian Fittipaldi	121
8.	Gil de Ferran	108
9.	Jimmy Vasser	104
10.	Greg Moore	97
11.	Tony Kanaan	85
12.	Bryan Herta	84
13.	Patrick Carpentier	61
14.	Roberto Moreno	58
15.	Hélio Castroneves	48
16.	Mauricio Gugelmin	44
17.	P. J. Jones	38
18.	Cristiano da Matta	32
19.	Scott Pruett	28
20.	Robby Gordon	27
21.	Al Unser Jr.	26
22.	Richie Hearn	
23.	Mark Blundell	9
24.	Jan Magnussen	8
25.	Michel Jourdain Jr.	7

* Montoya won the championship on a tiebreaker, seven wins to three. He was named "Rookie of the Year."

The postrace press conference was incredibly somber for (left to right) Christian Fittipaldi, Adrian Fernandez, and Max Papis. *Kazuki Saito*

CHAPTER 16

AFTERMATH

Wally Dallenbach's career as Chief Steward for Championship Auto Racing Teams and the FedEx Championship Series wasn't supposed to end this way. On the Friday night of the Marlboro 500 race weekend, he was feted at the popular annual event organized by CARA Charities called "Runway Madness," where one of his famous cowboy hats was auctioned for $9,500 to benefit Paul Newman's Hole in The Wall Camps.

"That's a big one for me—a nine-thousand-dollar hat," Dallenbach said. "I bought it in Aspen for $160."

Instead of celebrating the end of a distinguished second career, Dallenbach was investigating the death of one of Indy car racing's most popular and promising young drivers, in a graphically violent accident that played out live on cable television to more than two million viewers.

"I was trying to retire for the second or third time," Dallenbach told his biographer, Gordon Kirby. "That was going to be my last race, and I met each driver before the race to shake their hand. I had a lot of interaction with Greg through his career. I shook his hand, gave him a hug, and fifteen minutes later, he was dead. I took my place in the control tower at the exact moment he crashed. I saw it on television and the way he went in, I knew it was bad. I had to go look at the car. Those are tough moments."

Even before the checkered flag fell, Dallenbach canceled the podium celebration, and the top three finishers were told to proceed to their pits with the rest of the field. That's when they and the rest of their fellow competitors learned that their friend and rival hadn't survived a crash that occurred some three hours earlier, just ten laps into a 250-lap marathon.

"That's a low point," recalled Jimmy Vasser. "I remember Greg crashing, but we never talked about it. Nobody said anything to me on the radio, but I think others had somehow during the race gotten wind of what was going on. I was told coming down Pit Lane after the checkers. As I pulled into the box, Tom Anderson said on the radio, 'Greg didn't make it.' I couldn't believe what I was hearing. I had kind of forgotten he had crashed at the start. It was a five-hundred-mile race. I said, 'What do you mean by he didn't make it? Didn't make what?' Then it dawned on me because Tom was broken up in his delivery. I mean, Richie Hearn had virtually the same accident. Just the angle, I guess. It was just the most horrible racing day that I've been a part of, from the driver's seat for sure."

A crowd of about one hundred people gathered in and around Montoya's pit stall, where the new CART champion was given a bright red "4 for 4" hat commemorating Target/Chip Ganassi Racing's fourth consecutive triumph in the FedEx Championship Series. Montoya was not smiling. Over the California Speedway public address system, CART Chaplain Hunter Floyd led the remaining spectators in a prayer service for the deceased Greg Moore.

Gary Gerould was in tears when he was handed the unenviable task of interviewing Montoya for the live ESPN broadcast. "It's really bad, really bad that it's happened again this year," Montoya said. "Greg was a great guy, and I'm really sorry for his family and everything. He didn't deserve to die."

What Montoya accomplished on the racetrack in 1999 was unprecedented and unexpected. So were the circumstances he was presented with in the immediate aftermath of his achievement. The gravity of the moment left a lasting impression on the young champion.

"I never did really get to celebrate," Montoya revealed, much later in his life. "I was kind of close to Greg—not as much as Dario and the other guys, but we got on really well and everything. It was tough. It was a tough break for Greg. But at the end of the day, you need to understand that in racing, it's gonna happen whether you want it or not. That's the reality of it, and you need to be comfortable with it. It sucks, but it's the truth. There's no way around it. You're either comfortable having a shunt and you're comfortable knowing that it might happen . . . but at the same time, the way I look at it, it could happen on the road. It could happen going to the track—look at Nicky Hayden, who got run over on a bike. You just need to be alive. You can't stop living because something like that could happen."

On the broadcast, team owner Chip Ganassi's voice broke when he accepted Gerould's acknowledgement of his fourth straight title. "I'm just not ready for a championship, I'm not ready for today's activities," Ganassi said. "I'm ready to congratulate my pal here for what a great job he did driving. And I want to certainly . . . Greg was a friend of all of ours, and I'm a little bit speechless right now, to tell you the truth."

Race winner Adrian Fernandez respectfully declined a television interview request and sequestered himself with other drivers, including championship runner-up Franchitti, in a track meeting room. None of them were prepared for what they just heard about Moore.

"When I stopped in the pits, the first guy that came into my cockpit was Kevin Diamond, the team PR," Fernandez remembered. "He said, 'We have bad news—we've lost Greg.' At that point, I completely forgot about the win, the whole thing, and inside the car and inside the helmet, I just started crying like a baby. I just bawled. There's a picture of me coming out of the car where I was really crying, because I just couldn't stop thinking about Greg and his dad. I remember when I went to his memorial, when I hugged his father, I couldn't let him go for five minutes. I was just crying because I could feel his pain. They were such a great pair of guys, a father and son doing things together. Just to feel the pain he was feeling and to think about all that, it just broke my heart. I mean, Greg really hit me hard. To this day, it's always very hard to think about that very dark day."

Franchitti fell sobbing into his father George's arms on Pit Lane when he was told the news of his close friend's demise. "I'm sorry, son," George Franchitti said. "Greg is dead."

Twenty-five years down the line, the decisive pit stop still weighs on the mind of Team Green crewman Dave Popielarz. "Dario came up to me after the race and just hugged me because of Greg," he said. "The feeling was 'Nothing matters.' The team took it as: 'Win as a team,

DARIO FRANCHITTI

"I don't remember anything, really, about that weekend. I remember Greg having his scooter accident. I don't even remember if I tried to talk him out of driving. The first thing I remember was stopping the car after the race and being absolutely furious at what had happened. I was angry about the problem with the wheel nut or whatever. But actually, I was angry at myself because I had fucked it up earlier in the season. No championship is one moment.

"I got out of the car, and I think it was my dad who told me, or Jack Christiansen. Normally it would have been Poppy as well, but he was just so devastated at everything that had happened. I was walking back through that gate at the end of Pit Lane when Jack told me, and I never walked through there again without thinking about this for however many years I went back to that fucking track.

"I don't know how I would have reacted if I had won the championship and found out that Greg had died. It's never, 'Oh, I lost the championship that day.' No—I lost my best friend. I kind of get that Juan said he never celebrated, because when I won the 2011 championship when Dan Wheldon died in Las Vegas, I didn't ever celebrate. I don't even think about that. I get it.

"What I do remember is I was stopped by the police on the way back to the hotel for speeding. Ashley and I were going back, I think in a little S2000 that Honda had given us, and I was driving like a dick. I got pulled over, and I think Ashley convinced the cop to give me a break because my best friend had just been killed.

"To me, that's when it stopped being fun. Right then [snaps finger]. That's a very selfish thing to say, I guess, but from that point on, it was just never the same. At that point in my life, I was driving cars I loved driving. Those cars were fucking cool. There's shot of us on the wall at the Ganassi shop, of Monty and I at Mid-Ohio, and the tires are all curved under. Whoa! I met Ashley; I was loving life. And Gonzo got killed at Laguna, and it was like, 'Oh my God. Wow.' And then of course, Fontana, and it just ripped everything apart."

lose as a team.' Nobody ostracized me or pointed the finger at me or anything like that. But I got back to the shop, and I can't say I really felt great. There was no animosity, none at all. But I did feel like I had kind of let the team down. I felt bad about mouthing off to Dario and the team at Laguna. There was no friction, it was just a dumb thing to say. Then to stomp on your cock afterwards, you really look like a fool. I left Team Green not too long after and went to Mo Nunn Racing. It was an opportunity and a new team. I had the chance to become a crew chief; I thought you had to go up to do better. I was so wrong!

"Honestly, at the time, I was one of the fastest guys in the Pit Lane," Popielarz continued. "I was at the top of my game. I didn't stop going over the wall, but I never felt that fast again. Just like good drivers drive on confidence, I didn't drive on confidence anymore. I changed the wheel nut and made sure it was in the gun, set it down . . . all this is maybe two-tenths slower, but it wasn't that ragged supercross edge that those guys ride on. Now, I'm making sure there is no error." Poppy's last over-the-wall pit stop came in 2020, when he crewed for James Hinchliffe.

———

Perhaps befitting the mood after the events of Halloween 1999, the lights in the California Speedway press conference room were dim to the point of near darkness. CART CEO Andrew Craig, California Speedway President Scott Atherton, and Doctors Jeff Grange and Steven Olvey were the first to address the media. Olvey quickly dispelled the notion that the scooter incident that left Moore with broken bones in his hand played a role in the accident.

"We did have a brace made for his hand," Olvey said. "It was very small, just to keep the fracture comfortable. We tested him yesterday afternoon in the car to see how it went, and he was very excited about it afterwards. He felt fine. We re-X-rayed it and re-examined him at that time. We again saw him in the morning—by we, I mean myself and Dr. Terry Trammell, who really makes the orthopedic decisions. He and I examined [Moore] again this morning. He felt very comfortable, the finger looked good, and it looked good on X-rays. So, we allowed him to compete in the warm-up. In other words, we had several steps in this process. He ran in the warm-up without any difficulty whatsoever, and we again examined him following the warm-up. He was extremely excited about racing and very confident. He felt the hand would give him no difficulty.

"We feel very strongly that the hand was not related to the cause of the accident," Olvey concluded.

The press conference for the top three finishers was an incredibly emotional affair. Only race car drivers truly know and understand the risks that come with their chosen profession. Over the years, circuit and car safety improved considerably. But in 1999, the SAFER Barrier had not yet been invented. Doctor Robert Hubbard and Jim Downing were more than a decade into their struggle to gain acceptance from sanctioning bodies for the patented head and neck restraint they were developing called the HANS Device. Motorsport was considerably safer than it had been in the 1960s and '70s, and driver deaths were comparatively rare. But the CART community had been confronted by two tragedies in the space of just fifty days, including the passing of one of the series' most popular and promising drivers.

Adrian Fernandez, Max Papis, and Christian Fittipaldi all had red, swollen eyes. So did press conference moderator Mike Zizzo, whose voice barely rose above a whisper when he simply opened the forum for questions.

After a long pause, veteran Indy car journalist Gordon Kirby finally spoke, barely able to get the words out as he asked the trio if they could share any thoughts and memories of Greg Moore.

"It's so hard, because Greg was such a good friend of ours," Fernandez began. "We've been racing awhile and shared so many good moments inside and outside the racing track. This is a tragedy for all of us, and I can't express . . ."

He paused and broke down. "The win, it doesn't mean anything," he finally managed to continue. "I'm sure his dad is hurting right now. I will remember Greg as a great gentleman and a great friend and a fantastic race car driver."

Papis, who was one of Moore's closest friends, was deeply affected by the accident. "He's up there in the sky," Max sobbed. "This is a message God sent to us. There is no word, there's nothing, no satisfaction will pay this back. We need to understand why things happen, and I don't want to accept them. Now my prayers are with Ric and all of Greg's family."

Third-place finisher Christian Fittipaldi could barely contain his frustration and anger that another of his colleagues had passed on. "Obviously, it is a very bad moment for all of us, no doubt about it," he said. "Prayers to Greg and his family.

"We're in this to practice a very nice sport, not to kill ourselves," Fittipaldi added. "This year we had two losses. My thoughts go to Team Penske also. It's been a very difficult year, and we can't let things like this happen. We're not out there to give our lives. I have no words. Greg will be missed a lot everywhere."

ADRIAN FERNANDEZ

"I was the first one to speak to the press and the world after the race was finished. It was horrible. I had four or five situations like that, and this was probably the hardest one. Unfortunately, my race career has been marred by some deaths while I won races. Another was with Jeff Krosnoff at Toronto in 1996, and that was my first time that I lived an experience like that. We didn't know anything had happened until after we celebrated at the podium, so that came late. The other one that was very hard was Michigan in '98 [when three fans were killed by a wheel that flew off Fernandez's wrecked car]. That was very hard. The shock for me there was my family was there in the grandstand, too.

"When I talk to people about those days, I say in a lot of ways we were gladiators who happened to drive. We knew how dangerous it was. The cars were becoming really fast, the engines really powerful. The qualifying laps on the ovals, it was getting dangerous. I always tried to do my best with safety in terms of things that I could control as a driver. I looked at my position in the car, where I could hit my knees or my feet or my elbows. I knew it was a dangerous era. The cars were unbelievable to drive, they were just a blast. But they were incredibly fast. There was no SAFER Barrier, and in 1999 nobody had a HANS Device. It's just amazing and, honestly, I do feel like a survivor to have lived through this era. From what I started racing to when I stopped, whether in testing, qualifying or races, we lost fourteen drivers while I was there. That's a lot."

The end of the season always brings a succession of press conferences, most celebratory. The process tends to drag. On this day, it seemed endless. True to form, Montoya's appearance before the media was brief.

"I'm really sad for what happened to Greg, sorry for his friends and family," Juan began. "It's really nice to win it. It took a long time, even with all those wins."

He said he had a sideways moment in the prerace warm-up that required extensive car setup changes. "Right at the end, the car wanted to go in another direction. It was good because it was before the race." He worried about a rattle from his engine in the closing laps. "I thought I'd heard it before, but it went louder. But nothing broke." He chuckled about team owner Ganassi's energetic and sometimes frantic coaching over the radio. "I knew where we had to finish, and we got there.

"I was trying to win it," Montoya concluded. "All those wins, I'm kind of glad that it finished that way. It wouldn't have been fair if I had twice as many races as he's won."

Chip Ganassi was sometimes brusque to the point of rude. In 1999, he was forty-one years old, wrapping up his first decade as a team owner, and in Indy car racing he was still often seen as a brash upstart who was emerging as the dominant heir apparent to the likes of Roger Penske and Carl Haas. At this heartbreaking moment, Ganassi rose to the occasion as he spoke with eloquence and compassion reflecting on his organization's record-setting fourth consecutive CART-sanctioned championship.

"Juan and the team had a great year," he said. "Certainly, we tried to throw it away in a couple races, but in the end, we were rewarded. I think that will be the closest championship ever. I'm damn glad this year is over.

"We don't want our light to shine at the dimming of others," he continued. "Team Green—let's not underestimate the charge they made in the second half of the season. Believe me, ladies and gentlemen, you have your whole life to dream about days like today, and you're never prepared for what ultimately happens.

"Someday, when we get a rest from this day, there will be time to talk about what a great driver Juan Pablo is, what a great team this is, what great sponsors, and all that. But right now, it's time to think of our pal

Greg. Right now, he's at that big racetrack in the sky and he's probably a lot happier than all of us."

Ganassi paused to regain his composure. "I've known Greg for I guess five or six years, maybe longer. I think everyone who's ever driven one of these cars could tell you that maybe he's just not burdened with these things anymore. Senseless things we do like shock absorbers and wings and rules and fights. Our sport seems, I think, fairly insignificant at times like this."

Ganassi made a final plea. By the end of 1999, Indy car racing was not only split, it was broken. Greg Moore's death was the ultimate blow.

"Maybe this is a good time to take a step back," Ganassi said. "I think everybody in the sport needs each other. Maybe this is a time to get back together like it used to be."

Mario Andretti spoke for the racing community when he assessed Moore's death and the impact it made on the sport.

"That's when you realize how cruel the sport could be, to take away someone like Greg," Mario said. "He was just really coming into his own in his career, and I think he had all the ingredients as a person or individual. He was a good-looking kid, he was charming, he had everything going for him, and he was taken away. Those were the tragedies; there were too many in our sport. He was certainly one of them, and at the worst possible time, too, when there was much more awareness in the sport. We were beginning to edge more toward safety, but not enough."

Greg Moore, 1975–99. *Michael Levitt*

CHAPTER 17

INSTANT LEGACY

As Canada's most established and popular active Indy car driver, the nation's media sought out Paul Tracy to reflect on the passing of his countryman, Greg Moore.

"I spent a pretty sleepless night, and my wife and I had a hard day," Tracy told TSN SportsCentre via satellite link from Los Angeles, some twenty-four hours after Moore's fatal crash. "Just a few days ago, my wife cooked dinner for the three of us, and we ate in our motorhome. I've never had anything hit so close to home.

"It's a tough way to lose him, but he was out there doing what he loved to do," PT continued. "The last memory I have of him was talking on the grid. I don't know if he was teasing me or messing with me, but he used to call me 'Legend,' or 'Ledge' for short. He said, 'Hey Ledge, I'll see you up front halfway through the race!' That was it, really. He was out there trying to get to the front, giving it all he had."

Wally Dallenbach met with reporters and revealed his early conclusion that Moore's death was caused by angle of impact, not speed. Dallenbach said Moore's fastest lap in the race was 219 miles per hour and that the impact in the fatal accident was 154 g, the highest ever recorded in racing. "The bottom line is our cars are very safe," he said. "I've been in this thing for thirty-four years. It's part of our sport, sad as it is. It never disappears."

Dallenbach stated that CART and California Speedway were already looking into ways to prevent any kind of similar occurrence in the future. "I think we'll consider paving the track at least two-thirds of the way down into the infield coming off Turn Two," said Dallenbach. "When a car jumps out at 220 mph, nothing can help a driver until they make contact. All the advantages leave when a car enters the grass, and the surface road was six inches lower than the grass. Greg's car tripped because it was like a flat rock skipping across a still pond. It dug in and inverted itself.

"We'll also look at putting tires in front of the wall and maybe another independent row of tires fifteen feet in front of that one. Basically, try and build a catcher's mitt," Dallenbach added. "The tires aren't there now because we haven't perfected tire walls for cars going in at an angle. You've got to be careful and design a system that doesn't rip the car apart. All the corners at Brazil are more than ninety-degree turns. That track is almost a triangle and the tires there serve as a catcher's mitt. They greatly reduce the impact."

Dallenbach remained pragmatic as he reflected on Moore's passing. "The day before, he hurt himself on his scooter, and he and his dad came up to me and asked for special permission to prove to the doctor that he could drive with a cast on his finger," Wally said. "If I had told him he couldn't run, he might be alive today.

"But that wasn't the reason for his accident. Greg told everybody he was going to go from last to first, but even Superman can't do everything. Greg was a big fan of the mentality that if you're in trouble, put the throttle to the floor and you'll eventually get your way out of it. He did that once on the backstretch at Elkhart Lake and got away with it. Sometimes that works and sometimes it doesn't."

Moore's 1998 and '99 teammate Patrick Carpentier confirmed Dallenbach's analysis of the fatal crash. "I remember in Japan one time he spun and lit up the rear tires and would spin them like crazy and sometimes would avoid hitting the wall," Carpentier said. "And that's what he tried to do at Fontana. We could see that with the data that we had. He floored it once he started spinning and was wide open. I guess he didn't have enough revs or whatever it was, because instead of spinning around, it somehow accelerated the car toward the impact. That's why the impact was so big. That trick he did so many times didn't work that time.

"Greg was so good, and I never, ever, ever thought that he could die in a race car," Patrick added. "When Gonzalo Rodriguez passed away a few weeks before at Laguna Seca, we were all like, 'He's a rookie, something happened under braking, he pushed the brake and the throttle at the same time, you can't make mistakes like that.' So, as drivers, we kind of had a reason why it happened. But Greg was out of the blue, because he always got out of it."

Coming little more than twenty-four hours after the tragic death of a popular young star, CART's annual year-end Awards Banquet was a subdued affair. Around a thousand guests turned out at the Century Plaza Hotel in Los Angeles to honor PPG Cup Champions Juan Montoya and Target Chip Ganassi Racing, and to honor the memory of Greg Moore and Gonzalo Rodriguez. An even more last-minute honoree was former NFL great Walter Payton; the co-owner of Payton-Coyne Racing died earlier that day at the age of forty-six from complications of a rare liver disease.

For Michel Jourdain Jr., then twenty-three, the events of October 31 and November 1, 1999, were overwhelming.

"I think I was running decent before I had a car problem, I don't remember what," Jourdain recalled. "As I was coming out of the car, I knew it was probably my last race with Dale. I loved Dale and the guys. So, it was already a sad moment. I was finally having a decent race, then everything went in the shit, and then it only got worse. Dale told me to stay in the pits. They wanted to do a moment of silence or something because Greg passed away. That's a moment none of us will ever forget. Every one of us has our own story. We were all close with Greg. He was so much fun, and so good. It was terrible.

"You remember that he broke his finger the day before in a scooter accident," he continued. "I had an engine problem in qualifying, so we both started in the last row. For some reason, he took longer to get back to the grid than everybody else, but he came by when I was already getting strapped in, and said, 'Be safe and have fun.' Then he got in the car.

"For me, that was like a farewell for life, and a message that stuck with me forever. It wasn't about that day; it was what he wanted me to have forever. I've had nightmares and dreams about that moment, because it came just a few weeks after Gonzalo. It was hard for everybody, not only us as drivers, but the whole community. We all spent so much time with him.

"The next day, Walter Payton passed away," Jourdain concluded. "I was doing a Swift factory tour with Al Arciero when Dale Coyne called me to tell me about Walter. I think outside my family, Walter and Jimmy Vasser were two people who influenced me a lot. Walter was so strong-minded and just nice. He changed my life, really had a big influence. When we were teammates, Jimmy helped me with a lot of things. I believe, had Rahal stayed a two-car team with Jimmy in 2003, we would have been unbeatable. So, it was just a terrible year—guys dying, friends dying. And when you're twenty-three years old, it's too much."

CART had long intended to showcase its partnership with Quokka Sports by livestreaming the four-plus hour banquet in entirety on CART.com, a remarkable leap of faith at a time when only a small percentage of American homes had the internet and computer technology to reliably view the coverage.

"We would not have had this banquet tonight," said host Larry Henry during his opening remarks. "CART wanted to cancel it, but it was Greg's father, Ric, who said, 'No. Greg would want you to celebrate a new champion.' That's why we're here tonight."

"In many respects, it was a vintage year for [Indy] car racing," noted Henry's co-host—the author of this book. "We had a lot of unbelievable moments on the racetrack this year and some fantastic achievements. Juan Montoya with a remarkable rookie campaign—absolutely sensational. Seven race wins, a number of pole positions, and absolutely dominant on several occasions. Let's not take away from Dario Franchitti and what he did with Team Kool Green. He took the fight with Juan down to the absolute wire. We had great performances all season long from his teammate Paul Tracy, young stars like Hélio Castroneves . . .

"It's unfortunate that in a lot of ways, the 1999 season will mostly be remembered for the tragic events of the last six [*sic*] weeks."

After an opening greeting from CART CEO Andrew Craig, Scott Pruett, the outgoing president of the Championship Drivers Association, was the first to speak.

"This is a very tough time for all of us," Pruett said. "First, our hearts and feelings and well wishes go out to Gonzalo's family, as well as Walter Payton's."

He apologized for not preparing any notes before continuing. "When tragedy hits, by nature, the first thing we do is try to look for an answer . . . something that will make it make sense for all of us," said Pruett. "We all want to do it, in an effort to ease our own pain. The reality is it hasn't changed. We lost someone very special to us. There are no words to express my feeling, and certainly what we all are feeling. Greg seemed like such a young boy. He was racing Indy Lights at age seventeen and we all watched him coming through the years with determination and the vigor of a champion. He captured our hearts as a friend, competitor, and a good sportsman. We grieve now not only for who he was, but for what he would have been—a true champion.

"As drivers, we share much more than our desire to win," Pruett continued. "We understand in our heads the danger of racing, but it's tough for us to really feel it in our hearts. That's just one of the things that makes all of us drivers kindred spirits. When one of us falls, it rips that place open in our hearts."

Pruett struggled to hold back sobs. "My heart goes in sympathy to Greg's family and loved ones. And those here, especially Dario, Tony, Max, [CDA Director] Jon Potter, and the medical team. Greg was a very good friend of all of ours, and part of our family. Greg's memory and everything that made him such a great guy will live on in all of us forever.

"One thing I have learned in my years about loss is that you do need to take the time to grieve, for him and his family. That's it."

Father Phil De Rea and CART chaplain Hunter Floyd then led a fifteen-minute memorial service prior to the banquet meal. While the on-site guests dined, the CART.com coverage rolled on, with Larry Henry and I conducting live interviews. Bobby Rahal offered some poignant remarks.

"Last night I sat down with Jimmy and Max and Tony Kanaan and Paul Tracy. Dario was in there," Rahal said. "They were asking me what I felt, and I told them, 'You know, you guys have to tell everybody what Greg was all about. Tell them why he was a great friend of yours.' Greg had a tremendous spirit. Tremendous maturity for a young man of twenty-four. I always marveled at his maturity. It's a tremendous loss for us all, both from a professional, but also very much so from a personal standpoint.

"But I think we all recognize that Greg represents something very special," continued the former champion racer turned team owner. "Obviously we regret what happened. Nobody revels in that at all. Knowing Greg, you know what he was doing. He was hanging it out, going to the front. That was what Greg Moore was all about, and I think you have to celebrate people for what they are—not what you think they may have been, or what you like to think they were, but really for what they are. Greg was a go-getter, and he could light up the stage. I'll tell you what, there aren't very many people like that."

Wally Dallenbach was next to join us. "I don't know if the cowboy hat is going up in the closet, but that's almost three hundred races in twenty years," he noted. "It's kind of a relief to know that I'm finally going to cut bait and get to make a little lifestyle change. I'm very happy over the last twenty years with what we accomplished for the sport, and I'm looking forward to the future.

"Greg is like a son to me, and I think he's been like a son to everybody," Wally added. "He was always a star of ours, and he always lit up the room wherever he was—especially the driver meetings. He always had a quip of his own. Obviously, we will always miss him, but Greg had the privilege of doing what he liked best."

After dinner and dessert, Craig introduced the emcee for the main program, ESPN host Roy Firestone. In retrospect, it's a blessing that CART had contracted Firestone, who was respected as a serious and scrupulously fair interviewer in his Emmy Award–winning program *UpClose*, to serve as host rather than one of the more snarky and irreverent ESPN presenters like Kenny Mayne, or a comedian or novelty act. Firestone was completely respectful of the moment, and his opening remarks exuded class and compassion.

> Tonight was to be a festive occasion, a chance to honor and celebrate and indulge ourselves. It also marks the end of a glorious season—a season of joy, of great accomplishments. And we will do all of those things. But our hearts are heavy tonight, and for many of us, the mood is grim. We were going to entertain you tonight, maybe do some ribbing and toast the best of each other, but that will have to wait for another day.

Instead, I'd like to take just a few moments to tell you something about living. It's best when it's enjoyed with eyes wide open, when glory and pain are experienced without apology, without hesitation. In the last few weeks in the sports world, we lost some great people. Wilt Chamberlain, Payne Stewart, Greg Moore, and before him, Gonzalo Rodriguez. Just this afternoon, Walter Payton. Only the last three had something to do with racing, but every one of them had a great deal in common. They were men who left us way too early. That's certainly a tragedy. But they were also men who lived life with passion. They attacked life, and ladies and gentlemen, that is a legacy.

There will be men and women who shudder at these losses and maybe cower down and wonder why. Some will tell you not to fly private planes, or not to drive fast cars. They told Walter and Wilt that they lived their lives with too much on their plate, and I know because I heard it. The people who say these things, I think, live their lives in terror of their own mortality. They live in regret. In truth, I think, most of them live their lives in some kind of misplaced envy. Nothing is owed to you—not in sport, not in everyday life. We can live with justifiable caution, but we cannot be obsessed with fear.

Tonight, we celebrate those who celebrated life—men and their dreams, many of them fulfilled, many of them yet to come. But whose short lives remind us about our goodness and our greatness in ourselves. So, I say—we all say—run, and race, and fly, and laugh, and smile. And weep unabashedly—not a lament for the days of despair, but for the light and the pleasure and the passion. Let's also remember this. Most of those who we remember, and who we yet honor tonight, are people who were less interested in the love of power, but in the power of love. On that note, let us proceed.

The program led off with a mind-numbing series of contingency awards, broken up by some levity when the vastly experienced Paul Tracy received the award for Most Improved Driver. A countdown of the top ten drivers was capped by season champion driver Montoya and his entire Chip Ganassi Racing team taking the stage for a concluding toast.

Jimmy Vasser, who finished ninth in the standings, gave the first notable speech. "Congratulations, Juan—little did we know about your potential as a rookie," he began. "Chip got paid to take you on, much to the bewilderment of many, but you're a great champion and we're both with a great race team. Four consecutive championships are unprecedented and unfathomable."

He razzed Franchitti, who was seated with his then fiancée, the Hollywood actress Ashley Judd. Greg Moore had introduced the two at his friend Jason Priestley's wedding nine months earlier.

"Got your big movie star girlfriend there," he chided Dario. "Bro-filing. Changing your name at hotel registration."

He turned more serious. "A lot of these things are what Greg told me, and we're here to celebrate this evening that way," Vasser said. "Unfortunately, tonight, we're also here in a different manner. I know the family of Gonzalo Rodriguez is here [his sister, Maria, and cousins Laura and Bob Bryant were at the banquet], and our hearts were very heavy at Laguna Seca and they're extremely heavy now.

"Personally, I've had an awful lot of tears over the last twenty-four hours and an awful amount of laughs," he continued. "Every time I think about Greg, it was always about a laugh. It was always 'coming to Vegas' this or 'organizing a party' that, getting the guys together. It was always a smile. Paul Tracy was telling me—and he was absolutely right—Greg never worried about where he qualified. Just like yesterday—he didn't even qualify, he was dead last. But he was so excited about the race. That's just the way he was, he was always smiling, and he just cheered you up.

"I didn't realize how much I loved Greg until today and yesterday, and that's because he gave so much love all the time. I know we're not supposed to be up here talking about Greg, but I really can't help it. My heart is very heavy and it's difficult to lift it out of my stomach right now. I guess sometimes there's just no answers. But he loved what he was doing, and he was just a great guy. He'd want us all to kick ass next year."

As usual, Tracy masterfully mixed humor with vulnerability. "I hope someday I have a heart as big as Jimmy does, because what he said tonight was something very special," Tracy noted. "I think he said everything for the drivers."

Tracy shared his own first and last memories of Moore. "I'd just started racing Indy cars in 1993 or '94, and I was with the Penske Racing team," he said. "I'm flipping through the newspaper in Canada and there in the sports section is this kid from the West Coast. It says, 'The next Paul Tracy.' He was a little skinnier than me, a little taller than me . . . kind of the way I wish I looked. Kind of had the same haircut, the same glasses. He was breaking into the scene, and his dream was to race Indy cars against Scott Goodyear and myself, who were already at that level.

"On the grid yesterday, Greg's last words to me were 'I'll see you at the front.' I just want to say back to him, 'I'll see you again soon someday.' I can tell you, that guy had more talent in his pinky finger than most of the guys in this room. He's going to be missed by everybody, and it's a hard day for everybody. There's a couple other guys here who were really good friends with him, and we're going to miss him."

Foremost among Moore's closest friends was Dario Franchitti. A check for $500,000 did absolutely nothing to numb the pain of losing the CART championship, much less losing his pal. The result of the championship never entered his mind.

Dario did his best to inject a little light. "Well . . . third last year, second this year. We're getting there slowly," he said. "I just want to say to Juan and Chip—well done, guys. It doesn't get much closer than that. You guys deserve it, and it really was fun.

"I want to thank my friends who have stood up here tonight and said such wonderful things about my good friend Greg, who's no longer here. I think if he was here tonight, his words would be, 'Hey dude, where's the party afterwards?' Finally, I want to thank Wally for being a father to all of us and looking after us. I think you realize what kind of a man Wally is when you see tragic events like when Gonzalo died at Laguna and when Greg passed away yesterday, the way he's strong and looks after us."

When he came offstage, Franchitti granted one of the only one-on-one interviews he conducted in the immediate aftermath of Moore's death for our CART.com webcast.

"I don't think I've thought about anything at all in the sense of the race," he said. "Since I was told about what happened to Greg . . . to be honest, it doesn't interest me. You know, there's more to life than that, and Greg showed me that, basically. We had a lot of fun, and I think he said a similar thing to Paul: Last words were 'I'll see you at the front,' and he gave me a hug. He wished me well for the race. And I told him, 'Yeah, I'll see you there.'

"That's the way I want to remember him. Since I've been in this championship and I met him, he's been my greatest friend out here and I'm going to miss him. We've had some good races together, and we're going to get out there again next year and stand on it just as hard and try and do it for him."

On the livestream, I followed up by saying: "I'm still a young man when it comes to this motorsports business, but Dario Franchitti possesses a remarkable quality of professionalism and class that I've seen in few people. He's a true champion, and it's an absolute shame that we didn't have two champions this year."

Instead, it was time to celebrate the achievements of Montoya and Chip Ganassi Racing. Montoya's speech lasted less than a minute.

"I want to thank Chip," he said. "He gave me a great opportunity of being here, and I used it the best I can. I think this is going to be a very good future; this trophy means a lot to me. I want to thank Dario for the clean competition we had all year long. Very good side-by-side racing. I think with Michael we had a tough time in the beginning . . ."

He smiled, but before he could complete his thought, he turned serious. "I want to thank everyone. I want to thank Target and Honda. It's too much for me. I don't even realize I won the championship. You know, it's just too much."

And then he left the stage, leaving Ganassi to round out the show.

"I guess I want to close by saying that I've heard a lot of people up here tonight mentioning the racing family and how close-knit it is and how tight it is," Ganassi said. "Incidents like the few we've had this season, including yesterday, show us how much we need each other and how much we can pull together when what we really need is a family. Quite frankly, I think we all do need each other, and events like yesterday show that.

"Maybe one way to talk about it is, I was talking with one of my teammates yesterday—John Wheeler, who is our chef on our team," Chip concluded. "We were talking about what makes a great team, and John was talking about karma, and how our team has this karma going. I think in open-wheel racing today, we lack a little bit of karma, or a little bit of mojo, if you will. We need to get that back. And one way to get that back is to put this sport back together under one roof.

"I would hope each and every one of you work toward that goal."

Roger Penske reached out to Hélio Castroneves within hours of Greg Moore's death.
Indianapolis Motor Speedway

CHAPTER 18

BACK TO BUSINESS

Long before the checkered flag flew to end the 1999 Marlboro 500, when it was confirmed that Greg Moore had perished in a single-car accident on lap ten of 250, Marlboro Team Penske understood the implications. Indy car racing's most historically successful team, mired in a three-year slump, suddenly needed to hire a new driver on zero notice, from a limited market. While the race was still ongoing, a meeting with Hélio Castroneves was quickly arranged through Kika Garcia, a longtime Brazilian public relations manager who started working in the CART series with Emerson Fittipaldi in the 1980s.

"Unfortunately, the scenario with Greg happened," Castroneves said. "I didn't know how serious it was until my engine blew up. And then Andrea Montermini, the Italian driver—I knew him, he was there with one of the teams. [Montermini drove the No. 36 All American Racers Eagle/Toyota in 1999 at Vancouver, Laguna Seca, Houston, and Surfers Paradise but was not in the car at Fontana, where Raul Boesel drove.] He asked if I knew what happened, and I said no, and he said, 'Greg Moore passed.' So again, my whole weekend was worse to terrible.

"Right after the race, Kika Garcia came to me and said, 'Look, they want to talk to you.' I'm like, 'They who?' And she says 'Roger.' Oh wow. They wanted to meet at their hotel at seven forty-five. I said 'Sure.' But my mind that weekend, it was so blurry, it was so foggy. Because of the weekend already, before even the accident with Greg Moore happened, I was already a wreck, obviously. My future was going downhill."

Tim Cindric was engaged in his first weekend on the job as President of Penske Racing. Cindric had turned down the opportunity to call strategy for Alex Barron's No. 3 car in the race at Fontana, hoping to take more of an observational role to help him determine a path forward for the struggling team. He found himself thrown in at the deep end.

"We sat down and talked to Gil de Ferran after it all happened with Greg," related Cindric. "We knew that we needed to have a plan in place immediately to be sure. Marlboro had been on the fence because there hadn't been any success. So, we all huddled up. There's that balance between being respectful to Greg and being respectful to the people that are already counting on you—i.e., the team, to go forward. It's kind of a weird balance because on the one side you're grieving Greg's situation, and on the other side, we have a responsibility to our team and our partners to be sure that we have the best plan in place under the circumstances.

"We met with Gil, and we all talked about who was available," he added. "Hélio seemed like the best available. That's all it came down to. We grabbed him and met with him that night, and off we went. My first race on the job, and I'm meeting with Roger and Hélio in a hotel room after Greg passes away. It's really surreal how it all came together."

Castroneves was twenty-four years old, spoke little English, and his manager Emerson Fittipaldi was not present at Fontana. Hélio had been walking the paddock trying to find anyone willing to talk about a drive for the 2000 season. Suddenly, he was being pursued by the sport's biggest team—and he didn't understand or recognize what was unfolding before his very eyes.

"I called my sister, who was there, and told her I had no idea what was happening," Hélio recounted. "I was learning, I can't understand English. We went to the hotel and Gil was there, Roger, Cindric, and Teddy Mayer and Dan Luginbuhl. Roger said, 'Hey, I know it's a very tough situation.' I said, 'I don't know Roger, I have no idea.' I was saying 'I'm sorry, I don't know, I don't know' because I wasn't understanding anything. Finally, he said, 'Well, if it's not going to be you, it's going to be someone else.'

"I'm like, 'Alright, I need to find an attorney,'" Castroneves continued. "I didn't even have an attorney, because everyone screwed me over what I had with Carl Hogan. I had to find another attorney. I found Alan Miller through Derrick Walker. He used to represent Derrick, and when I was negotiating with Walker, he said 'I cannot negotiate with you because I am representing Derrick Walker.' After that, I called him and said, 'I don't know if this is still a conflict of interest.' He said, 'No, it's not. I can help you out.'

"And that's how everything started. That's where we really started our conversation with Penske. I guess I was the only guy available with potential at that time. Cindric told me they had never hired anybody who hadn't won a race. That was their system. I was one of the first ones, and that was because of the circumstances, to be in a Penske without winning a race."

Indeed, the loss of Moore—expected to perform as a co-No. 1 driver with de Ferran—and the recruitment of the relatively unknown Castroneves changed the complexion of Penske's future preparation and goals moving forward.

"After meeting with Hélio, I looked at Roger and said I was pretty sure that if he comes and drives for us, you need to work with Gil, and I'll try and figure out this kid," said Cindric. "Roger understood only half the words Hélio was saying. I've said it before, Hélio knew maybe fifty words of English. His sister was at this meeting, and RP thinks it's his girlfriend. He looks at me and goes, 'Who's the girl? This girl doesn't need to be in this meeting.' It's his sister. 'Well, why does he need his sister?' Because she speaks better English than he does.

"That changed the dynamic going forward, because it was going to take some time to get Hélio up to speed. Gil was the one kind of poised to put the team on his back."

While the eleventh-hour recruitment of Castroneves quickly solved a problem for Penske, it created a major setback for Bruce McCaw and the effort to create a new Mercedes-powered entry under the Mo Nunn Racing banner. Nunn had agreed to leave Chip Ganassi Racing and delayed his retirement. The original PacWest Racing shop at 150 Gasoline Alley in Indianapolis was being prepared to house the new effort until Nunn could arrange to move into a more spacious and modern location. The McCaw group was suddenly faced with its own driver hunt.

"We really thought we had a package together until Greg's accident," McCaw revealed. "I saw Hélio that day; I had spoken to him at that race about going forward. After the accident, Roger panicked and grabbed Hélio. I mean, just threw him in a trailer and said, 'You're going to drive for us!' He left us and Mercedes totally out in the cold. Mercedes just didn't have the balls to stand up and tell him he couldn't do it. They owned his contract; they had him. They had already forgiven a bunch of debt to Hogan in the assignment of the contract, and now here's a shareholder who goes out and goes around them. That was a bad deal, and it left us at a critical time without a driver for the Nunn effort. We had to find somebody else and finally got Tony Kanaan, who I think was a pretty good selection. Tony was a solid driver, and I have a lot of respect for him.

"There was a lot of funky stuff going on with Hélio's contract," McCaw added. "They were playing a lot of financial games with taxes, and that was one of the reasons why we didn't have a contract done, because they didn't want to take the income in the US and didn't have all their ducks in a row. A couple years later, he and his sister got tied up in a big investigation. Hélio has had a remarkable career. It's interesting, when I see him today, he's always very open and gracious. I think he knows I was there at a key time for him. But for a long time, I didn't like being around him because I was pissed. I thought he had really stuffed us."

There's not a rule book or operator's manual for responding to a tragedy. On a collective and an individual level, the CART community found it difficult to get back to the task of racing. The four-plus months between the 1999 season finale and the 2000 championship opener at Homestead-Miami Speedway seemed to drag on forever. And the fact that several of Greg Moore's most sensational performances came at Homestead meant that he would never be far from anyone's mind.

"That was a tough winter, because what happened came in the last race of the year," said Patrick Carpentier. "Often as race drivers, you just want to get back in the car to put things behind you, forget it, and create some fresh memories. The fact that it was the last race, and we had the whole winter . . . it was very different, and very sad. It was a tough, tough deal. I remember I bleached my hair blue and was pissed off that whole winter. My wife, even today, she remembers that was a tough winter, because I would often want to do things by myself."

Max Papis also remembers struggling in the winter of 1999–2000. But he eventually found himself at peace with what happened to his close friend Moore.

"I went to my family and thought about and talked about if it had happened to me," Papis related. "I really made up in my mind—and I truly believe it as of today—Greg got into Turns One and Two, he lost the car, he floored it, and it was like, 'Look at this, motherfucker! I caught—' and *BOOM* . . . he was somewhere else. I put in my mind that he was smiling and reviewing that spin, like usual being that cocky bastard, telling us, 'Look at what I did! Look how I saved it.' But he never woke up to tell us that. He woke up in a different place."

Dario Franchitti was probably the driver who was the most emotionally impacted by Moore's death, given their close friendship. Over the winter, Franchitti sometimes questioned whether he would ever have the desire to get back into a racing car, and the day he did, he suffered one of the hardest crashes of his career. On February 9, 2000, during CART Spring Training at Homestead, a failure of the right-rear spindle sent Dario's Team Green Reynard into the Turn Three wall. The Scot was taken to Jackson Memorial Hospital in Miami and diagnosed with several non-displaced fractures of the pelvis and hip and multiple small contusions of the brain from the single-car accident.

"Dario had a normal neurological examination and he's in good spirits," said Dr. Steve Olvey, CART's Director of Medical Affairs. "We'll try and get him up on crutches, and he'll undergo intensive physical therapy for about six weeks so he doesn't lose agility or muscle mass. We won't make a decision on his driving for three or four weeks."

The Homestead 2000 crash was an emotional setback for Franchitti, and he now recognizes that he likely sustained a concussion that went undetected. "After Greg was gone, I said to Barry Green, 'I don't know if I want to do this anymore. I need to go away and think about this,'" Dario related. "Barry being Barry, he said 'Take as much time as you need, pal.' And then the first time I got back in the car at Homestead in early 2000, the car broke, and I broke my pelvis in the crash. But the pelvis thing wasn't that big. It was the head injury. I've never fully recovered from that head injury, and I can say that now. It was massive. You're down, and that was a kick to the gut. It took a long time to climb out of that hole."

When Franchitti crashed at Spring Training in 2000, Wally Dallenbach was enjoying a hot dog outside a Homestead Speedway concession stand while chatting with a friend. Wally was free to roam the grounds while cars were on track because earlier that morning, CART's Vice President of Competition J. Kirk Russell was named the organization's new Chief Steward, putting an official end to Dallenbach's eighteen-year reign.

Russell joined CART as Technical Director in November 1978; his duties during his tenure included general administrative responsibilities as well as overseeing CART's competition department. He was a long-time safety advocate who was instrumental in several advances in race car and facility safety, including the deformable tire wall successfully utilized at Emerson Fittipaldi Speedway in Brazil.

"People have been coming to me for decisions for the last twenty years," said Dallenbach. "I'll be out here this year at all the races to provide Kirk with advice if he asks for it, but it's his call now."

Franchitti was able to regain enough fitness to compete in the 2000 season opener, where he finished eleventh. But he endured one of only two winless seasons in his seventeen-year career and finished a distant thirteenth in the standings.

Perhaps appropriately, and certainly to the delight of almost everyone, Max Papis earned his first Indy car win in that race at Homestead. He dedicated the victory to his friend Greg Moore—and on that day, the legend further popularized by Canadian racer James Hinchcliffe of "Red gloves rule" was born.

"I put Fontana behind me; I'm very compartmentalized how I operate," Papis remarked. "I was very motivated. I qualified something like fourteenth because I almost crashed in Three and Four, trying to get through wide open. In the race, I was noticing the car was pretty free, and I was doing everything I could to stay in the top five. All of a sudden, I saw Paul Tracy backing up and struggling more than I did. I found the energy, and I saw him getting backed up by traffic into Turn Three. I drove so deep into Turn One that I almost crashed. If you watch the video of how I passed PT, the rear wiggles three or four times. But I saved it and won the race.

"I never planned a celebration," Max added. "I crossed the start-finish line, and going into Turn One, I had in my eyes an image of Greg smiling. I opened the radio, and I said, 'Greg, I love you.' That was the first time I ever used red gloves. Greg always used to tell me that superheroes wear red gloves. So, I called Ric after the race and told him 'Red gloves rule.' That's been a motto ever since. It's something very important to us. I miss Greg, but his legacy is truly and sincerely with me."

The healing process continued throughout the 2000 season. CART created the Greg Moore Legacy Award to honor "the driver who best typifies Moore's legacy of outstanding talent on track as well as displaying a dynamic personality with fans, media, and within the CART community." The 2000 recipient was Hélio Castroneves.

"I was uncomfortable through the beginning, through some time, until I went to Toronto in 2000," Hélio recalled. "I won the pole at that race, and there was an award named after Greg Moore. His mom gave me the trophy. And I had a conversation with her in my broken English, saying, 'I'm so sorry, I don't know what to say . . . I feel so bad in this position. And ironically, I'm here now. This is supposed to be your son.' And she's like, 'Nope. You have our blessing. It's your place. He is in a much better place.' Those words were like opening the gate to keep it going, and I'm so thankful, of course. That award I won in Toronto was a blessing in disguise."

The uplifting omens continued as the 2000 season unfolded. Vancouver, as Moore's home race, was arguably the emotional highlight of the year, as Paul Tracy and Dario Franchitti scored an enormously popular one-two for Team Kool Green. "The vibe that was here this weekend was fantastic," Tracy said. "Everybody was really happy and upbeat. It was a great festival all week, and there was no sadness. Everybody was just celebrating, and I think Dario and I will have a big celebration tonight."

The return to California Speedway, where $1 million was again on offer at the Marlboro 500, was naturally rather subdued. A strange race of mechanical attrition saw only six cars running at the finish. Christian Fittipaldi won the race over Roberto Moreno, who landed the No. 20

Patrick Racing ride following the death of the intended driver, Gonzalo Rodriguez. Gil de Ferran finished third for Team Penske to claim the 2000 CART championship.

A group of Greg Moore's Maple Ridge friends traveled from Canada to attend the 2000 season finale. Al Robbie staged his own memorial for his late friend by spraying graffiti on the wall where Moore crashed.

"Rick Rice, the ESPN cameraman, drove us out to that corner of the track on his golf cart on the Saturday night," Robbie said. "We jumped over the fence. All the people who had their RVs there knew what we were doing, so they kept quiet about it. We just spray-painted 'SEE YOU UP FRONT' on the inside wall. Troy Lee put that on a helmet decal, because that was the last thing Greg said to Paul Tracy before they got in the car.

"Track security found it and painted over it, but you could still see it. I rode around in Jimmy Vasser's truck with his buddy Kenny on the parade lap for the drivers—we all hopped in other guys' trucks—and they all knew we had done it. It was pretty cool, because they all enjoyed it."

Dario Franchitti finally found a sliver of joy at Fontana when he won an Indy Racing League–sanctioned four-hundred-miler at California Speedway in 2005. Franchitti's Andretti Green Racing teammate Tony Kanaan appeared to pull ahead of Dario's draft into the lead exiting Turn Four on the final lap. But he audibly lifted from the throttle, allowing Franchitti to claim the laurels.

"Tony hasn't told me much, but it definitely looked like he lifted," Franchitti said. "I'll ply him with alcohol tomorrow night and try to get the answer."

Kanaan claimed his Honda engine faltered when he used his push-to-pass function at the crucial moment. When pressed, he denied he handed Franchitti the victory.

"It's my word against yours," Kanaan said.

Franchitti broke down in tears in a post-race interview when asked about winning at the track where Moore was killed. He turned a series of smoky donuts at the site of Moore's fatal accident.

"It's kind of sweet winning here," Dario said. "I lost a good friend here six years ago."

Twenty years down the line, Franchitti is still convinced Kanaan gifted him that race win.

"He got a run on me at the last corner, and he and I had these new Honda engines that were different to everybody else," Franchitti said. "He got to the inside of me, and he says he hit the Pit Lane limiter button, but I think he lifted so I could win. We then went around to Turn Two and did donuts. I kept every win helmet, and that one just says 'Fontana—at last.'"

Three-time Indianapolis 500 winner Dario Franchitti celebrates his 2012 victory.
Indianapolis Motor Speedway

AFTERWORD

FAST FORWARD

A private memorial for Greg Moore was held Wednesday, November 3, 1999, in Vancouver, with a public Celebration of Life the following day in Moore's hometown at Maple Ridge Baptist Church. "Our entire family is overwhelmed by this tragedy," said Ric Moore in a statement. "Losing a child is never easy, no matter what their age. However, we are equally overwhelmed by the genuine kindness and compassion of all those who are sharing this very personal loss with us. Greg touched so many lives here at home and throughout the racing world, and I want everyone to know just how much their thoughts and prayers mean to us during this very difficult time. To know that your son was respected and admired by so many means a great deal to us."

Wally Dallenbach's retirement was short-lived. His successor, Kirk Russell, found himself unsuited to the duties of CART Chief Steward, so Dallenbach stepped back in with the intention of grooming former driver Chris Kneifel to assume the role in 2001. Wally ended up staying on as Chief Steward Emeritus for the Champ Car World Series through the end of 2004. Dallenbach finally enjoyed twenty years of leisure in his beloved Colorado before passing away in April 2024.

Max Papis won twice more for Team Rahal in 2001, but his open-wheel career stalled. He turned his attention to NASCAR, where thirty-six Cup Series starts netted a single top-ten finish. However, Papis put his limited time in NASCAR to good use: His Max Papis Innovations firm now supplies nearly 100 percent of the steering wheels for the Cup Series field. He also serves as a Steward for IndyCar.

Juan Pablo Montoya went on to a surprisingly diverse career and was successful in everything he raced. In May 2000, Chip Ganassi Racing was the first team to break ranks with CART and field cars in the Indianapolis 500. The Ganassi team's superior pit stops helped Montoya make a mockery of the Indy Racing League competition, as he led 170 laps to take an easy win over Buddy Lazier, who would go on to win that year's IRL championship. Following the 2000 CART season, in which Montoya won three CART races in a Lola/Toyota in addition to the IRL's Indianapolis 500, Montoya moved to a much more competitive Williams F1 team now equipped with BMW engines. JPM caused a stir by passing World Champion Michael Schumacher to lead in only his third F1 race. Montoya won seven Grands Prix between 2001 and '06 before making a surprise move to NASCAR—once again with Chip Ganassi's team, where he ran seven full seasons and claimed a pair of road course wins in the Cup Series. Juan's eclectic career then took him back to Indy cars, where he won the 2015 Indianapolis 500 for Team Penske. He remained with the Penske organization and won three races and the 2019 IMSA Daytona Prototype International (DPi) championship for Acura Team Penske. Montoya continues to occasionally race sports cars and is actively involved in helping advance his son Sebastian's racing career.

Team Penske followed Ganassi Racing back to Indianapolis in 2001, achieving Roger Penske's first ever one-two finish at IMS as Hélio Castroneves bested Gil de Ferran. With Tim Cindric's role expanded to lead all of Team Penske's participation in IndyCar, NASCAR, and IMSA, the organization remains a perennial front-runner across multiple forms of racing and now boasts twenty Indy 500 wins and seventeen championships through USAC, CART, IRL, and IndyCar sanction.

Castroneves stepped into the seat intended for Greg Moore and turned an unfathomably unfortunate opportunity into a long and successful career with Team Penske. Castroneves won his first Indy car race at Detroit in June 2000; he spontaneously stopped his car on track and climbed a chain link catch fence in celebration. Over the next two decades, Castroneves had many opportunities to perform his trademark fence climb after Indy car race wins, but he never captured a championship. He maintained honor for CART by winning the 2001 Indianapolis 500, repeating that feat in 2002, but this time it was a win for the other side given Team Penske's transfer in loyalty from CART to the IRL. In 2009, just weeks after he was acquitted of US federal tax evasion, Hélio won the Indianapolis 500 for the third time. Castroneves finally did earn a season title—the 2020 IMSA Daytona Prototype International championship for Acura Team Penske, the last year of his Penske employment. Like Indy car's greatest generation of drivers, Hélio didn't want to quit, and he pursued a new opportunity with Meyer Shank Racing. In 2021, he joined A. J. Foyt, Al Unser, and Rick Mears in the exclusive club of four-time Indianapolis winners. Castroneves was part of the winning team at the IMSA Rolex 24 at Daytona for three consecutive years and finally stepped down as a full-time Indy car driver after the 2023 season to take a minority ownership role in the Meyer Shank team, with plans to continue competing in the Indianapolis 500 in the hopes of becoming the event's first five-time winner.

Gil de Ferran won the 2000 and 2001 CART championships in Team Penske's extensively modified Reynard/Hondas. De Ferran moved with Penske to the IRL full time in 2002; he won the 2003 Indianapolis 500, then retired from Indy cars at the end of 2003 after winning his final race at Texas Motor Speedway. He never departed the sport, creating an Acura sports car team for which he codrove, before serving as an advisor to Honda's Indy car and Formula 1 programs. He later worked as an advisor to Zak Brown and McLaren's Formula 1 and Indy car teams until stricken by a massive and fatal heart attack in December 2023 at the age of fifty-six.

CART mainstays Team Green and Mo Nunn Racing were next to return to the Indy 500 in 2002; Tony Kanaan took to IMS like a duck to water, leading comfortably for Nunn before crashing on oil. Paul Tracy passed Castroneves for the lead in Turn Three on the 198th lap, but IRL officials ruled that the pass occurred after the caution was displayed for an accident that was simultaneously occurring behind them in Turn Two. The decision to declare Castroneves the winner was seen as highly political. Barry Green spent more than $500,000 on his appeal, which was denied not by an independent arbiter, but by IRL founder Tony George. Soon after, Green sold Team Green to a group consisting of his brother, Kim Green, Michael Andretti, and Kevin Savoree, and essentially walked away from racing at the end of the 2002 season.

Tony Kanaan joined Andretti Green Racing in 2003 and quickly emerged as one of the top stars in the IRL and later in the unified IndyCar Series. In 2004, he completed every lap of every race and finished outside the top five only once on the way to the IRL championship. Kanaan won the 2013 Indy 500 for KV Racing and then finally landed a ride with Chip Ganassi Racing, where he ran the full IndyCar schedule through 2019. He won just one more race after his Indy victory, but he could always count on being competitive at IMS, making his final Indy 500 start four years later with the McLaren team. TK remained with McLaren as a driver advisor and consultant before moving into the role of team principal in 2025.

After forming Andretti Green Racing in late 2002, Michael Andretti announced he would retire from driving following the 2003 Indianapolis 500. He nominated Indy Lights race winner Dan Wheldon as his replacement. Though he never won the 500 behind the wheel, Michael's forty-two career Indy car race wins ranked him third on the all-time list for many years behind A. J. Foyt (sixty-seven) and Mario Andretti (fifty-two). Michael enjoyed much more success as a team owner at Indianapolis, winning the 500 five times with drivers Wheldon, Franchitti, Ryan Hunter-Reay, Alexander Rossi, and Takuma Sato. Andretti bought out partners Savoree and Kim Green in 2009 and renamed the team Andretti Autosport. He diversified the organization into many forms of racing, including IMSA sports cars, Formula E, Australian Supercars, and Extreme E off-road. In 2022, Michael began the process of trying to break into Formula 1 as an all-American constructor; he encountered resistance from existing F1 teams, but his efforts gained credibility in late 2023 when he announced a partnership with General Motors to supply Cadillac-badged engines beginning in 2028. He finally sold his ownership stake in Andretti Global in late 2024.

———

Al Unser Jr. raced full time in the IRL through the end of the 2003 season; an attempted mid-2004 comeback stalled when Unser announced his retirement after just three races, though he reappeared to run the Indianapolis 500 again in 2006 and '07. Unser won three IRL-sanctioned Indy car races, the last coming in 2003, but his personal life continued to unravel as he battled alcohol addiction. Unser was arrested for several impaired driving offenses, as luridly conveyed in his memoir *A Checkered Past*. Al Jr. worked for several years with Future Star Racing to identify and groom young drivers; he is living a sober life in Indianapolis, involved in an active role with the Vintage Indy organization.

———

At the end of 2003, CART declared bankruptcy. The assets of the championship were acquired by team owners Gerald Forsythe and Kevin Kalkhoven, who operated what was called the Champ Car World Series through early 2008. Between 2002 and '04, most CART teams, along with engine manufacturers Honda and Toyota, moved into the Indy Racing League. Newman/Haas Racing, Forsythe Racing, and Dale Coyne Racing were the only notable teams to remain in Champ Car for the long haul. In February 2008, Kalkhoven and Tony George announced a "reunification" or "merger" that absorbed the remains of Champ Car into the IRL.

———

When Champ Car folded, Gerald Forsythe immediately disbanded his team, honoring the contracts of all staff and driver Paul Tracy. Tracy won the 2003 CART championship for Forsythe after turning down a lucrative offer from Honda to go to the IRL with Andretti Green Racing. PT was CART/Champ Car's most recognizable and outspoken star after the 2002–4 exodus to the IRL, but Forsythe's abrupt withdrawal in early 2008 left the charismatic Canadian on the sidelines without a ride and he made just nineteen post-unification Indy car starts between 2008 and '11. Tracy won a total of thirty-one Indy car races and continues to make waves on social media and during his occasional driving appearances.

———

Jimmy Vasser stayed on the CART side to the end, making his final start in the last pre-unification race for the 2.65-liter turbo engine formula—the 2008 Long Beach Grand Prix. By then, Vasser had already delved into team ownership in conjunction with Champ Car series leader Kevin Kalkhoven. Known under several names, the Kalkhoven-Vasser team netted seven race wins, including the 2013 Indianapolis 500 with driver Tony Kanaan. Kalkhoven was also responsible for bringing Australian driver Will Power to America to race Indy cars in late 2005. By the end of 2024, Power was IndyCar's all-time leader with sixty-nine pole positions. He won the Indy 500 in 2018, IndyCar Series championships in 2014 and '22, and stands third on the all-time list with forty-four race wins. Vasser and business partner James "Sulli" Sullivan currently field a factory-backed Lexus team in the IMSA sports car championship. Kalkhoven passed away in 2022.

———

Dario Franchitti remained loyal to Andretti Green Racing and Honda and therefore made the switch to the IRL in 2003, though he missed most of the season after breaking his back in a motorcycle accident. He was in jeopardy of losing his ride in late 2006, but he bounced back to win the Indianapolis 500 and the IRL championship for AGR in 2007. Franchitti then made the shocking decision to try NASCAR with Chip Ganassi Racing. He instantly disliked the cars, then was sidelined for the summer when he broke his ankle after being swept into another driver's accident at Talladega. Attending the 2008 Detroit Grand Prix in September as a spectator rekindled Dario's enthusiasm for the open-wheel scene, and he returned to the unified IndyCar Series in 2009 to team with Scott Dixon at Ganassi for the most fruitful period of his career. Franchitti won three consecutive IndyCar Series championships from 2009 to '11, along with the 2010 and '12 Indianapolis 500, putting him in the rarified three-time winner's club. A jarring crash on a forgettable Houston street course in 2013 caused head injuries that meant a premature end to Dario's driving career, though he continues to participate in vintage racing events. He is also the lead development driver for Gordon Murray Automotive.

———

Franchitti and Tony Kanaan were close friends with their Andretti Green Racing teammate Dan Wheldon, who won the 2005 IRL championship but was killed during the 2011 IndyCar Series finale at Las Vegas Motor Speedway. The race was immediately stopped, but it seems lessons from Greg Moore's passing in similar circumstances a dozen years earlier went unlearned as IndyCar turned Wheldon's death into a spectacle. After a brief press conference confirming the fatal outcome of the accident, the scoring pylon showed only Wheldon's No. 77, and the drivers were told to drive five slow laps in Indianapolis-like three-wide formation as a tribute to their departed colleague, while the participating teams all stood in line on Pit Lane as "Amazing Grace" and "Danny Boy" were played through the public address system. In a tragic parallel to 1999, Franchitti lost one of his closest friends in a racing accident during the final event of the season while embroiled in a fight for the championship. On this occasion, Franchitti prevailed over Will Power.

After his Indy Lights win at Chicago Motor Speedway in 1999, Scott Dixon signed a long-term contract with PacWest Racing. He defeated Townsend Bell to become the 2000 Lights champion and was promoted to PacWest's CART team alongside Mauricio Gugelmin. Dixon used canny strategy and the fuel saving ability of a veteran to take a victory at Nazareth Speedway in April 2001, making him, at the time, the youngest ever winner of an Indy car race. Chip Ganassi Racing assumed control of Dixon's contract in mid-2002, and the Dixon-Ganassi combination proceeded to rewrite the Indy car record books. At the end of 2024, Dixon had won six Indy car championships, achieved a record 142 podium finishes, and ranked second on the all-time list behind only A. J. Foyt with fifty-eight race wins, including the 2008 Indianapolis 500.

Chip Ganassi Racing (twelve), Team Penske (six), and the Andretti organization (four) have won every IRL- or IndyCar-sanctioned championship since 2003.

In 2015, a feature film titled *Gonchi: la película* was released that documented Uruguayan national hero Gonzalo Rodriguez's attempts to break into Formula 1 and the short but happy time he spent racing Indy cars prior to his tragic death at Laguna Seca Raceway.

On November 4, 2019, Penske Corporation announced it had reached an agreement to acquire the Indianapolis Motor Speedway, the INDYCAR organization, and IMS Productions from the Hulman-George family. The transaction was completed in January 2020. A new entity called Penske Entertainment Corp. now serves as an umbrella company over the Speedway, the IndyCar Series, and all Indy car–related activities.

Alex Zanardi endured a miserable comeback to Formula 1 in an uncompetitive Williams-Supertec, failing to score a single championship point in 1999. He was released from his contract at the end of the year. Zanardi returned to the CART series in 2001 to drive a Reynard/Honda for Mo Nunn in his second year of team ownership. Zanardi was having his best race of the season at Eurospeedway Lausitz, on September 15, 2001, when he spun exiting Pit Lane and slid up onto the track, where his car was struck broadside at roughly 200 miles per hour by a car driven by Alex Tagliani. Remarkable rescue work by the CART Safety Team and Doctors Terry Trammell and Steven Olvey saved Zanardi's life, but both of his legs were amputated above the knee.

In July 2002, Zanardi traveled to the CART race at Toronto to receive the Greg Moore Legacy Award. He received a standing ovation from the media when he walked into the press conference on his prosthetic legs. "The award is named after a guy that was not only a great race car driver," Zanardi said. "I would say we were really similar in the way we were driving, both very aggressive. I think both were never content with the result. Always wanting to do something more. We were very, very competitive. I can't say we were close friends, but we were friends, and for sure, we had a great deal of respect for each other." Zanardi then returned to Eurospeedway Lausitz in May 2003 and "finished the race" by driving thirteen laps at speed in a Reynard Indy car equipped with hand controls. He went on to successfully compete in specially modified touring cars for BMW in several international championships before switching his focus to hand cycle racing. Zanardi won the hand cycling class of the 2011 New York City Marathon and two individual gold medals and a team silver in the 2012 Paralympic Games in London. On June 19, 2020, Zanardi sustained critical head injuries when he crashed into a truck during a hand cycle training run for the Obiettivo Tricolore road race in Italy. After facial reconstruction and lengthy rehabilitation, he was able to return home in December 2021 but has withdrawn from public life. His courageous story continues to inspire fans globally.

The Indy car community and racing fans around the world celebrate the memory of Greg Moore every year on Halloween.

Greg Moore (second from left) inspired lifelong friendships with his fellow drivers. *Michael Levitt*

EPILOGUE

THE SPIRIT OF GREG MOORE

I believe the 1999 CART FedEx Championship Series produced the most compelling single season of Indy car racing in the sport's long history. A twenty-race international slate of events that featured nine ovals, seven temporary circuits, and four permanent road courses ended in a tie between Juan Pablo Montoya and Dario Franchitti—two promising young drivers who would go on to make a lasting impact in motorsports around the world. Twenty-three of the twenty-four drivers who started the '99 season with a full-time ride won at least one Indy car race in their career; collectively, they won fourteen Indy car championships and 276 races, including thirteen at the Indianapolis 500.

"To me, that was the biggest year I've done in racing, including NASCAR and everything, in terms of how popular it was," said Patrick Carpentier. "You'd catch a plane, and people would talk to you about the race and how it went. I do some Formula 1 announcing for Canadian TV, and the guys who are the top commentators used to cover the CART series in those days. To this day, they still say that was the greatest form of racing that ever existed. People could pass, there were a lot of midfield battles, and it was hugely popular worldwide. I think at one point even F1 was concerned about how popular it was. It was a perfect mix, and even though we had big crashes, that car was pretty safe for the speeds we were doing. It was a fun club to be part of.

"A group of guys came in during the 1990s, and man, they were talented," he added. "A lot of good drivers. We didn't envy anything to F1 at that time, because the CART series had some of the top drivers in the world with Zanardi and all these guys. Unfortunately, Dario got into a crash toward the end, but they were so talented that they could push their careers for many, many years. How long they lasted in the sport is proof of how popular they were, and that's probably why those guys are so well known, because they were the stars when the series was really at its highest level."

While the 1999 CART season was mostly notable for the rise of Montoya and the continued excellence of Chip Ganassi Racing, it tends to be remembered even more for the deaths of drivers Gonzalo Rodriguez and Greg Moore. It was a year in which the tragedies outweighed the triumphs. And that's a sad thing, because the most important aspect of that star-crossed '99 campaign is that it truly confirmed the arrival of a new generation of stars who went on to represent and grow the sport for the next twenty years or more. It was an extremely vital year, and the key participants recognize that fact.

"Whether it's coincidence or not, I think 1999 was the crucial year for my career—and Hélio too, actually," observed Tony Kanaan. "By then people realized I was getting results with a small one-car team, and people were saying, 'Imagine how he could do if he goes to X team?' I think '99 changed all our lives, for the good and the bad, because we lost Greg. I think '99 is the year to write the book—you are spot on.

"I mean what an era, as far as being a kid, having your best buddies around, doing what you love in the coolest sport in the world, making a shitload of money in a prime time of your life, and being able to brag about it and make fun of your friends when you pass them at 200 miles per hour. If there was anything positive about that year, it involved the four of us—Dario, Greg, Max, and me. I was the new kid. We grew our relationship. It was big. We were already friends, but we just tightened that up. I was doing well here and there, but talking with Dario, talking with Greg, it helped. That was very special. None of the people nowadays, those young kids today have no idea."

If Indy car racing's "Greatest Generation"—consisting of A. J. Foyt, Mario Andretti, et al—carried the sport from the 1960s into the 1990s, the core group of young drivers that emerged through the CART championship in the late '90s made a similarly long-lasting impact. A quarter of a century later, Hélio Castroneves and Juan Pablo Montoya still race competitively, and Kanaan is slated to serve as a relief driver for NASCAR star Kyle Larson at Indianapolis if needed in May 2025. Franchitti mixes a slate of vintage car racing with TV commentary for the FIA Formula E championship and a driver/engineer advisory role for Chip Ganassi Racing.

Scott Dixon, who arrived on the scene in 1999 in the CART-sanctioned Indy Lights series and graduated to the top level in 2001, has compiled an Indy car record every bit as impressive as A. J. or Mario, with fifty-eight wins and six championships. The only other drivers who started racing Indy cars in the 2000s among the sport's all-time elite are Will Power (forty-four wins and a record seventy poles since 2005), and Josef Newgarden, who has collected thirty-one wins from 2012 to present, and like Power, is a two-time series champion. Alex Palou, born in April 1997, a month or so before Greg Moore won his first Indy car race, racked up eleven wins and three championships in his first five seasons.

Parallels are sometimes drawn between Moore and Dan Wheldon, who was killed in a multicar accident on the eleventh lap of the final race of the 2011 IndyCar Series season at Las Vegas Motor Speedway. Like Moore, Wheldon had just signed a contract to drive for a top team—he inked a deal that very morning to return to Andretti Autosport in 2012, the team with which he claimed ten of his seventeen Indy car race wins and the 2005 IRL championship. But Wheldon was almost a decade older than Moore when he perished, and he had already reached the pinnacle of the sport, including a pair of wins at Indianapolis. The most successful phase of his career was already thought to be behind him, whereas Moore's was most certainly ahead.

Moore's death at California Speedway on October 31, 1999, created one of Indy car racing's all-time "What if?" scenarios. What would he have achieved paired alongside Gil de Ferran in Marlboro Team Penske's No. 3 car starting in 2000? Castroneves, who replaced him, became Penske's longest-tenured driver, winning thirty Indy car races including three of his four victories in the Indianapolis 500 in a twenty-one-year career with America's most successful racing organization. Separated in age by just eighteen days from Moore, Hélio showed plenty of potential as a young Indy car driver in 1998 and '99. But he wasn't viewed as a can't-miss prospect.

"It's always going to be controversial," commented Tony Kanaan. "I think Greg would have dominated. Look at what Gil and Hélio did. It's only hypothetical, but I think he could have won as many 500s as Hélio did, to be honest. Greg was the king of the ovals. You know that—you lived it. But some others might say, 'C'mon, you're crazy.' Because they've never seen it. I think he would have changed history. But easy for us to say, because at the end of the day, it didn't happen. He's not around."

"Anything Hélio did, plus 30 percent," declared Papis. "And then he would have moved over to NASCAR and achieved his dream of racing stock cars, because that's what he wanted."

"We've all speculated about that, whether it was Tony and I, Max and I, Jimmy," added Franchitti. "We've definitely had that 'Can you imagine?' conversation. We always just sort of shake our heads and say, 'We would have all been fighting for second place.' I never thought about this until Gil died, but can you imagine Greg's talent with Gil's analytical approach—and his talent as well—in that Penske organization? Greg in those cars, whether it was the Reynard-Hondas that were just so much better than everything else, or in Roger's IRL cars at the Speedway . . . I don't know how many races, championships, or 500s he would have won, but it would have been a lot. It would have been quite something, and I think he would have rewritten the record books. That talent in those cars would have been something special. And it would have been lovely to see it."

The biggest "What if?" about Moore is the record he might have compiled at the Indianapolis Motor Speedway, whether in an Indy car or a stock car. The only race he ever contested at IMS was an International Race of Champions event in August 1999, in which he crashed. Team Penske has claimed ten Indianapolis 500 wins since 2001, with three going to Castroneves (2001, '02, and '09).

"I can't fathom that Greg Moore and Alex Zanardi never drove in the Indy 500," said Jimmy Vasser. "That's a tragedy to the sport. I'm sure you could point out other people that also didn't, but they're the two from that era. It's hard to believe. You could maybe make the case that it wasn't as important to Zanardi as it would have been for Greg. Taking away nothing from Zanardi's oval prowess, but Greg Moore was arguably one of the greatest oval drivers of all time."

Tim Cindric, who served as Castroneves's race strategist for his three Indianapolis wins with Penske, is another who believes Moore could have rewritten the Indianapolis record book.

"Greg couldn't wait to run at the Indy 500," Cindric related. "All his skill sets, you knew that kid was going to be a star there. And he was young enough in his career where he hadn't really missed the Indy 500 yet. De Ferran's career was just starting, and he missed five years of the Indy 500. Then you look at those who won during that period in the late '90s; really Kenny Bräck is the only one that emerged to win races when we were all together. None of the rest of those IRL guys left a mark.

"It's interesting to think about what could have been, and what might not have been, relative to Hélio," Cindric added. "He's obviously been a huge part of the sport as well. Those guys emerged through that era, but unfortunately, some of them had five or six years of their career being stars at Indy taken away from them."

From the very start, Castroneves handled the difficult scenario of slotting into a car intended for Greg Moore with dignity and class. In the process, especially thanks to his long-term success at Indianapolis, Hélio became one of Indy car racing's biggest stars. The popularity of Kanaan, and especially Castroneves, demonstrates that even in a diminished capacity from its greatest days in the 1960s and '70s, the Indianapolis 500 still retains star-making ability. For decades, winning the Indianapolis 500 four times was Indy car racing's holy grail, the crowning achievement that cemented A. J. Foyt's status as a legend. Castroneves was already a fan favorite before he equaled the historic tally first set by Foyt and later matched by Al Unser and Rick Mears (in far fewer starts).

Aside from his tax evasion situation, the only real adversity Castroneves encountered in his career was the controversy of the 2002 Indianapolis 500. The record book will always declare Hélio the winner, but some continue to place an asterisk on the second of his four triumphs, believing that Paul Tracy had passed Castroneves and was ahead on the track when the critical final caution flew on lap 198 of 200.

"Hélio doesn't want to talk about the '02 race," sayid Tracy. "He was gifted a race, and he'll take it. I guess if the roles were reversed and I was gifted something, I wouldn't give it up either. He won on a technicality in a court, on fine print in a rulebook. It was a highly political time, and they didn't want another guy from CART coming in and winning the race again. But I know what it feels like to win the Indy 500. I know what it's like when you're a kid in the driveway shooting hoops, dreaming of that situation with one second to go. You release that three-point shot right before the buzzer goes off and you drain it. That's what it was like pulling off that pass on the outside with one lap to go. I know what that feels like in my heart, and that's probably more important to me than having a tarnished and dusty trophy on the shelf."

It's interesting to wonder how it would have all played out had Greg Moore been in that No. 3 car in the 2002 Indianapolis 500. He might have lapped the field, or he might have crashed on the third lap. There's no doubt that whoever would have won—or been declared the victor by officials—Moore would have organized the party. That's the effect he had on his fellow drivers—to race as hard as possible on the track, then laugh about it afterwards, no matter what the outcome.

"I think we raced each other harder, just to make fun of each other later," said Kanaan. "There was no mercy. But you know what? That was the right way. We raced hard, probably extra hard. We never really crashed into each other, but I would say there was an extra nudge, a little bit closer. But I knew, and they knew we wouldn't do anything stupid. I knew I could go that extra inch closer, because they wouldn't do anything silly to me."

It was Moore who created that dynamic, which fueled the drivers desire to race each other hard on the track, while still somehow taking care of each other. It was Moore who encouraged the others to allow themselves to become genuine friends. For a young man, he taught a lot of life lessons.

"When I think about then, I really believe the unspoken and inner knowledge was that what we were doing was really dangerous," said Max Papis. "That created that bond outside the track. It all started with me landing in Melbourne in 1997 for the first race with Greg. I introduced myself. We started talking, and I realized there was a person with a great sensitivity and kindness outside.

"He built relationships. Even nowadays, I talk to Ric every few weeks. He created something that goes beyond the sport. Greg is not here anymore, but he is here with me. As we are talking, I am standing in Phoenix beside the Penske trailer, and I feel his legacy is here with me."

To this day, there is a great deal of love and respect between the generation of drivers who arrived in Indy car racing in the late '90s and served as the face of the sport through its most difficult political years. It's a kind of closeness that the Foyt, Mario, and Unser generation couldn't have understood in their driving days.

"You talk about the hardcore years before us when they raced any kind of shit and tried to kill each other," said Kanaan. "They made history and they're badasses, they're legends. Then a new generation comes where we're just as fast, but we're more outgoing. It's just a new generation. Any generation has to be better than the previous one, or it's the end of the world, right? But our generation became friends, which is not very common, because racing was never about being friends. You don't have friends because you have to beat everybody.

"We were vocal, but we truly were friends—it wasn't a marketing stunt. It was not very well taken by the old-timers. A. J. would call us sissies and other stuff we can't write. We can debate, because every generation changes history at some point. But we did it too. We kept dominating. We came in really young; we kept ourselves in shape. We made the owners say, 'Why would I change him? This guy is as good as he was as a rookie, but he's still in great shape and has so much experience.' We made it so, for a long time, there was no place for newcomers."

Unlike Kanaan, Castroneves, and Montoya, who continue to occasionally compete at the top level to this very day, Franchitti did not have the luxury of ending his full-time racing career on his own terms. His history of concussions finally caught up with him, and it seems dreadfully unfair that one of the greatest drivers in the history of Indy car racing had his career ended by an accident not of his own making on a forgettable street course. But he refuses to complain.

Not a day goes by when Dario doesn't think about Greg Moore and the times they shared together on and off a racetrack for a few years in the late 1990s. They'll always be linked, like they were from the very first day they met while watching CART testing on the Homestead road course in early 1997.

"You go in my office in my house in London, and there's an oil painting of Greg," Dario smiled. "It's just huge, and he sits and stares at me every day when I'm in that office. I talk to my kids about him, and I tell them the stories. When Austin Cindric did the Greg tribute helmet recently, that was cool, and it shows that still, to this day, he has that effect on people. People still come and talk about those years, about those cars.

"It was something special. It was a special group of people and relationships that were made then. We've all got a lot of gray hair now, but we still have that in common. We went to war in a way. To build a trust level that you need with these guys at Michigan and Fontana when you're wheel to wheel, you had to know who you were racing against."

ACKNOWLEDGMENTS

I had a great ride covering Indy car racing full time from 1993 to 2018, including fifteen years with ESPN.com. For that, I am indebted to my friends and colleagues Robin Miller, Gordon Kirby, and David Phillips—my compadres in the so-called "CART Gang of Four"—along with John Zimmermann, K. Lee Davis, and Jeff Olson, plus Paul Pfanner and Laurence Foster and the crew at Racer Communications. Raise a glass of milk to Steve Shunck, who works harder than anyone to sustain the legends of Indy car's original "Greatest Generation" and the Indianapolis 500.

The International Motor Racing Research Center in Watkins Glen, New York, was an invaluable resource for filling the gaps in my original reporting. It's sobering to reflect on the amount of media coverage Indy car racing once enjoyed from newspapers and specialty publications, including *On Track*, *Racer*, *Indy Car Racing*, and *AutoWeek*. I also enjoyed using the Greenwood (Indiana) Public Library as a comfortable base to work from on days my son was attending classes at the nearby airport.

Bruce McCaw continues to be an important advisor and supporter, and I will always be thankful for his friendship. I hesitate to call any of the drivers I worked with or covered a friend, but I think it says a lot that Dario Franchitti, Tony Kanaan, Hélio Castroneves, and Juan Pablo Montoya were extremely candid and trusted me to tell their stories in this book. I'm also grateful to Jimmy Vasser, Paul Tracy, Michael Andretti, Tim Cindric, Adrian Fernandez, Max Papis, Patrick Carpentier, Al Robbie, Michel Jourdain, Bryan Herta, Steve Horne, Dave Popielarz, and especially Mario Andretti for their contributions to this project.

I'll always be thankful that my parents encouraged me to pursue my passion, though they probably would have pushed me down a different path had any of us foreseen the challenges of a freelance career focused on a form of racing that often seemed hell-bent on destroying itself. Much love to my sister Mary-Kate, who from the day she was born was always my best friend and biggest cheerleader.

Lastly, kudos to Lee Klancher and the team at Octane Press for once again turning a crazy concept into reality on the printed page.

John Oreovicz
Speedway, Indiana – April 2025

AUTHOR'S NOTE

The narrative of this book is based on the author's original reporting from 1999. The first-person sidebars represent current day reflections from key figures on events as they unfold in the season timeline. Unless specifically noted, these quotes are from interviews conducted specifically for this book, with the remainder from the author's personal interview archive. Alternate sources are cited when used.

Hélio Castroneves, John "Oreo" Oreovicz, and Tony Kanaan have collectively won five Borg-Warner trophies. *John Oreovicz Collection*

Dario Franchitti and author John Oreovicz. *John Oreovicz Collection*

John Oreovicz interviews Juan Pablo Montoya in Vancouver in September 2000. *John Oreovicz Collection*

INDEX

Photo section pages are indicated with a "*P–*" before the page number.

PLAYERS